CROSSCURRENTS *Modern Critiques*

**Oliver Evans,** Associate Professor of English at San Fernando Valley State College, is teacher, poet, critic, and translator. His numerous articles have appeared in *Partisan Review, Yale Review, Sewanee Review, Critique,* and *Prairie Schooner.* His books include a volume of poetry, *Young Man with a Screwdriver;* a descriptive study, *New Orleans;* a Machiavelli translation, *La Clizia;* and a critical biography, *The Ballad of Carson McCullers.*

CROSSCURRENTS *Modern Critiques*
Harry T. Moore, *General Editor*

*Oliver Evans*

# Anaïs Nin

WITH A PREFACE BY
*Harry T. Moore*

Carbondale and Edwardsville

SOUTHERN ILLINOIS UNIVERSITY PRESS

FEFFER & SIMONS, INC.
*London and Amsterdam*

*For Eve and Harry Finestone*

ANAÏS NIN virtually invented a type of novel. To say this is not to say that her books of fiction cannot be read like any others, but rather it is said to emphasize her originality.

And for these books she has virtually invented a language, at least a special way of using available language. This is not to say that she doesn't communicate understandably; the statement is made to stress her uniqueness.

Miss Nin, delicately petite and delicately beautiful, is a pronouncedly feminine type of woman. To characterize her work we might best use the elemental word female, for Anaïs Nin is not one of those women authors who write like men. Her work is subtle and complex, sensuous, and with soundless depths. It takes the reader in and out of dreams.

Besides her imaginative writing there are also her Diaries, two of which have so far been published (expertly edited by Gunther Stuhlmann). These journals stand apart from autobiographies and confessionals as Miss Nin's novels and stories stand apart from other examples of their genres.

When she first began submitting her work to commercial publishers, she had no luck. But she did better with booksellers; with money advanced by Frances Steloff of the Gotham Book Mart, Miss Nin bought a small press and began printing her own books. I first had the pleasure of meeting her and her husband at Ben Abramson's Argus Book Shop (late 1945 or early 1946), when they came to

Ben's loft on West 46th to see him about taking some of the books, which he of course did. I had known some of Miss Nin's early work, particularly her 1930 book on D. H. Lawrence, for whose second edition in 1964 I have had the privilege of writing the preface.

Oliver Evans in the present book describes how he discovered Anaïs Nin's work at the Gotham in early 1945. This subsequently led to his meeting the author and to the writing of the present book.

It is a timely volume, for since her days of printing her own material, Miss Nin has indeed triumphed. She is reviewed on the front pages of the book sections, and her writings are taught in universities. And her first editions now command high prices.

Mr. Evans' study is penetrating, thorough, and valuable. We welcome it into the Crosscurrents / Modern Critiques series as we welcome Miss Nin herself, from whom Mr. Evans quotes at sufficient length to show readers unfamiliar with her work just how fine it really is, so that they will turn to her own books for more of such prose. Meanwhile, readers of Anaïs Nin will find themselves indebted to Mr. Evans for this excellent critical study.

HARRY T. MOORE

Southern Illinois University
November 11, 1967

# ACKNOWLEDGMENTS

THE AUTHOR wishes to thank the San Fernando Valley State College Foundation and Faculty Research Committee, who awarded him a grant that, by temporarily freeing him of teaching duties, enabled him to complete this book. Thanks are also due to Mrs. Arthur Blackburn and Mrs. Nellie Almquist, who kindly relieved him of some of the secretarial labor involved.

The author and the publisher wish to thank Anaïs Nin for allowing them permission to quote from the pamphlets *Realism and Reality* and *On Writing*, and from the unpublished version of her Diary, which had not, at the time this book was being written, yet been published. They wish also to thank the Swallow Press for use of extensive extracts from *House of Incest*, *Winter of Artifice*, *Under a Glass Bell*, *Ladders to Fire*, *Children of the Albatross*, *The Four-Chambered Heart*, *A Spy in the House of Love*, *The Seduction of the Minotaur*, and *Collages*. For permission to quote from reviews, they are grateful to the editors of *The Chicago Review*, *Critique*, *Partisan Review* for Elizabeth Hardwick's review of Anaïs Nin © 1948 by *Partisan Review*; *The New Republic* for Isaac Rosenfeld's "Eternal Feminine," reprinted by permission of *The New Republic*, © 1944 Harrison-Blaine of New Jersey, Inc.; *The Hudson Review* for Vernon Young's "Five Novels, Three Sexes, and Death," reprinted by permission from *The Hudson Review*, Vol. 1, No. 3 (Autumn, 1948), copyright © 1948 by The Hudson Review, Inc.

O. E.

# CONTENTS

IN THE SPRING of 1945, after my discharge from the Air Force, I went to live in New York. My two years of military service I considered wasted except for a few poems I had somehow managed to produce—poems that afforded a temporary escape from the appalling monotony of barracks life—and I was anxious to start living again. I chose New York because it was full of what the places where I had been stationed were empty of: color, movement, variety, life; and like so many other young men there with literary leanings I found part-time jobs with book agents and publishers. Though precarious and underpaid, this work was ideal for my purpose: I did not want a full-time job; I wanted to revel in my new liberty, to live in the shining city as fully and as freely as possible.

One day as I was browsing in the Gotham Book Mart my eye fell upon an odd-looking little book entitled *Under a Glass Bell*. It was obviously the product of a small amateur press, a collection of short stories with wildly fanciful engravings by an artist named Ian Hugo—but as I leafed through it, reading a paragraph here and there out of what was at first mere idle curiosity, I became increasingly absorbed and astonished. The prose was wonderfully clear and simple, the images accurate and spontaneous. I had never heard of the author, Anaïs Nin, but I decided I must have the book. That evening and the remainder of the week I ate a little more lightly at the Automat than I would otherwise have done, but the sacrifice was justified:

I was getting something that did not come out of a slot, and though it is hard for me to say precisely what it was, it somehow involved the idea of freedom. For as I read the stories in this book I was struck, more than anything else, by their extraordinary airiness; by the impression they gave of being somehow dimensionless, and thus illimitable, unconfined, and unrestrained; and by their serene independence of the conventions of ordinary fiction. I suppose it was inevitable, reading her at that particular time in the shining city, that I should have made some sort of connection between the freedom of this author's technique and that of my own personal situation. In any case, ever since that spring, seventeen long years ago, Anaïs Nin has constituted for me a symbol of freedom, excitement, and discovery.

It could not have been much later than this, perhaps the following year, that I saw her name, again in the Gotham Book Mart, on the cover of a pamphlet entitled *Realism versus Reality,* which turned out to be an essay defending her theory of fiction. My copy of this pamphlet (which unfortunately is out of print) disappeared at least ten years ago, but I remember that in it she accused the ordinary realistic novel of superficiality, of being concerned with only the external aspects of existence and character. It was not enough, she declared, merely to record the actions and words of a character, since much of the time people act and speak to conceal their deepest feelings, and the realists who believed they were depicting the natural man were only depicting impersonations. The novelist of the future was to concern himself not with realism but with reality, with discovering the secret self (or selves) beneath the apparent one, with exposing the hidden behind the obvious motive. Thus dreams, daydreams, and fantasies become enormously important as clues to the inner self; the process of free association is more revealing than that of conscious thought; and we learn more about the characters from interior monologues than from the speeches which they exchange with one another.

These ideas were not altogether new to me; they were in the air at the time. I knew that they represented the application to literary theory of some of the principles of Freudian psychology, and that they had already been practiced, at least to a certain extent, by Proust, Joyce, Woolf, and even Faulkner. But I had never seen them stated in so many words, with such directness and clarity, and they enabled me also to view the strange little stories in *Under a Glass Bell* (for notwithstanding my delight I *had* found them strange) in the light of their author's intention—an opportunity for which any reader should be grateful, particularly in the case of a writer as unconventional as Miss Nin, whom it would obviously be unjust to judge by standards she neither respects nor acknowledges. I felt, too, that her prophecy concerning the future of the novel might possibly, some day, be fulfilled.

In 1947, tiring of hack work, I accepted a teaching job at a Midwestern university where I remained for three years and published my first book, a collection of poems, *Young Man with a Screwdriver*. During this time I read only one of Miss Nin's works, a short story titled "Hejda" which appeared in George Leyte's beautiful but short-lived *Circle*. It depicted, with unusual penetration, the relationship of an Arab girl and her Roumanian artist-lover in the Paris Latin Quarter, and it made a profound impression on me; I still think it one of her very best. I was especially interested in her theory of characterization, of arriving, sometimes in a very few words, at the *essence* of a character, either by means of symbol, or by a deliberate flatness, an abstractness of statement that is somehow peculiarly effective.

A part of her wants to expand. A part of her wants to stay with Molnar. This conflict tears her asunder. The pulling and tearing brings on illness.

Hejda falls.

Hejda is ill.

She cannot move forward because Molnar is tied, and she cannot break with him.

Because he will not move, his being is stagnant and filled with poison. He infects her every day with this poison.

I spent my summer vacations in New Orleans, and it was here, in either 1948 or 1949, that I conceived the idea of a group of little stories with a French Quarter setting in which I would attempt to practice some of Miss Nin's theories. Conveniently for me, Mr. Tennessee Williams, whom I had met in the summer of 1939 and who was spending the summer in a big old apartment on Orleans Street, was suddenly called to New York before the expiration of his lease, and very generously gave me the use of his place, which was ideal for working. I never finished the project, and only one of the stories has ever been published, but the experience enabled me to appreciate some of the problems inherent in Miss Nin's method and to give me a new respect for her achievement.

Meanwhile I continued to hear rumors about this author: that she had written the preface to Henry Miller's *Tropic of Cancer* (it does not, for some reason, appear in the American edition); that she printed her own books on a second hand foot-power press; that she was breathtakingly beautiful; that she had been a fashion model and also a professional dancer; that she had written a book on D. H. Lawrence; that she had practiced psychoanalysis under the direction of Otto Rank; that since early adolescence she had been writing a monumental diary which, according to Henry Miller in T. S. Eliot's *Criterion*, "will take its place beside the revelations of St. Augustine, Petronius, Abelard, Rousseau, Proust and others" (it was then, in 1937, in its fiftieth volume and is now in its one hundred and third). I had, quite understandably, some difficulty in reconciling these rather disparate bits of information into a single image, and thus Miss Nin, besides being a symbol of freedom, became for me also a symbol of the enigmatic.

The enigma was dispelled when, in 1950, I left the Midwest to teach at the City College of New York and had an opportunity to meet this legendary creature. At least it was partially dispelled: Miss Nin is still something of an enigma to me—but then, as she herself never tires of pointing out, does not every personality present a mystery? Certainly there was no doubt of her beauty. The rumors, however, had not prepared me for the special quality of her charm: I had expected a febrile intelligence, vehement gestures, Niagara-like monologues, eccentricities of dress and behavior. The woman I met was singularly collected; she spoke but little, and her speech had the curious precision of multilinguists; her diminutive, shapely form was clothed simply but elegantly. Her blue-green eyes were enormous and you felt they did not miss very much—they gave the impression of being as innocent as they were beyond surprise, like the eyes in the portrait of Beatrice Cenci that is attributed to Guido Reni.

It was Tennessee Williams who introduced us, and that year I saw a good bit of Miss Nin. We discovered we had a number of friends in common, like Gore Vidal and Olive Leonhardt, and I showed her my poems and New Orleans stories, some of which she was kind enough to read on a radio program. Then I left for Europe, where I remained several years, out of touch with Miss Nin and with most of my American friends. But wherever I went—Paris, Rome, Barcelona, Tangiers—I continued to hear her name mentioned in literary circles, usually with admiration. If Miss Nin's is not a popular audience, it is at least an international one.

Fiction such as Anaïs Nin's poses a peculiar problem for the literary critic, for the critic is essentially a rational creature, and he must use the language of rational discourse. Miss Nin's primary appeal, however, is not to the rational but to the emotional at its deepest level—"I intend the greater part of my writing," she has said, "to be received directly through the senses, as one receives painting and music"—to what, for lack of a more precise term, we call the intuitive; and to the unconscious. As such, it approaches that condition of poetry which Jerome Rothenberg had in mind when he observed recently that in a successful poem we have the phenomenon of the unconscious speaking directly to the unconscious. In an experience of this kind, the sensitive reader is apt to be gratified without quite knowing why; and the critic is at a loss, faced with a reader who has not so responded, to demonstrate exactly what it is to which he *should* have—what it is to which he is insensitive.

Karl Shapiro exaggerated and oversimplified the problem when he declared some years ago that criticism is meaningless because the critic is forced to use rational discourse to explain the nonrational. This is the Crocean cul-de-sac which holds the poem to be totally inaccessible to the reader, and Murray Krieger, who substitutes for rational and nonrational the terms propositional and contextual, is closer to the truth when he says, "The critic must try to grasp the contextual within the terms of the propositional while trying to avoid the generic, conceptual world of experience to which this discourse, as propositional, must lead . . . The procedure is muddy and self-defeating, but it *does* proceed."

I have attempted to proceed in this fashion here. I think there is little doubt that contemporary criticism to a large extent lacks the necessary apparatus to deal with the kind of effects Miss Nin is interested in creating, but this does not require that the critic abdicate his role. Certain injustices, admittedly, are bound to be done the author, but this is the risk which every writer necessarily runs who, like Miss Nin, abandons the traditional forms of fiction.

With Eliot, I conceive the primary function of criticism to be illumination rather than judgment. It is, or ought to be, constructive in the broadest sense; the good critic will not dissipate his energies in the discussion of bad literature. This does not mean, of course, that he will note only the excellencies of his subject, for, though his choice of it implies a vote of confidence, once that vote is cast his conscience must not cease to function. But what the critic primarily does is to discover value where the less experienced and less specialized reader does not, and attempt to share his discovery; this is at once the justification and the necessity of that kind of criticism which is explicational. The critic of the future will differ from ours not so much in his approach as in the possession of such equipment as will facilitate that approach and make it ultimately more profitable.

Finally, because this book was conceived as criticism rather than criticism of criticism, I have omitted any discussion of Anaïs Nin's first book, a critical appreciation of D. H. Lawrence.

OLIVER EVANS

Northridge, California
June 1, 1967

Anaïs Nin

## 1 GENESIS OF A FICTION
### THE DIARY

ANY DISCUSSION of Anaïs Nin's work must properly begin with her Diary, for from the first it has been the source of all her fiction. Long before she had any idea of becoming a professional writer she entered into this extraordinary record, begun when she was a child and now many thousands of pages in length, the raw materials from which she was later to fashion many of the situations in her stories and novels: innumerable impressions, characterizations, anecdotes, ideas, dreams, transcripts of conversations, and extracts from her correspondence. It was a vast and rather formless accumulation, overwhelming in its thoroughness, and all of it recorded with an attention to detail that bordered on the fanatical: there are whole pages devoted to the analysis of a mood, whole paragraphs concerned with the expression of a single nuance of feeling.

More than twenty-five years ago Henry Miller, to whom she had shown portions of the work, prophesied in *Criterion* that it would "take its place beside the revelations of St. Augustine, Petronius, Abelard, Rousseau, Proust and others." Ever since then rumors have flown thick and fast in the literary world concerning the nature of this gigantic undertaking. Gossip is generally inclined to be sensational, and literary gossip is no exception: it was whispered that the Diary recorded events so scandalous, and involving persons of such prominence, that it could not possibly be published during its author's lifetime. Most of these rumors had little or no foundation in fact. It is true that Miss Nin's journal contains passages which might conceivably shock persons of conventional morality, and it is certainly true that it mentions a great many famous people; but this is merely another way of saying that its author, who was privileged to be on intimate terms with some of the best minds of her generation, has been completely honest. If a diary has any value, it is that, for on any other basis it simply could not justify itself.

Now that portions of the work have been published, the public which imagined that Miss Nin was writing another *Life and Loves à la* Frank Harris has had occasion to learn how false was their impression—and, no doubt, to be disappointed. But for those whose expectations were less lurid, and particularly for those students of literature who are interested in seeing the relations between Miss Nin's fiction and her Diary, the publication of even this small a portion of it constitutes an event of first importance. It is with these relations, of course, that we are here primarily concerned,[1] but first it will be necessary to show how the Diary began and how it grew; the importance which it has occupied in the writer's life; and some of the changes which it has undergone, particularly in recent years.

She began the work, as has been said, in childhood—on board the ship which was carrying her mother, her two brothers (Thorvald and Joaquin) and herself from Spain to the United States. Her parents had separated, and the Diary was conceived as a sort of elaborate and never-ending letter to her father, whom she continued to love in spite of his desertion of the family: "At the core of my work was a journal written for the father I lost, loved, and wanted to keep . . . The journal is for my father but my mother does not let me mail it to him, she says it will get lost." It is possible that Mrs. Nin resented the child's preference of her father over herself, and the move to America may have represented an attempt, perhaps unconscious, to estrange her children from their father not merely by physical distance but by immersing them in an alien culture and obliging them to learn a language with which he was unfamiliar.

These early volumes were written in French, for, though fluent in that language and in Spanish, the child had not yet learned English. "It is a strange country, America," she noted shortly after disembarking in New York, "where the staircases move up and down and the people stand still." And again:

> In the subway a hundred mouths masticating, and Thorvald asks, "Are they ruminants?" . . . They eat oatmeal and bacon for breakfast. There is a remarkable shop called the Five and Ten Cent Store, and a library where you can borrow books for nothing. Men rub their hands and spit in them as they stand waiting for the elevators. The elevators travel so fast it is as if they were falling.

A passage written when she was only thirteen reveals that the young girl had already developed those tendencies toward introspection which are part of the necessary equipment of any imaginative artist.

> At times I have sensations which I cannot explain, impulses I cannot control, impressions I cannot shake off, dreams and thoughts contrary to the usual dreams and thoughts of others. When I read a book I discuss it with myself, I judge it, I find its virtues or its faults, I begin to think such deep thoughts that I get lost, weary; I no longer understand myself . . . Is there anyone who will understand me? I do not understand myself.

"Dreams and thoughts contrary to the usual dreams and thoughts of others." This sense of the uniqueness of her own character was accompanied by a sense of its complexity, as the following entry (remarkable because it anticipates what was to become one of her major preoccupations) illustrates.

> Time does nothing to my companions in school.[2] For me each day is a novelty, and it seems to me that my character changes every day. If I do rise at the same time, I have different impressions each day. Even if I wear the same dress, it seems to me that I am not the same girl. Even if I repeat the same prayers during one year, each time they appear different to my interpretation, and I understand them differently.

When she was at this age, her narrative impulse found its expression orally: "I tell Joaquin and Thorvald so many stories that my mother said my imagination is like Niagara Falls in its richness and continuous movement." Her journal, however, meant more to her than anything else, and already she was completely conscious of the function which it was performing in her personal life: "So that my dreams may be my own, so that they may never become real, so that I may always call them back to keep me company, to help me live, I keep them in the deepest part of my being or in the most secret part of my Diary."

When Miss Nin began to write fiction seriously, in the early thirties, she became uneasily aware of a certain conflict between it and the Diary. It was difficult to be faithful to both, and she was reluctant to neglect either for the sake of the other. It might be said that she had two consciences on this score, one personal and the other aesthetic. "I poured everything into the Diary," she wrote regretfully. "It channelled away from invention and creation and fiction." And she made the following resolution:

> Never write anything in the Diary which can be immediately described and written for the novel [3] . . . Never describe a scene which belongs in the novel, or in *House of Incest*. Only notes in the Diary, if I have no time to develop.

Another entry made during this period reads:

> Dear Diary, you have hampered me as an artist. But at the same time you have kept me alive as a human being. I created you because I needed a friend. And talking to this friend, I have perhaps wasted my life . . . Writing for a hostile world discouraged me. Writing for you gave me the illusion of a warm ambiance I needed to flower in. But I must divorce you from my work. Not abandon you. No, I need your companionship. Even after I have worked, I look around me and whom can my soul talk to without fear of miscomprehension? Here breathes my love of peace, here I breathe peace.

Certain friends who admired her literary gift, like the literary agent William Aspinwall Bradley, urged her to forsake the journal altogether. In 1933 she wrote:

> Everybody wants to deprive me of the journal which is the only steadfast friend I have, the only one which makes my life bearable, because my happiness with human beings is so precarious, my confiding moods so rare, and the least sign of non-interest is enough to silence me. In the journal I am at ease.

When Miss Nin underwent psychoanalysis, first with René Allendy and later with Otto Rank, both men attempted to lessen her dependence on the Diary by suggesting that it was no longer necessary since the father for whom it had originally been intended was no longer *in absentia*, and she saw him frequently during this period of her residence in Paris. As they saw it, the father fixation from which she had suffered since childhood was curable: the mystery and importance which he had assumed for her in his absence might now, through familiarity, be expected to disappear. "Leave your Diary," Rank advised, "That is withdrawing from the world." Whereupon she wrote with fresh determination: "I will not give all to the sketch book [*sic*] . . . Is this what Rank wanted, to throw me into my novels, books, out of the intimacy of the Diary?"

Again and again, under their combined influence, she tried abandoning the Diary, but always ended by returning to it. The habit of confiding in her faithful friend had become too firmly fixed for her to relinquish it altogether. "The period without the Diary," she confessed, "remains an ordeal." And, "Every evening I wanted my Diary as one wants opium." And so, in relation to her fiction, the Diary continued to serve as a vast storehouse of materials. Nor was this all: some of the stories, like "Birth," that were published independently, either in literary magazines or in her first collection, *Under a Glass Bell*, were taken almost word for word from the Diary.

Only within the last few years has Miss Nin succeeded in subordinating her journal to her fiction. Or perhaps it would be more accurate to say that her concept of the

Diary, in which she continues to write, has changed, and that it no longer performs the function which it formerly did. The need to confide and to confess is no longer an obsession with her, and what she writes in it now concerns herself less than it does her friends and her acquaintances: it has become, as she says, "a diary of other people." The autobiographical element, therefore, while still present, is relatively insignificant. From a personal point of view the change was probably healthy, and it was certainly desirable professionally, for the focus of her attention in the Diary is now where, for a novelist, it properly belongs: on the potential characters of her fiction. The Diary, in other words, has shown an increasing tendency to become a sketch book. As Gore Vidal comments, "The diary was begun as a substitute world and then, in time, it became a world and then later, when she was older and grown strong, she was able to step out of this personalized world and, though continuing her diary, become a full complete person, living outside as well as within." [4]

When we examine the relationship between Miss Nin's Diary [5] and her fiction, we find that most of the ideas and the obsessions which are present in the latter are present also, and naturally more explicitly, in the former. For example, the Whitmanesque thirst for experience which motivates the actions of her main characters, who are invariably women, and which results in their attempting to lead several quite different lives simultaneously, has the following personal source:

> Like June [6] I have infinite possibilities for all experience, like June I have the power to burn like a flame,[7] to enter all experiences fearlessly, decadence, amorality or death. The idiot and Nastasya are more important to me than the self-denial of Abélard and Héloïse. The love of only one man or one woman is a limitation. To be fully alive is to live unconsciously and instinctively in all directions, as Henry and June do.

The satisfaction of this thirst for experience involves the assumption of multiple identities:

> I have always been tormented by the image of multiplicity

of selves. Some days I call it richness, and other days I see it
as a disease, a proliferation as dangerous as cancer . . . My
first concept about people was that all of them were co-
ordinated into a WHOLE whereas I was made up of a
multitude of selves, of fragments. I know that I was upset
as a child to discover that we had only one life. It seems to
me that I wanted to compensate for this by multiplying
experience . . . Multiple personalities, multiple lives born
of an extravagant hunger.

The character who best personifies this ideal—or this
dilemma—is, of course, Sabina in *Spy in the House of
Love*, who sees in Duchamp's famous Surrealist painting,
*Nude Descending a Staircase*, a symbol of her own complexity.

> For the first time, on this bleak early morning through New
> York streets not yet cleaned of the night people's cigarette
> butts, she understood Duchamp's painting of a Nude De-
> scending a Staircase. Eight or ten outlines of the same
> woman, like many multiple exposures of a woman's person-
> ality, neatly divided into many layers, walking down the
> stairs in unison (*SHL*, p. 127).

Compare with this passage the following entry from the
Diary:

> I am like a person walking through a mirror broken in two.
> I see the split. One woman, stylish, fresh, blooming, is
> walking toward the Trocadero, and the other walks into
> nightmares which haunt the imagination.

The act of putting this theory of personality into practice, while rewarding in the sense that it resulted in an
increased richness of experience, nevertheless created certain problems of which Sabina, too, was painfully aware.
One difficulty was that the possession of multiple selves
could only be accomplished at the sacrifice of the single self,
and when Miss Nin wrote that on certain days she viewed
the split as "a disease, a proliferation as dangerous as cancer," it was of this danger that she may have been thinking.
Another problem was that the several selves showed a
distressing tendency to conflict and to compete with one
another, so that we find entries such as the following:

How difficult it is to be "sincere" when each moment I must choose between five or six souls! Sincere according to which one, reconciled to which one? . . . What happens when you try to live out not two sides of your nature but three, four, five, as many as there are relationships around you?

Finally, and perhaps most alarmingly, she felt that her writing was beginning to reflect the division. "My books are splitting too," she confessed to the Diary, "the dream on one side, the human reality on the other." She discovered pages in *House of Incest*, whose mood was deliberately hallucinatory, which, because of their realism, belonged instead in *Winter of Artifice*, on which she was working simultaneously.

It was here that Doctor Rank was once more able to be of service. She sought him out, as she says in the Diary, "because I felt torn apart by my multiple relationships, and I would have been able to live fully in each one—I had enough love and devotion for all of them—but they conflicted with each other." His advice was that she should live alone for awhile, "to disentangle my real self from all my "roles," to free myself of the constellation of interrelationships and identifications."

The belief in a "real" or basic self which for one reason or another chooses various dissembling roles came in time to supplant Miss Nin's earlier theory of separate selves, each with its own peculiar identity. It is easy to trace the process, both in the Diary and in the novels, but it was not accomplished without a certain struggle—a struggle that was analogous to the one which was simultaneously going on between the Diary and the novels. "What interests me," she declared in the former, "is not the core but the potentialities of the core to multiply and expand infinitely. The diffusion of the core, its suppleness and elasticity, rebound, ramifications. Spinning, encompassing, space-devouring, star-trodden journeys, everything around and between the core." And again, "It is no crime to play roles. I too am aware of the basic self. And once I have seen it, known it, I believe in it, no matter what appearances say." But though she came to "believe in" the concept of a basic self, she continued to be intrigued by the fictional possibilities of her earlier theory: "If we could only write simultaneously all the levels on which we live, all at once. The whole truth!" Much later, in the fifties, she wrote: "man is his own most elusive impersonater . . . we are all Walter Mittys as described by Thurber, going about our daily living while living a secondary, a third, a fourth life simultaneously, as heroes of amazing adventures." The difference between this and the earlier quotation, which implies that the "whole truth" is nothing more than the sum of its parts, is enormous: Walter Mitty *has* a real self, and the imaginary selves which he assumes merely serve to define and to comment upon it. Moreover, they are *imaginary* selves, which he does not make the mistake of trying to live out: he knows it would be impossible for him to do so, which is the reason he does not make the attempt. If he could live them out there would probably be no need for him to invent them. In Miss Nin's fiction the most emphatic expression of the theory that a basic self exists which can be revealed by the systematic removal of false selves is her latest novel *Seduction of the Minotaur*.

Rank believed not only that each individual possesses a basic self but also that women, collectively, possess a "real" self which, through their subjugation to the opposite sex, they have been obliged to conceal in order to please their partners. This, as he saw it, was the real theme of *House of Incest*,[8] which, according to him, represented the protagonist's "desperate attempt to find her true woman's self in this man-governed factory . . . The truth lies not in what woman actually appears to be but in what she has become through man and hence has accepted as an image of herself." This theory which, interestingly enough, Miss Nin had not consciously formulated prior to writing *House of Incest*, came to be one of her favorite theses. "Women," she wrote in the Diary, "are still occupied in making the world as the man wants it, and then trying as best they can to create the one they can breathe in."

Man also, Rank maintained, had a false image of him-self which concealed the true one. Proud of his science, of his empirical achievements, of what he believed to be an objective approach to reality—by contrast, that is, to woman, whose essential subjectivity he considered made of her an inferior being—he failed to realize that even his most rational maneuvers concealed a subjective basis. Man's faith in his objectivity, Rank felt, was an illusion, an illusion in which he needed to believe in order to sustain him in his role of superior being. The most objec-tive systems of thought, Rank insisted, can be exposed as having a subjective base.[9] Women, being under no such obligation, were more honest in this respect, and were therefore freer, since they were unencumbered by illusions of objectivity. "Women are so much more honest than men," Miss Nin wrote in the Diary. "A woman says: 'I am jealous.' A man covers it up with a system of philosophy, a book of literary criticism, a study of psychology." It is interesting to compare this passage with the following, from *The Four-Chambered Heart*:

> It saddened Djuna that Rango was so eager to go to war, to fight for his ideas, to die for them. It seemed to her that he was ready to live and die for emotional errors as women did, but that like most men he did not call them emotional errors; he called them history, philosophy, metaphysics, science (*FCH*, p. 72).

And this, from *Children of the Albatross*:

> It was then that he practiced as deftly as older men the great objectivity, the long-range view by which men eluded all personal difficulties: he removed himself from the pres-ent and the personal by entering into the most abstruse intricacies of a chess game, by explaining to her what Darwin had written when comparing the eye to a micro-scope, by dissertating on the pleuronectidae or flat fish, so remarkable for their asymmetrical bodies (*CA*, p. 96).

This concept of man, which one finds again and again in Miss Nin's work—particularly in *Cities of the Interior*—can also be traced directly to her association with Rank. "Man's language," she wrote in the Diary, "is this displacement from personal to impersonal, but it is another form of deception. The self is disguised; it is not absent, as they believe it is." In an interesting pamphlet, *On Writing*, published in 1947, she elaborated this theory of the difference between the sexes.

> Man has faced boldly the forces of nature outside of himself, has investigated them, mastered and harnessed many of them. But this conquest deprived him at the same time of his primitive, intimate contact with nature, resulting in a partial loss of his power and vitality.
>
> Woman has retained her communication with nature (even in its negative form of destruction) and could have remained the symbol of nature for man, because her language and her means of perception are more unconscious and non-rational. But she has failed to fulfill that role, partly because of her tendency to imitate man and adopt his goals, and partly because of man's fear of complete contact with the nature of woman (p. 18).

This fear in man, she went on to speculate, may have arisen "from his being not quite so certain that the forces of nature manifested through woman could be as easily mastered or harnessed" [as those manifested through non-human agents]. And she concluded: "This has led to the absence, or failure of relationship between men and women so prevalent today, and it is a dramatic proof of the absence of relationship between man and nature." There is something of Lawrence, as well as of Rank, in all of this, and it has a certain affinity also with the views about women expressed by Robert Graves in *The White Goddess*.

Again like Lawrence, Miss Nin constantly celebrates what is subjective and personal. "There is no objectivity," she declared flatly in the Diary, "there is only instinct." And like Virginia Woolf, what interests her primarily is the inner world of her characters, not the surface relationships in which they become involved. "It is necessary," she has written, "to travel *inwardly*, to find the levels at which we carry on, in a free-flowing, immensely rich vein, the uninhibited inner monologue in distinction to the controlled manner in which we converse with others." Her collected novels, appropriately entitled *Cities of the Interior,* are all concerned with these inward voyages whose destination is the self, and she is convinced that self-knowledge is indispensable to an accurate understanding of the outside world and should therefore have priority over it. The following entry from the Diary is typical:

> The inner hatreds of men are now projected outside. There are fights in the streets. Revolution in France, they say. None sought to pacify their own personal revolutions, so now they act them out collectively.

In her work it is always the male who, as a means of escape, becomes involved in causes and movements and seeks to know the secrets of the physical universe; and it is the woman who accepts the greater challenge, who turns her eyes inward and discovers the truth of her own nature and who seeks to function on the more significant level of personal relationships. Here is Djuna, in *Four-Chambered Heart.*

> She smiled at man's great need to build cities when it was so much harder to build relationships, his need to conquer countries when it was so much harder to conquer one heart, to satisfy a child, to create a perfect human life. Man's need to invent, to circumnavigate space when it is so much harder to overcome space between human beings, man's need to organize systems of philosophy when it is so much harder to understand one human being, and when the greatest depths of human character lay but half explored . . . Man turned his telescope outward and far, not seeing character emerging at the opposite end of the telescope by subtle accumulations, fragments, accretions, and encrustations. Woman turned her telescope to the near, and the warm (*FCH*, pp. 73, 164).

Djuna's ideas, which, we gather from the *Diary,* are also the author's, remind us irresistibly of Descartes' dictum, "Conquer yourself rather than the world," and even more forcibly, perhaps, of Whitman:

*The earth, that is sufficient,*
*I do not want the constellations any nearer,*
*I know they are very well where they are,*
*I know they suffice for those who belong to them.*

It is sometimes difficult to reconcile Miss Nin's intense subjectivism with her interest in psychoanalysis, and there is evidence in the Diary that her attitude toward the analytic process in general underwent considerable change as a result of her association with Doctor Rank. For, apropos of Henry Miller's passion for analyzing his wife's character, she had written: "What we analyze, will it die? You go about it like a surgeon with a scalpel. And as you cut you kill what you cut into." This is of course a romantic idea—one with which Lawrence was particularly obsessed.[10] But only a few pages later we find:

> The aim of analysis resembles the old Chinese definition of wisdom: the destruction of idealism. The basis of insincerity is the idealized image we hold of ourselves and wish to impose on others—an admirable image. When this is broken down by the analyst's discoveries, it is a relief because this image is always a great strain to live up to. Some consider the loss of it a cause for suicide.

That is, the function of analysis is to reveal the basic self and to enable the subject to live comfortably with it by relieving him of the necessity for conforming to an idealized identity. But the basic self is not unalterable, and this is yet another justification for analysis.

> Destiny can be directed . . . one does not need to remain in bondage to the first wax imprint made on childhood sensibilities . . . What we call our destiny is truly our character, and that character can be altered. The knowledge that we are responsible for our actions and attitudes does not need to be discouraging because it also means that we are free to change this destiny . . . You can alter the chemistry provided you have the courage to dissect the elements.

It is by means of such dissection, or analysis, that one arrives at the truth of his identity. And truth, according to

Miss Nin, has no worse enemy than romantic idealism. "Idealism," she declared in a passage whose context is the necessity for sexual liberty, "is the death of the body and the imagination. All but freedom, utter freedom, is death." Idealism, in fact, amounts to nothing less than neurosis, as she noted in a later passage.

> Neurosis a modern form of romanticism. Stems from the same source, a hunger for perfection. Many of the romantics destroyed themselves because they could not attain the absolute . . . they could not attain it because it was invented. The neurotic is the same. He will seek union with opposites, or perverse contraries, relationships to those who turn away; he will seek to conquer the unconquerable.

Partly through her experience with psychoanalysis, partly through her reading of André Breton and other Surrealists, Miss Nin at this period of her life in Paris became greatly interested in the use of dreams as literary material. Again it is easy to trace the growth of this interest through the pages of the Diary. After beginning *House of Incest,* she noted: "I have written the first two pages of my new book in a surrealistic way. I am influenced by *transition* and Breton and Rimbaud. They give my imagination an opportunity to leap freely." Dream-writing became the favorite subject of her conversations with Miller, conversations which often continued into the small hours of the morning. One of the problems that interested them was the function of dialogue in such writing.

> I said talk in the dream was only a phrase issuing from a million thoughts and feelings, only a phrase now and then formed out of a swift and enormous flow of ideas. Henry agreed with me that the verbalization of thought in dreams was short and rare. Therefore, we agreed, there must be a telescoping, a condensation in words. (Psychoanalysis describes the great condensation in dreams.)

The biggest problem faced by the writer who attempts to communicate the dream sensation, they decided, is that he must work with words, and the dream "happens with-

out language, beyond language." The art medium that
was best suited for reproducing the dream experience, they
agreed, was the film, whose language is primarily visual.
And what Miss Nin attempted to do in *House of Incest*
was, using a literary medium, to approximate something of
the effect of a Surrealist film.

> I said there was a need of giving scenes without logical,
> conscious explanations . . . I gave as an example of the
> silent mystery the feeling of the dream scenes from the
> *Chien Andalou* where nothing is mentioned or verbalized.
> A hand is lying in the street. The woman leaps out of the
> window. The bicycle falls on the sidewalk. There is a
> wound in the hand. The eyes are sliced by a razor . . . It is
> a silent movie of images, as in a dream. One phrase now
> and then, out of a sea of sensation.

But Surrealism interested her not merely as a literary
technique, nor even as a philosophy of literature and art; it
interested her (as it did also Breton) as a way of life.
Indeed, for the original practitioners of this group, it *was* a
way of life.[11] As she wrote in the Diary:

> The surrealists are the ones who believe one can live by
> superimpositions, layer upon layer, past and present, dream
> and actuality, because they believe we cannot live on a
> single line, and that the only way to transcend the contra-
> dictions of life is to allow them to exist in such transposi-
> tions.

This was, as we have seen, the identical ideal at which
Miss Nin had arrived independently, though not without
a few misgivings—"Richness or disease?" she had asked
herself. She and the characters in her fiction attempted to
put into practice the surrealists' concept of life, with the
strains and complications we have noted. Its realization
obviously required a maximum of freedom from the re-
straints of conventional behavior, and there is perhaps no
dictum in all the literature of Surrealism which is more
characteristic of the movement as a whole than Breton's:
"Only the word liberty can still produce a state of exalta-
tion in man." As Henri Peyre has observed: "Liberty, or

rather the pursuit of a total liberation, is the keyword of its [Surrealism's] doctrinal pronouncements." [12]

Surrealism also advocated living intensely at the heights and at the depths of experience. It shared the Romantic view that emotions, all emotions, were valuable in themselves—that the experience of pain was as indispensable as that of joy to the person desirous of leading a full life, and that the two were often curiously blended.[13] Both Miss Nin's temperament and her acquaintance with French romantic authors inclined her to accept this theory. In her Diary she had written a passage addressed to her father, whose attachment to the routines of everyday existence she deplored.

> I have a thirst for the marvelous, only the marvelous has power over me . . . Reality does not impress me. I only believe in ecstasy, in heightened living, and when ordinary life binds me, I escape in one way or another. No more walls. You try to live in both worlds: time for the marvelous and time for ordinary life. I choose the moon, even for breakfast. But no concessions to the quotidian . . . Mysticism of earth or heaven, but extremes.

Miss Nin's interest in Surrealism, both as a literary method and as a way of life, coincided directly, as we have seen, with her interest in psychoanalysis, and in this respect she was of course typical of a good many avant-garde writers of her generation. The influence of Freud on Surrealism has recently been noted by Gwendolyn M. Bays and others, but, as Miss Bays admits, the ultimate roots of the movement are to be found in French symbolism, which in turn was a latter-day manifestation of Romanticism.[14] Surrealism, indeed, is perhaps the most eloquent modern expression of the Romantic attitude to art and to life,[15] and its brief liaison with science in the early part of the present century may perhaps account for some of the paradoxical attitudes which even a desultory reading of the Diary will discover. Thus, is it not rather curious that a writer whose assumptions are as characteristically Romantic as Miss Nin's should declare neurosis to be "a modern form of romanticism" and to assert that "idealism is the death of the body and the imagination"?

The debt which Miss Nin's fiction owes to the Diary, however, is by no means merely a matter of ideas and attitudes. There are many specific similarities between the Diary and her fiction, the most important of which involve characters and situations common to both. The wise critic knows that most characters in fiction are amalgams—composite portraits of several persons whom the writer has known and observed, rather than faithful likenesses of any one of them. It will be sufficient for our purpose to mention three cases involving minor characters. The playwright Antonin Artaud, who figures prominently in the Diary and who was indubitably the largest single influence on the so-called Theatre of the Absurd, appears in "Je Suis le Plus Malade des Surréalistes" (*Under a Glass Bell*) as Pierre, the character with the "deep-set eyes of the man living in the caverns of his separation from the world" who wishes to start a Theatre of Cruelty. Though composites, the brother and sister described in the title story of *Under a Glass Bell* (and also in *House of Incest*) were partly suggested by actual acquaintances of Miss Nin's when she was living at Louveciennes, and a large part of their story appears *verbatim* in the Diary. Likewise with the lesbian violinist and her friends in *Winter of Artifice*.

Nor is the resemblance limited to characters and situations; it extends also to particular scenes, such as the house in *Children of the Albatross*, which the reader will recognize at once as Miss Nin's house at Louveciennes, about which she wrote in the Diary:

> There are eleven windows showing between the wooden trellis covered with ivy. One shutter in the middle was put there for symmetry, but I often dream about this mysterious room which does not exist behind the closed shutter.

Here is Djuna's house, in *Children of the Albatross*:

> She had chosen it too because its symmetrical facade covered by a trellis overrun by ivy showed twelve window faces.

> But one shutter was closed and corresponded to no room.
> During some transformation of the house it had been
> walled up.
>     Djuna had taken the house because of this window
> which led to no room, because of this impenetrable room,
> thinking that someday she would discover an entrance to it
> (CA, p. 26).

There is also a certain resemblance between the Louveciennes house and that described in *House of Incest*.

> In the house of incest there was a room which could not be
> found, a room without window, the fortress of their love, a
> room without window where the mind and blood coalesced
> in a union without orgasm and rootless like those of fishes
> (HI, p. 52).

Certain specific devices also, such as that of using an
abstraction for a character, or of substituting a particular
feature for the whole (as occurs in Part Two of *Winter of
Artifice*, where The Voice is a synechdocical representa-
tion of a psychoanalyst) can be traced directly to the
Diary:

> Will Slotnikoff says: I am having a love affair with a voice.
> A voice that gets to things so deep in me that I can't realize
> what is happening.

Compare with this the experience of Lilith, in *Winter of
Artifice*:

> Such simple words he [the analyst] said, yet Lilith left him
> feeling a great warmth towards him, something resembling
> love. She was falling in love with the Voice (WA, p. 146).

The metaphor of the labyrinth, which is present obses-
sively in Miss Nin's early work (until, in *Four-Chambered
Heart* and subsequent novels, it is succeeded by that of
floating objects) also had its inception in the Diary, which
is itself, in the story "Labyrinth" (*Under a Glass Bell*),
compared to a labyrinth, "I was eleven years old when I
walked into the labyrinth of my Diary . . . I was lost in
the labyrinth of my confessions, among the veiled faces of
my acts unveiled only in the Diary." In the same story,

which is really a kind of prose poem, the condition of soundlessness is likened to a labyrinth.

> I sank into a labyrinth of silence. My feet were covered with fur, my hand with leather, my legs wrapped in accordion-pleated cotton, tied with silken whips. Reindeer fur on my breast. Voicelessness. I knew that like the reindeer even if the knife were thrust into me at this moment, I would not even sigh.
>
> Fragments of the dream exploded during my passage through the moats, fell like cutting pieces from dead planets without cutting through the fur and cotton of this silence. The flesh and fur walls breathed and drops of white blood fell with the sound of a heartbeat. I did not want to advance into the silence, feeling I might lose my voice forever (*UGB*, p. 65).

The labyrinth is a metaphor not only for silence but also (in "Hejda") for speech as well.

> Her speech revealed and opened no doors. It was labyrinthian. She merely threw off enough words to invite one into the passageway but no sooner had one started to walk towards the unfinished phrases than one met with an impasse, a curve, a barrier. She retreated behind half admissions, half promises, insinuations (*UGB*, p. 87).

In "Hejda," however, the principal function of the labyrinth image is to define the personality of the protagonist.

> The passageways that led one to Hejda were as tortuous and intricate as the passageways in the oriental cities in which the pursued women lost themselves, but all through the vanishing, turning streets the eyes continued to signal to strangers like prisoners waving out of windows (*UGB*, p. 87).

Compare with this the following passage in the Diary:

> Certain cities of the Orient were designed to baffle the enemy by a tangle of intimate streets. For those concealed within the labyrinth its detours were a means of safety; for the invader it presented an image of fearful mystery. June must have chosen the labyrinth for safety.

By extension, the labyrinth is also used in "Hejda" to suggest the secretiveness of women generally, and it is associated with another of Miss Nin's favorite metaphors: the veil ("The unveiling of women is a delicate matter. It will not happen overnight. We are all afraid of what we shall find."). The image of veils and robes is almost as persistent in the early fiction as that of the labyrinth, and the act of removing them corresponds, symbolically, to the penetration of the heart of the labyrinth — to the revelation of the secret feminine self. Here is Hejda before her spiritual "unveiling."

> At seventeen she left the Orient and the veils, but she retained an air of being veiled. With the most chic and trim French clothes, which molded her figure, she still conveyed the impression of restraint and no one could feel sure of having seen her neck, arms or legs. Even her evening dresses seemed to sheathe her. This feeling of secrecy, which recalled constantly the women of Arabia as they walked in their many yards of white cotton, rolled like silk around a spool, was due in great part to her inarticulateness. . . .
>
> This covering of the body, which was like the covering of the spirit, had created an unshatterable timidity. It had the effect of concentrating the light, the intensity in the eyes. So that one saw Hejda as a mixture of elegance, cosmetics, aesthetic plumage, with only the eyes sending out signals and messages (*UGB*, p. 87).

In the Diary, Miss Nin had written of June Miller:

> June must be like one of those veiled figures glimpsed turning the corner of a Moroccan street, wrapped from head to foot in white cotton, throwing to the stranger a single spark from fathomless eyes.

Independently of sex differences, the labyrinth also represents, in Miss Nin's fiction, the maze of surface selves whose innermost chamber is the basic self, the core. And, in *Winter of Artifice*, the image is expanded to include a vertical as well as a horizontal dimension, and is used to suggest the passageways which lead, through various stages and layers of semiconscious experience, to the innermost unconscious center, the dream.

> The woman who walked erect during the day and the woman who walked and swam during the night were not the same. The day woman was like a cathedral spire, and the opening into her being was a secret. It was inaccessible like the tip of the most labyrinthian sea shell.
>
> But with the night came the openness (WA, p. 172).

Elsewhere in the same novel the dream experience is described as follows:

> The dream was composed like a tower of layers without end, rising upward and losing themselves in the infinite, or layers coiling downward, losing themselves in the bowels of the earth. When it swooped me into its undulations, the spiraling began, and the spiral was a labyrinth. There was no vault and no bottom, no walls and no return. But there were themes repeating themselves with exactitude.
>
> If the walls of the dream seemed lined with moist silk, and the contours of the labyrinth lined with silence, still the steps of the dream were a series of explosions . . . On the first layer of the spiral there was awareness. I could still see the daylight between the finger of eyelashes . . . The dream was a filter. The entire world was never admitted. It was a stage surrendered to fragments, with many pieces left hanging in shreds. At the tip of the spiral I felt passive, felt bound like a mummy. As I descended these obstacles loosened (WA, pp. 170–71).

The labyrinth metaphor persists throughout *Children of the Albatross,* where it is associated with memory (an association that had been anticipated by a passage in *Winter of Artifice* describing Proust's *À la Recherche du Temps Perdu* as "the endless book in which he made no choice [16] but followed the labyrinth of reminiscence") and finally disappears altogether. In *Ladders to Fire* Rango, at the seashore, "digs labyrinths in the sand," but the action appears to have no particular symbolic significance. The frequency of this metaphor, as well as that of the veil, in Miss Nin's early work may perhaps be accounted for by a trip which she made to Morocco in 1936, and which she describes in a portion of the Diary which has not yet been published.

It would be a mistake to imply that because the Diary is indispensable to an understanding of Miss Nin's fiction it is not valuable in its own right. In the tradition of European letters, the journal is a well-recognized and honored form: one thinks of Rousseau, of Pepys, of the brothers Goncourt, of Gide. No such tradition exists in this country, it is true, and yet Miss Nin's multivolumed achievement is of unusual interest, both literary and extraliterary. There is an almost incredible richness of style: images, among them some of the most accurate and ingenious in modern English, bloom with the profusion of orchids in a Brazilian jungle, and as casually; Surrealist fantasies which are as dazzling as the fireworks scene in *Seduction of the Minotaur* or the underwater explosion described in *Ladders to Fire*; excursions into the psyche as dizzying—and as terrifying—as Doré's illustrations of the *Inferno* or Piranesi's dungeon scenes. There are random insights, expressed with such simplicity that one wonders at never having seen them before in the same words: "It is the people who do not love themselves who need so much to be loved by the world. Their supply of admiration is so low it has to be replenished by the world." When she turns her gaze inward, the result is nearly always illuminating.

> I never go to the very end of my experiences. I did not take drugs with June, or rebel destructively as Henry does; I stop somewhere to write the novel. The novel is the *aboutissement*. I did not go to the very end with my father, in an experience of destructive hatred and antagonism. I created a reconciliation and I am writing a novel of hatred.[17] I write novels perhaps to supply the deficiencies of life itself.

If Miss Nin's fiction concerns itself with imaginative truth, her journal is concerned with truth of quite another kind, and one is, or ought to be, grateful for the complementary view of the world which it affords. As Henry Miller notes, "The diary is not necessarily more truthful than other forms of art, but the fact that it takes its stance *in truth* is of peculiar interest and importance." [18] Commenting on the compulsive quality of the writing ("more like the eruption of a geyser than a limpid flowing stream"), Miller states, "It is my impression that no woman has ever written in like manner, and very few indeed are the men who have had the courage to reveal the truth so wholeheartedly."

Historically, too, the Diary has value. Its inhabitants include personages who for the past thirty-five years have figured prominently in the cultural life of two continents: Antonin Artaud, Kay Boyle, André Breton, John Cage, Truman Capote, Theodore Dreiser, Lawrence Durrell, Maude Hutchins, Jacques Lipchitz, Henri Michaux, Henry Miller, Isamu Noguchi, Kenneth Patchen, Otto Rank, Man Ray, Yves Tanguy, Edgar and Louise Varèse, Rebecca West, Tennessee Williams, Edmund Wilson, Frank Lloyd Wright, Ossip Zadkine. Of real documentary value are the scene in which Miss Nin visits Dreiser at the Hotel Ansonia, the shrewd comparison she draws between Rebecca West and Henry Miller, the passages in which she analyzes her analyst (Rank), her portraits of Artaud and Zadkine.

Whether one agrees with Miller's judgment of the Diary that "no woman has ever written in like manner," or with his highly controversial views on the relative importance of fiction and autobiography,[19] one thing at least is certain: Miss Nin's journal is one of the most accurate factual descriptions in English of Bohemian life in Paris during the early thirties, and one of the most intelligent firsthand commentaries that have appeared in this country on the growth of literary Surrealism during those exciting years.

## 2 THE ROOM WITHOUT A WINDOW
### HOUSE OF INCEST

HOUSE OF INCEST was first published in 1936 in Paris by Siana Editions.[1] It is the most difficult of Miss Nin's books, but an understanding of it is essential to an appreciation of this author's later work. As she has commented, "It is the seed of all my work, the poem from which the novels were born." And again, on the flyleaf, "All that I know is contained in this book without witness, an edifice without dimension, a city hanging in the sky."

In our study of the Diary we noted that Miss Nin's general intention in *House of Incest* was to depict a series of psychological tortures, and that the plan of the book was suggested by that of Octave Mirbeau's *Jardin des Supplices*, which depicted a series of physical tortures. In *House of Incest* the tortures, while different from one another, are all conceived as having the same source: an incapacity to love fully and freely. This incapacity in turn is the result of self-engrossment, of a failure to transcend the narcissistic and homosexual elements which, the author believes, are characteristic of immature emotional relationships. Such relationships are, therefore, ultimately incestuous, which is why Miss Nin calls her book *House of Incest*.[2] The work as a whole dramatizes the agony of individuals trapped within this house, and the knowledge that they *are* trapped (for each of them is granted a degree of insight, just enough to make his situation painful) of course adds to this agony as they struggle, unsuccessfully, to escape.

The influence of Mirbeau's novel upon *House of Incest* was really superficial, for it did not extend beyond the general design of the book. More important influences were Lautréamont and Rimbaud, particularly the latter, and many passages in Miss Nin's book are strongly reminiscent of the *Saison en Enfer:* she has, in fact, several times referred to *House of Incest* as "a woman's season in hell." The influence of both these writers is seen in the surrealistic quality of the style, and in the profusion and brilliance of the images.

The composition of *House of Incest* did not take place in a straight line but in separately written fragments upon which Miss Nin later imposed an associational rather than an intellectual order. This accounts for much of the difficulty of the book, and for the failure of many readers to find in it a satisfactory "narrative line." [3] Actually the book has considerable unity, and a progression as well, as I shall presently show. For the moment it will be sufficient to understand that the dream experiences, the passages of surrealistic description, and the experiments in semiautomatic writing of which it is composed were conceived independently, very much in the way that poems are, and were later assembled into a whole. It was nearly three years in the writing.

The prologue has puzzled many readers at the same time it has impressed them with its haunting beauty. Because of its brevity, we may here reproduce it in full.

> The morning I got up to begin this book I coughed. Something was coming out of my throat: it was strangling me. I broke the thread which held it and yanked it out. I went back to my bed and said: I have just spat out my heart.
>
> There is an instrument called the quena made of human bones. It owes its origin to the worship of an Indian for his mistress. When she died he made a flute out of her bones. The quena has a more penetrating, more haunting sound than the ordinary flute.

Those who write know the process. I thought of it as I was spitting out my heart.

Only I do not wait for my love to die (*HI*, p. 11).

The surrealistic image in the first paragraph is a way of explaining the deeply personal quality of the book: it is not, that is to say, a mere invention or an intellectual structure, abstract and impersonal; its creation has been a traumatic experience involving the very source of life itself, organic and concrete. Its birth, like the birth of a child, has been a physical thing: she has here, so to speak, given birth to her heart, and her action in "yanking" at the "thread" corresponds, in this imagery, to the severing of the umbilical cord.

Similarly with the second image: the music which the poet creates is not the product of any ordinary instrument manufactured from such inert substances as metal or wood, but rather of one compounded from materials which are essentially human: it is personal and human, not abstract and synthetic. "Those who write know the process": Miss Nin may have been thinking here of D. H. Lawrence, by whom, as we noted in the first chapter, she has been profoundly influenced. At any rate the idea expressed here, that the successful literary artist puts not merely his head into his work but his very blood and bones as well, is very typical of Lawrence and indeed of the whole Romantic school.[4]

Here it is appropriate to remark that the alchemical symbols printed in all editions at the beginning of each of the seven sections, or movements, were chosen at random and serve no other than a decorative purpose.

It is convenient to consider the first movement as having three aspects, one of them involving the literal level of the narrative and the others the symbolic. Literally, then, what is being described is a prenatal experience: the author, who is also the narrator, the feminine "I" of the story, chooses images which suggest the freedom, the passive ecstasy, of the fetal condition. On this level, the sea corresponds, of course, to the "waters of the womb," a phrase Miss Nin was later to use in the story "Birth," and the final paragraph describes the act of birth.

On the first level of symbol, what the author describes in this movement is an ordinary dream experience. On this level, Atlantis, the submerged continent, corresponds to the basic self, the unconscious core of the personality which can only be reached by "the route of the dream" and "at night." The "rigid new city" with its "heaviest portals" represents the conscious self from which, when these portals slide open "on smooth-oiled gongs," one escapes into the primeval subaqueous environment whose fluidity contrasts with the "rigidity" of the "new city": "My bones move as if made of rubber. I sway and float, stand on boneless toes listening for distant sounds." According to this interpretation, the final paragraph refers to the moment of awakening from the dream, the return to the "new city." The materials of this movement, incidentally, had their origin in actual dreams. Miss Nin, who, coincidentally, was born under the astrological sign of Pisces, has confided that her dreams are frequently of water; thus she writes in the opening paragraph: "I am of the race of men and women who see all things through this curtain of the sea, and my eyes are the color of water." [5]

The second symbolic level is more general. Sentences such as "I remember my first birth in water" and "My first vision of earth was water veiled" tempt the reader to wonder whether the author is referring not merely to the dream experience of an individual but also to a kind of generic experience common to all mankind—even, perhaps, to all the forms of life which can be arranged on the evolutionary scale. On this level, the Atlantis symbol represents something which resembles the Jungian concept of the collective unconscious, or even the Hindu-inspired "Oversoul" of Emerson and the "Original Source" of Plotinus and the Neoplatonists; and the return voyages which we are occasionally enabled to make to it correspond to those sporadic contacts which, atavistically, we can presumably succeed in establishing with our psychic origins. The final paragraph of the movement, thus viewed, refers to the separation of the individual soul from the universal soul, to resume its independent identity. This interpretation is not really so remote from the overt intention of the book as might at first appear, since the various movements depict successive stages in the failure of love, and these stages are completely consistent with the Neoplatonic theory of Emanations, which postulates a "ladder of love."

The second movement is the longest and most ambitious in the book. It describes the infatuation of the narrator for another woman, referred to as Alraune [6] in the earlier editions and as Sabina in the later. In this attraction, which is never translated into physical terms, even on the realistic level, there is a strong element of narcissism: the narrator sees, or imagines that she sees, in Sabina the other half of herself, and thinks that through union with her she can achieve wholeness. In reality, however, she is not in love with Sabina, but with herself; even the desire to be joined to her complement represents a form of self-love, and the wholeness that she imagines might result from this union is not a real wholeness. When one makes the beloved a part of oneself a dependency is created,[7] while in a truly mature relationship the beloved is allowed to have a separate existence. And so the attempt ends in failure; it is the first of the agonizing dramas acted out in the *House of Incest*. It is appropriate that it should come at the beginning of the book, since the kind of love (or rather of pre-love) which it describes is characteristic of adolescence, and the types of incest which it involves are basic and elemental:    as *a*] love of the self, and    *b*] love of the self in the form of another woman.

The movement has three parts. The first (pages 18–28) [8] describes the meeting of the two women and the initial ecstasy of the relationship. The second (pages 29–31) is concerned with the personality split which results from the abdication of the self in favor of the beloved, and also the strenuousness of the effort involved in attempting to maintain a separate identity. In the third part (pages

31–34) there is a deliberate withdrawal from the beloved and an attempt to retreat into the isolation of the self—an attempt which results in agony even greater than that caused by its division.

The characterization of Sabina is not merely that of an individual; she has a symbolic significance as well, which emerges out of the contrast between her and the narrator, who thereby also acquires the identity of a symbol. She is the predatory female who somewhat resembles in her destructiveness the *femme fatale* archetype, with the important difference that she is destructive *naturally* rather than out of calculation. The wiles which she practices upon her victims are as necessary to her as the air she breathes and the food she eats: from them she derives her psychological nourishment. Her opposite is the earth-mother archetype, which is the identity assumed, in the context of the movement, by the narrator, and together they represent the dual aspect of woman. This explains the sun-moon imagery which is the subject of some of the most beautiful passages in the book: the narrator is associated with the sun (a fertility symbol) and with warmth generally, while Sabina is associated with the moon—beautiful, but barren and cold—and is also described in a series of steel images, testimony at once of her coldness, her invulnerability, and her destructive power.

The symbolism, however, involves more than an opposition between two readily recognizable feminine archetypes. Sabina symbolizes not only the destructive aspect of woman but also the unconscious human mind, primitive, untamed, and unevolved. Her behavior is instinctive, irrational, impulsive—therefore antisocial and uncivilized. The narrator, on the other hand, represents the conscious mind, the intelligence which controls, restrains, and evaluates: her behavior is deliberate, rational, inhibited, governed by consideration for others—therefore civilized. The two characters taken together thus represent the dual aspect not merely of woman but of the human psyche generally.

Sabina's identity is less complicated than that of the

narrator, who has a "night self"—though she will not
allow it to dominate—as well as a "day self." She does not
*deny* the night self, but seeks instead to control it. The
implication here is that neither of the two selves is self-
sufficient, and that the attempt of either one of them to
stand alone must end in frustration and failure: the life of
impulse and the life of inhibition must coexist and complement each other, just as in the other symbolic context
the "total woman" is a compound of destructive elements;
the moon has its value as well as the sun. It is her
realization of this that causes the narrator to long for
union.

> I become you. And you become me . . . You will see love
> which was excluded from the passions given you, and I will
> see the passions excluded from love . . . For an hour you
> will be me; that is, the other half of yourself. The half you
> lost. What you burnt, broke and tore is still in my hands: I
> am the keeper of fragile things and I have kept of you what
> is indissoluble (*HI*, p. 27).

So far from repudiating Sabina's jungle world of instincts and primal passions, the narrator freely acknowledges its power, and even deprecates, in this connection,
her own relative ineffectiveness.

> Sabina, you made your impression upon the world. I passed
> through it like a ghost. Does anyone notice the owl in the
> tree at night, the bat which strikes the window pane while
> others are talking, the eyes which reflect like water and
> drink like blotting paper, the pity which flickers quietly like
> candlelight, the understanding on which people lay them-
> selves to sleep? (*HI*, p. 26).

But though she has respect for Sabina's world and is
willing to join her there, the narrator, because her identity
is essentially rational, will not relinquish altogether her
contact with consciousness and with civilization.

> Your lies are not lies, Sabina. They are arrows flung out of
> your orbit by the strength of your fantasy. To nourish
> illusion. To destroy reality. I will help you: it is I who will
> invent lies for you and with them we will traverse the

world. But behind our lies I am dropping Ariadne's golden thread—for the greatest of all joys is to be able to retrace one's lies, to return to the source and sleep one night a year washed of all superstructures (*HI*, p. 26).

And, just as she agrees to accompany Sabina into her world of night, the narrator, in a kind of ode or aria whose language has a warmly sensuous quality—"Come away with me, Sabina, come to my island. Come to my island of red peppers sizzling over slow braseros, Moorish earthen jars catching the gold water . . ."—invites her friend to accompany *her* into the world of sunlight.

Here it may be wise to warn the reader that he is not expected to see, in this wooing of the unconscious by the conscious mind, or of the *femme fatale* by the earth-mother, any elaborate Allegory of the Psyche: these passages justify themselves, insofar as they have justification, as lyrical expressions—even, perhaps, as conceits of a semi-whimsical character. The symbolism involving the dual aspect of woman and the human mind is essentially a device for dramatizing the predicament of the protagonist, who mistakes for a genuine love-object a reflected image of herself in another woman. And the symbols *are* appropriate: the relationship between the two feminine archetypes and the conscious and unconscious mind is incestuous in that, in each case, they are different aspects of the same entity—members, that is, of the same family.

Returning, then, to the narrative level, we find that the protagonist early in the course of the relationship suffers a loss of identity through the strenuousness of her effort to achieve unity with her friend: this is the first torture. Identities become exchanged and confused ("Does anyone know who I am?") but are unable to fuse simultaneously: "I am the other face of you . . . Only our faces must shine twofold—like day and night—always separated by space and the evolutions of time." The struggle is described quite explicitly.

I see two women in me freakishly bound together, like circus twins. I see them tearing away from each other. I can hear the tearing, the anger and love, passion and pity. When the act of dislocation suddenly ceases—or when I cease to be aware of the sound—then the silence is more terrible because there is nothing but insanity around me, the insanity of things pulling, pulling within oneself, the roots tearing at each other to grow separately, the strain made to achieve unity (*HI*, p. 30).

This agony is followed by an attempt at withdrawal: the protagonist realizes that in order to retain her sanity she must grow separately, must use her own lungs. Threatened with loss of her self, she attempts to find it in the isolation of a hotel room, but this experience proves to be merely another form of torture.

A room with a ceiling threatening me like a pair of open scissors . . . I lie on a bed like gravel. All connections are breaking. Slowly I part from each being I love, slowly, carefully, completely . . . I part from them all. I die in a small scissor-arched room, dispossessed of my loves and belongings, not even registered in the hotel book (*HI*, pp. 31–32).

The torment is increased by her realization that withdrawal and solitude can never adequately compensate for the failure of love.

At the same time I knew that if I stayed in this room a few days an entirely new life could begin—like the soldering of human flesh after an operation. It is the terror of this new life, more than the terror of dying, which arouses me (*HI*, p. 32).

So aroused, she rushes from the room in a state which borders upon lunacy, and the movement ends with a series of feverish images of despair and anxiety: the self, deliberately barricaded against invasion by others from without, now suffers invasion from within in the form of nightmares: a ship whose sails have been ripped; black seas filled with hissing purple serpents; trees deadened and withered by pain; a white prison-house shaped, ironically, like an egg and approached by a cactus-bordered path.

In this brief movement, which is really a continuation of the second, the dream of withdrawal comes to a climax: the narrator retreats further and further from earthly life, and the images, appropriately, are astronomical. The section may thus be viewed as a kind of excursion into space—only it is inner rather than outer space.

The nightmares continue ("The dream! the dream! . . . It brushes by me with bat wings when I open human eyes and seek to live dreamlessly"), but here they present themselves in images of dissociation involving a sense of distance ("I feel the distance like a wound. It unrolls itself like a rug before the steps of a cathedral for a wedding or a burial.") And the distance is conceived vertically as well as horizontally: "I rise, I always rise after the crucifixion, and I am in terror of my ascensions." And again, "Everything for me took place either in the belfry where I was alone with the deafening sound of bells calling in iron voices, or in the cellar where I nibbled at the candles stored away with the mice."

Miss Nin's researches into anxiety neuroses serve her to good purpose in this movement. Thus, the paragraph on pages 39–40 describes the hypersensitivity so often encountered in cases of this type, as well as the sensation, almost equally common, of the kind of total awareness that enables the individual, as in a mystic vision, to view the past, the present, and even the future as one continuous whole, and to "remember" not merely in the Jungian sense of participation in a collective unconscious, but also in the sense that he can identify with previous forms of existence, even nonhuman existence: "I am constantly reconstructing a pattern of something forever lost and which I cannot forget . . . I remember the cold on Jupiter . . . Bands of ammonia and methane encircling Uranus. I remember the tornadoes of inflammable methane on Saturn. I remember on Mars a vegetation like the tussock grasses of Peru and Patagonia, an ochrous red, a rusty ore vegetation, mosses and lichens."

Even in this state of extreme withdrawal, the narrator is conscious of having retained from her relationship with

Sabina the habit of lying ("I am enmeshed in my lies, and I want absolution.") It is as if the Ariadne's thread referred to in the preceding movement as connecting her with reality had here been broken. But her lies have a different source from Sabina's: their purpose is to shield men from the truth they cannot bear to face; they are *mensonges vitales*,[9] and the images in which they are described have a protective, even a maternal quality: "I cannot tell the truth because I have felt the heads of men in my womb." This paragraph, the penultimate of the section, is not easy to justify, even by the logic of association; though not precisely an irrelevance, it does, I think, constitute an intrusion.

The fourth movement, and the two which follow it, depict the agony of a brother-sister relationship, a relationship which, on the physical level, is, like that of Sabina and the narrator, never consummated. Jeanne's [10] crippled leg is the outward sign of her moral infirmity, the badge of her deviation: [11] it symbolizes the perverse and guilty passion from which she cannot free herself. She is, at the same time, a superior individual, possessed of dignity and even a certain nobility, with eyes that are "higher than the human level." Though she sings "I love my brother," the narcissism which is frequently at the root of such relationships is revealed by the telltale gestures with which she regards herself in the mirror. And she too is the victim of hypersensitivity: the passage on page 45, in which she describes to the narrator her marriage, reminds one of Poe's description of Roderick Usher, another incestuous lover who suffers from a similar exacerbation of the nerves.[12] Here, of course, the sound of the bells is particularly painful because, longing for her brother, Jeanne does not wish to hear them.

Because of her suffering, she too is tempted to withdraw from the earth, and the request which she makes of the narrator ("Please give me that heavy book. I need to put something heavy like that on top of my head. I have to place my feet under the pillows always, so as to be able to stay on earth. Otherwise I feel myself going away, going

away at a tremendous speed . . .") reminds one strongly
of the latter's predicament in the previous two movements; it is for this reason that she is enabled to sympathize with Jeanne—they are, in fact, sisters in suffering.
But Jeanne, at the same time that she welcomes this
sympathy, fears the narrator because she has made her the
confidante of her terrible secret. The narrator seeks to
console her ("The fear of madness will burn down the
walls of our secret house and send us out into the world
seeking warm contact") but she will not let herself be
comforted, haunted as she is by images of dissociation.

> When I sit before my mirror I laugh at myself. I am
> brushing my hair. Here are a pair of eyes, two long braids,
> two feet. I look at them like dice in a box, wondering if I
> should shake them, would they still come out and be ME. I
> cannot tell how all these separate pieces can be ME . . .
> When I shake hands I feel that the person is so far away
> that he is in the other room, and that my hand is in the
> other room. When I blow my nose I have a fear that it
> might remain on the handkerchief (*HI*, pp. 47–48).

Since Jeanne will not permit herself any physical expression of her passion, she must resort to furtive means of
gratification: she must kiss her brother's shadow rather
than the man himself, and the passage describing this
gesture is one of the most moving in the book, as it is also
one of the most beautifully written.

> When my brother sat in the sun and his face was shadowed
> on the back of the chair I kissed his shadow. I kissed his
> shadow and this kiss did not touch him, this kiss was lost in
> the air and melted with the shadow. Our love of each other
> is like one long shadow kissing, without hope of reality
> (*HI*, p. 48).

The role played by the narrator in the three movements
dealing with Jeanne and her brother requires a word of
comment. She is not here, as in the first two movements,
the central character, but she is involved in their drama of
suffering, and the nature of her involvement is interesting.
It will be remembered that in the preceding section her

affinity with Jeanne has been suggested in two ways: the tendency, which both experienced, to withdraw from the earth, and the feeling, which both of them also shared, of loss of identity expressed in images of dissociation. The implication cannot be ignored that the relationship in which the narrator stands to the brother and sister, and more particularly to the latter, is also partly of an incestuous character; there is thus a family resemblance not merely in the sense that they are all three sufferers, but also in the sense that their suffering, ultimately, has the same source: self-love. The *genus* is identical; it is only the *differentia* that distinguish them: the narrator, that is, loves herself in the form of another woman; Jeanne loves herself in the form of her brother. It is in acknowledgment of this affinity that Jeanne, at the beginning of the present movement (the fifth) leads the narrator "into the house of incest," where indeed they are all of them at home.

The model for this house was an actual one in Switzerland, owned by an eccentric of Miss Nin's acquaintance, whose inhabitants actually conversed with one another by means of small windows built into the walls so that, as in the book, "one might talk in the dark from room to room, without seeing each other's face." As a symbol of incest this house is valuable in two ways: it suggests the guilt of which its occupants are forever conscious, and also the prison-like sense of their isolation. The unreality and the lifelessness of their situation is emphasized by the fact that the main windows open "on a static sea, where immobile fishes had been glued to painted backgrounds." "Everything," she continues, "had been made to stand still in the house of incest, because they all had such a fear of movement and warmth, such a fear that all love and all life should flow out of reach and be lost." Jeanne's predicament here reminds us somewhat of Quentin's, in Faulkner's *The Sound and the Fury*, who is enamored of his sister and who would like to live with her forever in a place outside of time—as Cleanth Brooks puts it, "in some cozy private niche in hell." [13]

The "room which could not be found" corresponds to

the secret which the guilty pair keep hidden from the outside world and perhaps, at times, even from themselves. It is airless, viewless, and is described as a place "where the mind and the blood coalesced in a union without orgasm and rootless like those of fishes." It is a place not merely of sterility but also of exclusiveness, the "fortress of their love." The painting of Lot and his daughter referred to on page 40 is, since it represents a classic case of incest, more than a mere decorative detail and is obviously appropriate to the situation.

The movement closes with a series of three symbols: a clock, a thicket of "decapitated trees," and a forest of plaster eggs. The clock on which one cannot find "the truth" refers both to the secrecy of the relationship, the guilt that cannot squarely be faced and recognized, and to the timelessness of this special world. The trees, with their "truncated undecagon figures," whose natural forms have been distorted into artificial and arbitrary forms, into "intellectual contortions," symbolize the unnatural relationship of the brother and sister. This passage, in which the wailing natural forms rebel against the shapes they have been made to assume, is one of the most effective in the book.

> The torso of a tube-rose, the knee of Achilles, tubercles and excrescences, the foot of a mummy in rotted wood, the veined docile wood carved into human contortions. The forest must weep and bend like the shoulders of men, dead figures inside of live trees. A forest animated now with intellectual faces, intellectual contortions. Trees become man and woman, two-faced, nostalgic for the shivering of leaves. Trees reclining, woods shining, and the forest trembling with rebellion so bitter I heard its wailing within its deep forest consciousness. Wailing the loss of its leaves and the failure of transmutation (*HI*, p. 56).

The source of these images was a visit which Miss Nin paid to the studio of Ossip Zadkine in Paris,[14] just as the source of the final symbol, of the eggs, was the sculpture of Brancusi. These eggs, being of plaster, are (like the egg-shaped prison house in the second movement) a parody of genuine eggs, thus a comment upon the sterility of the House of Incest.

The sixth movement, and the final one devoted to the brother-sister relationship, begins with an imaginary drama in which Jeanne loses her brother and succeeds, with the help of the other occupants, in discovering his whereabouts: he has concealed himself from her in the above-mentioned secret room which symbolizes their guilt. The main window in this room has its blinds tightly closed; it is "without light like a closed eye, choked by the hairy long arm of old ivy."

The sister is the aggressor in this relationship. She suffers actively, he passively, and her discovery of his hiding place represents, perhaps, her recognition that the only way in which they can fulfill their love is in the actual act of incest—an act which the fact of his concealment proves his reluctance to commit. Anguished by this knowledge, Jeanne, in the passage at bottom of page 60 (which recalls the one on page 46, previously mentioned) makes a conscious gesture of withdrawal: the "death" referred to is, of course, a spiritual death—death-in-life. This rejection is exactly analogous to the rejection of Sabina by the narrator in the second movement, and the analogy is quite conscious: the author is seeking to represent the actions of people trapped in impossible situations and making desperate efforts to escape their certain doom. For the sake of symmetry, these movements of attraction and withdrawal, which the characters make, follow a definite pattern almost like that of a formal dance, and indeed after the initial frenzy of the search this movement has a strongly stylized quality. Consider, for example, this minuet-like gesture:

> They bowed to one part of themselves only—their likeness.
> —Good night, my brother!
> —Good night, Jeanne! (HI, p. 61).

The passage wherein, in this after-life which is really a form of death-in-life, Jeanne encounters her brother "asleep among the paintings" is analogous to that in the third movement wherein she kisses his shadow. Rather than love the woman, he will worship her portrait.

> I fell in love with your portrait, Jeanne, because it will never change. I have such a fear of seeing you grow old, Jeanne; I fell in love with an unchanging you that will never be taken away from me. I was wishing you would die, so that no one could take you away from me, and I would love the painting of you as you would look eternally. (*HI*, p. 61).

Here we are reminded not only of Faulkner's Quentin [15] but also, and perhaps even more strongly, of Wilde's Dorian Gray.

The final movement begins with another dance-like gesture, this time on the part of the narrator, who takes refuge in her work (the book referred to in the opening paragraph is *House of Incest*) from the suffering in which she has participated vicariously through her involvement with Jeanne and her brother. Even within the privacy of her book, however, she cannot escape the suffering created by her own hypersensitivity, the "seeing too much"; her overstimulated imagination is still busy seeing "a tragedy in the quiver of an eyelid, constructing a crime in the next room."

> As I move within my book I am cut by pointed glass and broken bottles in which there is still the odor of sperm and perfume (*HI*, p. 62).

This too is incestuous activity: she has transferred the interest she has taken in Sabina and the siblings (which, as we have seen, was really a form of self-interest) into an interest in the characters of her own creation—one of whom is, of course, herself disguised as the narrator. The lies referred to at the top of page 67 are the lies of fiction, the "fairytale" which disguises the truth, and she is once more conscious that they are indeed lies. It is this consciousness, this Ariadne's thread connecting her with reality, that is her immunity against madness: "I am wrapped in lies which do not penetrate my soul, as if the lies I tell were like costumes." But the solitude of the artist can also be painful, as she soon discovers.

It is in the final pages of *House of Incest* that the resemblance to Mirbeau's *Jardin des Supplices* is most apparent. We are introduced to three "exhibits," all of them depicting extremes of psychological anguish whose source is self-obsession. Exhibit A is the paralytic whose actions cannot keep pace with his ambitions and who is thereby rendered immobile.

> I want to tell the whole truth, but I cannot tell the whole truth because I would have to write four pages all at once, like four long columns simultaneously, four pages to the present one, and so I do not write at all [16] (*HI*, pp. 67–68).

Exhibit B is the extreme example of hypersensitivity: lacking a skin, there is no contact, however gentle, which he can endure without suffering.[17] His extreme agony justifies the crucifixion image according to which he is the "modern Christ, who is crucified by his own nerves." Here it should be commented that the dialogue among the paralytic, the modern Christ, and the narrator suffers for lack of a gloss which would identify the speakers more clearly. Exhibit C, the armless dancer whose motions have no relation to the music which she cannot hear, is the woman who has been crippled by her possessiveness: "I was punished for clinging. I clung. I clutched all those I loved; I clutched at the lovely moments of life; my hands closed upon every full hour." Her dance is evidence of the extent to which she is out of phase with normal life and love: ignoring the music which is real, she is doing a crazy jig to some tune in her own head.

It will be noted that the suffering of the various occupants of the House of Incest is enhanced by their realization that they have not found the instrument which will free them from their predicament, the key which will release them from their cells. As the modern Christ says, "If only we could all escape from this house of incest, where we only love ourselves in the other, if only I could save you all from yourselves." But they lack the courage to make the effort, and believe themselves incapable of it.

> But none of us could bear to pass through the tunnel which led from the house into the world on the other side of the walls, where there were leaves on the trees, where water ran beside the paths, where there was daylight and joy. We could not believe that the tunnel would open on daylight: we feared to be trapped into darkness again; we feared to return whence we had come, from darkness and night. The tunnel would narrow and taper down as we walked; it would close around us, and close tighter and tighter around us and stifle us. It would grow heavy and narrow and suffocate us as we walked (*HI*, p. 70).

Nevertheless, they know that beyond the tunnel daylight does exist:

> Yet we knew that beyond the house of incest there was daylight, and none of us could walk towards it (*HI*, p. 70).

The knowledge that they are their own prisoners is perhaps the greatest torture of all.

AS PUBLISHED BY Dutton in 1948,[1] *Winter of Artifice* consisted of two parts, entitled "Djuna" and "The Voice"
respectively, and this is the form in which most readers are
now familiar with the story. As originally published by the
Obelisk Press in 1939, however, *Winter of Artifice* consisted only of the first part; "The Voice" was conceived as
a sort of sequel to the earlier story and was thus joined to
it in the later edition.[2]

Actually there is little connection between the two
parts: "Djuna" is the story of a romance between a girl
and her father—a romance which, like that in *House of
Incest*, is never consummated physically—while "The
Voice" is the story of a psychoanalyst's relations with his
patients. The only link between the two is the character of
Djuna, who figures in the latter as one of the Voice's
patients. The reader is expected to infer that she has
sought analysis as a result of the traumatic experience with
her father; it is in this sense, and in this sense only, that
"The Voice" can be considered a sequel to "Djuna."
Actually the title *Winter of Artifice* as applied to both
stories is rather misleading, since it has reference only to
the romance between the girl and her father.

Readers of the *Diary*, seeing certain resemblances between it and *Winter of Artifice*, may be tempted to identify the character of Djuna with the author, but here a
word of warning becomes necessary. Though (especially at

this stage) Miss Nin's fiction relies heavily upon her journal, it is important to remember that it is still fiction: Djuna, her father, and the analyst of "The Voice" are all composite portraits, and the reader must not make the mistake of identifying them completely with any of the real-life individuals by whom they were undoubtedly suggested but who are present in them only partially. For unless this caution be observed, the charge made by Vernon Young in *The Hudson Review* (Autumn, 1948) is only too pertinent: "The critical vocabulary balks at the very concept, fiction, for has one not been told that Miss Nin's work is drawn from a massive and never-ending diary? One is morally blackmailed at the start, since, by this entangling alliance, strictly *literary* criticism is almost proscribed." [3]

Part One begins by describing the reunion in Paris between father and daughter after a separation of twenty years, a reunion for which the girl, during all this time, has never ceased to long romantically: she has cast him in the role of Prince Charming, a role which, when she meets him again, he seems to play to perfection—on the surface, at any rate. Finding her beautiful and intelligent and thus fulfilling *his* image of *her*, he is similarly attracted. The two enjoy a brief ecstasy in an idyllic setting at Valescure, in the south of France, but the idyl is interrupted by scenes of mutual jealousy. Returning to Paris, they attempt to continue the relationship; the daughter, however, gradually becomes disillusioned when she realizes how little her real father corresponds to the idealized creature of her imagination, and sadly abandons the relationship. Occasional flashbacks (such as the one describing her arrival in New York as a child, taken almost word for word from the *Diary*) relieve the straightforward progression of the narrative.

To some readers it may appear that the relationship between Djuna and her father was actually consummated, and indeed it is possible so to interpret the story. This, however, was not the author's intention, and the careful reader will note that in one of the scenes at Valescure she refers to Djuna as "the *mystical* [italics mine] bride of her father." It is true that they speak the language of lovers—which, of course, they are, but in exactly the same sense that Jeanne and her brother are lovers in *House of Incest*. Readers were misled by this dialogue and by the reference to Djuna's pregnancy and stillborn child: since there is no reference to a husband or to another lover, except the oblique one on page 74 (Swallow edition), it might naturally be assumed that the child is her father's. But Miss Nin did not intend for the reader to reach this conclusion; and the lack of such a reference, which would have cleared up the matter, is, she has conceded, a structural flaw in the story. The omission could, perhaps, be justified in terms of the theory of the antinovel, in which she was interested at the time, and which held it unnecessary to account, in conventional realistic manner, for every action in the story—the ideal being rather to focus on the concrete details of single scenes and to abstract or omit the remainder. Certainly in this age of psychoanalysis, when the tendency of young girls to worship their fathers (and to attempt, usually unconsciously, to supplant the mother) is acknowledged to be a recognizable pattern of adolescent behavior, no reader need be shocked at the intensity of Djuna's feelings, nor be obliged to conclude that the affair found physical expression. In Djuna's case, because of the circumstance of her having been separated from her father for two decades, the pattern was merely prolonged beyond the period of adolescence, and the force of her passion was a cumulative thing, twenty years in the making.

In any case, and granting the possibility that *Winter of Artifice* can, like *The Turn of the Screw*, be read in two ways, physical love is not what the story is *about*. The reader who finds the question of whether Djuna actually slept with her father to be important is missing the point of the book. *Winter of Artifice* is perhaps the least sensational of Miss Nin's works—a wistful, coming-of-age story with a stern underlying moral: that it is fatal for the lover to invent an a priori image of the beloved, since the strain of living up to this image destroys the ease and naturalness of the relationship.[4] One is reminded here of the statement in the *Diary*, "Idealism is the death of the body and the imagination." The lover who does this—and inevitably every lover does, in varying degree—is guilty not only of injustice but even of positive cruelty to the object of his passion. When Djuna discovers that her father is not the *beau ideal* of her fantasies, that he is unfaithful (so that she is obliged to supplant not merely the mother but other women as well) and shallow, she is crushed; but in reality she has only herself to blame for having harbored an impossible illusion. On the other hand, the indignation which the father feels when he discovers his daughter has a life of her own, whose interests exclude his, is misplaced, for his error consists in imagining that his daughter's personality was identical to his own.

At this point the reader may wonder why, if this is indeed the theme of the story, Miss Nin did not select a more "normal" pair of lovers to dramatize it than a father and his daughter. But just as in *House of Incest* (to which the first part of *Winter of Artifice* bears a much closer resemblance than it does to the second part), Miss Nin's theme in this story is the failure of love, and the reason for this failure is exactly the same as it was in the earlier one: in fashioning the beloved after his own wishes, the lover, rather than worshiping the loved object in and for himself, is actually worshiping *a part of himself*, so that the situation contains elements of incest *ab initio*. Thus, the choice of a pair of incestuous lovers to dramatize this general predicament—which is nothing less than that of the human condition—is, symbolically, exactly right. Djuna's infatuation for her father thus represents, like the relationship described in *House of Incest*, one of the stages of pre-love.

The process by which Djuna becomes disenchanted furnishes the narrative thread along which are strung all the incidents that comprise the story. The difficulty begins when her father reads the diary she has been keeping during all the years of their separation.

He observed that after two years of obsessional yearning for him she had finally exhausted her suffering and obtained serenity. After serenity she had fallen in love with an Irish boy and then with a violinist. He was offended that she had not died completely, that she had not spent the rest of her life yearning after him (WA, p. 79).

Perceiving his jealousy, she adopts the following strategy:

When she became aware of his jealousy she began immediately to give him what he desired . . . she began to relate the incidents of her life in a deprecatory manner, in a mocking tone, in such a way that he might feel she had not loved deeply anything or anyone but him. Understanding his desire to be universally loved, to be at the core of every life he touched, she could not bring herself to talk with fervor or admiration of all she loved or enjoyed. To be so aware of his feelings forced her into a role. She gave a color to the past which could be interpreted as: nothing that happened before you came was of any importance.
The result was that nothing appeared in its true light and that she deformed her true self (WA, pp. 79–80).

A note of dishonesty has crept into the relationship, and the discord increases when she makes a curious discovery,

What he noted in her diary were only the passages which recalled their sameness. She began naturally to think that he loved in her only what there was of himself, that beyond the realm of self-discovery, self-love, there was no curiosity (WA, pp. 83–84).

Here, of course, we are back once more to the theme of *House of Incest.*

Her doubt recurs in the long stream-of-consciousness passage (pages 84–88) [5] which attempts to convey, in a series of surrealist images of which perhaps the most striking is that in which Djuna passes a violin bow between her legs "drawing music out of her body," something of the effect of an orchestra playing in unison—it is, we are told, the orchestra of their desire, and they dance to it together. Nevertheless she finds herself asking,

Can we live in rhythm, my father? Can we feel in rhythm, my father? Can we think in rhythm, my father? (WA, p. 88).

But it is in the train on which they are returning to Paris that she finally realizes the truth. She has been trying to conceal it from herself by means of the lying imagination, but it can no longer be denied.

> By certain signs she recognized all her pretenses. Every time she had pretended to feel more than she felt, she experienced this sickness of heart, this cramp and tenseness of her body. By this sign she recognized her insincerities. At the core nothing ever was false. Her feelings had never deceived her. It was only her imagination which deceived her. Her imagination could give a color, a smell, a beauty to things, even a warmth which her body knew very well to be unreal.
>
> In her head there could be a great deal of acting and many strange things could happen in there, but her emotions were sincere and they revolted, they prevented her from getting lost down the deep corridors of her inventions. Through them she knew. They were her eyes, her divining rod, they were her truth (WA, pp. 89–90).

The passage is very typical, and in it we recognize the combined influence of Lawrence ("In her head there could be a great deal of acting . . . but her emotions were sincere") and Rank ("At the core nothing ever was false").

Back in Paris, she enters the period which she refers to as the "winter of artifice."

> There was no change in his love, but the mask was back again as soon as he returned to Paris. The whole pattern of his artificial life began again. He had stopped talking as he talked down south. He was conversing. It was the beginning of his salon life. There were always people around with whom he kept up a tone of lightness and humor. In the evenings she had to appear in his salon and talk with the tip of her tongue about every thing that was far from her thoughts (WA, p. 95).

One might speculate that Djuna here shows signs of jealousy herself, and the real source of her dissatisfaction may well be a reluctance to share her father with his friends. It is clear at any rate that she is still emotionally involved; otherwise she would sever the relationship. In her heart she realizes that she is making a mistake, and that the romance is doomed, but she cannot as yet bring herself to leave. The distance between them is widening, however, to the point where she can analyze the situation quite objectively. For instance, she recalls an occasion when, in Valescure, her father eased a sore foot by removing one of his shoes.

> As he pulled off his sock she saw the foot of a woman. It was delicate and perfectly made, sensitive and small. She felt as if he had stolen it from her: it was her foot she was looking at, her foot he was holding in his hand . . . To this foot she could have said: "I know you." She recognized the lightness, the speed of it. "I know you, but if you are my foot I do not love you. I do not love my own foot" (WA, p. 91).

Immediately after this she is conscious of a confusion of identities which recalls the relationship in *House of Incest* between the narrator and Sabina. The situations are completely analogous, since both are forms of self-love.

> A confusion of feet. She is not alone in the world. She has a double. He sits on the running board of the car and when he sits there she does not know where she is. She is standing there pitying his foot, and hating it too, because of the confusion. If it were someone else's foot her love could flow out freely, all around, but here her love stands still inside her, still with a kind of fright (WA, pp. 91–92).

The torture is almost as intense as in the other book, and has the same source.

> There is no distance for her to traverse; it chokes inside of her, like the coils of self-love, and she cannot feel any love for this sore foot because that love leaps back into her like a perpetually coiled snake, and she wants always to leap outside of herself. She wants to flow out, and here her love lies coiled inside and choking her, because her father is her double, her shadow, and she does not know which one is

real. One of them must die so that the other may find the boundaries of himself. To leap out freely beyond the self, love must flow out and beyond this wall of confused identities. Now she is all confused in her boundaries. She doesn't know where her father begins, where she begins, where it is he ends, what is the difference between them (WA, p. 92).

The passage concerning the father's foot is an excellent example of Miss Nin's ability to see the significances that lie in the ordinary, and to explore and develop them with a poet's imagination.

As Djuna's separation from her father increases, she is able to see the less pleasing aspects of his personality: his uncompromising rigidity, his vanity, his fanatical meticulousness and devotion to detail, his fear of life, his shallowness, his faithlessness, the ruthlessness which he conceals beneath the perfect manners. His worship of discipline is perhaps the chief source of their incompatibility: her nature is essentially uninhibited, and she is conscious of his disapproval even when he does not voice it. To express this consciousness, Miss Nin again resorts to the orchestra image.

> You held the conductor's baton, but no music could come from the orchestra because of your severity. As soon as you left my heart beat in great disorder. Everything melted into music, and I could dance through the streets singing, without an orchestra leader. I could dance and sing (WA, p. 100).

The difference between their temperaments is defined in relation to their respective concepts of music: to him it means discipline; to her, liberation.

> Motion was music. Her father was the musician, but in life he arrested music. Music melts all the separate parts of our bodies together. Every rusty fragment, every scattered piece could be melted into one rhythm. A note was a whole, and it was in motion, ascending or descending, swelling in fullness or thrown away, thrown out into the air, but always moving.
>
> As soon as she left her father she heard music again. It was falling from the trees, pouring from throats, twinkling

from the street lamps, sliding down the gutter. It was her faith in the world which danced again. It was the expectation of miracles which made every misery sound like part of a symphony. Not separateness but oneness was music (WA, p. 99).

Occasionally, now, they are capable of conscious cruelty to each other. Djuna says, "I don't mind what you think of me," and when she tells him she is pregnant his reply is simply, "Now you are worth less on the market as a woman." It is not so much that she is jealous (though, reading between the lines, it is difficult to escape the conclusion that she is) as that she resents his attempts to deceive her, "She did not mind his philandering, but she was eager for the truth." She reproaches him, saying, "I thought we were above questions of good and evil. I am not saying you are bad. That does not concern me. I am only saying that you are *false* with me." At this he flies into a rage, and the break is permanently effected.

When Djuna was a small child, her father went away on a concert tour, and the girl threw herself upon him clutching his coat and crying, "Don't leave me!" In a beautifully written passage, Miss Nin endows this gesture with a symbolic meaning for the mature woman.

> It was so hard for her to believe that this father she was still trying to hold on to was no longer real or important, that the coat she was touching was not warm, that the body of him was not human, that her breathing, tragic desire had come to an end, and that her love had died. *Today she held the coat of a dead love* (WA, p. 118).

And Djuna's stillborn child is also made to serve a symbolic purpose: just as the child died in her body, the little girl who fell in love with her father also dies.

> The last time she had come out of the ether it was to look at her dead child, a little girl with long eyelashes and slender hands. She was dead.
> The little girl in her was dead too. The woman was saved. And with the little girl died the need of a father (WA, p. 119).

As a novelist Miss Nin's favorite subject is the myriad emotional influences which her characters exert upon one another: she has an obsessive interest in depicting the nuances of feeling, which are forever changing as the relationships she describes pass through their successive stages. In this respect, at least, none of her works is more successful than *Winter of Artifice* (Part One). The characters of her fiction are defined not in terms of their relation to their environment, or to any abstract principle or idea, but of their relation to one another personally, as individuals. Because this relation is seldom constant or really predictable, her most memorable characters are never static; they are capable, like the people we meet in our everyday lives, of occasionally surprising us. And in this connection it is interesting to compare the characterization of Djuna with that of her father. Djuna, who is of course the real protagonist, undergoes considerable change; the father, hopelessly set in his ways ("congealed," as Miss Nin says, "into an attitude") is incapable of change—incapable, certainly, of changing into the image she has invented of him—and stasis, in fiction as in life, is death. This is not to say that he is uninteresting (for a corpse he is amazingly lifelike), only that the task of creating him was simpler. Actually he is very real, with his *Tabac Blond*, his gold-tipped cigarettes in their filtered holder, his lumbago, his perfectionism, his carefully manicured nails, his elegant gloves, his feelings of guilt, his fear of life (disguised as fear of death) symbolized by his compulsive habit of washing his hands.

> He washed his hands continuously. He had a mania for washing and disinfecting himself. The fear of microbes played a very important part in his life. The fruit had to be washed with filtered water. His mouth must be disinfected. The silverware must be passed over an alcohol lamp like the doctor's instruments. He never ate the part of the bread which his fingers had touched.
>
> Her father had never imagined that he may have been trying to cleanse and disinfect his soul of his lies, his callousness, his deception. For him the only danger came

from the microbes which attacked the body. He had not
studied the microbe of conscience which eats into the soul
(WA, pp. 110–11).

But it is the reality of a photographic image—registered,
to be sure, with remarkable accuracy on a sensitive plate,
though it might be objected that the hand-washing gesture, in this age of psychological awareness, is too much of
a cliché. In a sense, of course, it is appropriate that the
father's character should be immovable: stasis, as we have
noted, is death, and the author is using him quite consciously as a death symbol: "She always left his house with
a feeling of having come near to death because everything
there was so clearly a fight against death." In any case, it is
in relation to the father that the character of Djuna is
defined for us.

> He had chosen to live on the surface, and she to descend
> deeper and deeper. His fundamental desire was to escape
> pain, hers to face all of life. Instead of coming out of his
> shell to face the disintegration of their relationship he
> eluded the truth. He had not discovered as she had that by
> meeting the person she feared to meet, by reading the letter
> she feared to read, by giving life a chance to strike at her
> she had discovered that it struck less cruelly than the imagi-
> nation. To imagine was far more terrible than reality, be-
> cause it took place in a void, it was untestable . . . To fight
> a real sorrow, a real loss, a real insult, a real disillusion, a
> real treachery was infinitely less difficult than to spend a
> night without sleep struggling with ghosts. The imagination
> is far better at inventing tortures than life because the
> imagination is a demon within us and it knows where to
> strike, where it hurts. It knows the vulnerable spot, and life
> does not, our friends and lovers do not, because seldom do
> they have the imagination equal to the task (WA, p. 106).

This insight of Djuna's (and there are others which are
equally wise) might be used to discredit the criticism
which is frequently made of Miss Nin's work, that it is not
sufficiently "down to earth." A more legitimate criticism,
perhaps, is that it is often lacking in a sense of humor—a
point made by Elizabeth Hardwick in a generally unsym-

pathetic review.[6] Her characters, in this novel at any rate, take themselves with intense seriousness, as do Lawrence's and Poe's—and indeed those of most romantic novelists. And speaking of Poe, the resemblance of Djuna's father to Roderick Usher is unmistakable.

> Noise was his greatest enemy. His nerves, as vibrant as the strings of a violin, had endowed or cursed him with uncanny hearing. A fly in the room could prevent him from sleeping. He had to put cotton in his ears in order to dull his oversensitive hearing (WA, p. 77).

And like the brother in Poe's story, which also has an incest theme, Djuna's father is a scholar of esoterica—an authority on the music of remote periods.

But if there is little humor there is a great deal of compassion,[7] and here Miss Nin is much closer to Lawrence than to Poe. Even in the extremity of her disillusion, Djuna is enabled to feel pity for her father, and the author's compassion includes both of them—as it included all the characters in *House of Incest*. And humor, to be sure, is not entirely lacking—Miss Hardwick was mistaken there—though it is humor of a sly, sophisticated, and intensely feminine sort. Thus when the father boasts to Djuna that his indifference to a woman enamored of him caused her to burst into tears, ruining her make-up, Djuna knows he is lying.

> When a woman weeps the rimmel comes off, but not the lipstick, and besides, all elegant women have acquired a technique of weeping which has no such fatal effect on the make-up. You wept just enough to fill the eyes with tears and no more. No overflow. The tears stay inside the cups of the eyes, the rimmel is preserved, and yet the sadness is sufficiently expressive. After a moment one can repeat the process with the same dexterity which could fill a liqueur glass exactly to the brim. One tear too much could bring about a catastrophe, but these only came uncontrolled in the case of a deep love (WA, pp. 107–8).

I have said that Miss Nin is a romantic, but is this a romantic observation? It sounds more like DeMaupassant, or even Colette, but the quality of the humor is really that of the eighteenth century, and would have delighted the author of *The Rape of the Lock*.

Part Two ("The Voice") opens with an impressionistic description of the "Hotel Chaotica," which was an actual building in New York where Miss Nin lived and practiced as a lay analyst. In the story, however, it is the Voice who is the recipient of the confidences that make up the bulk of the narrative, and here it is proper to recall our earlier warning against identifying these characters with individuals in real life. But even if we recognize that they are composites, and refuse them any but a fictional reality, a problem arises concerning the identities of Djuna and Lilith, for these, as we shall presently see, have not been sufficiently separated: in particular Lilith (who is the prototype of Lillian in *Cities of the Interior*) is inadequately defined, and to make matters even more confusing, one of the minor characters in "The Voice" is also named Lillian. This is undoubtedly the weakest of Miss Nin's longer narratives; the blurring may have been deliberate, but it can scarcely be called successful. Certain individual scenes are sharply realized, but, because the characters remain shadowy and elusive, the scenes do not add up to a unified whole.[8]

When the story opens, Djuna is undergoing analysis from the Voice, and the dialogue between them is one of the better parts of the story. She complains of a feeling of detachment in crowds: "I seem to be standing and watching this current passing and I am left behind. Why have I the feeling they all pass like the day, the leaves, the moods of climate, into death?" The Voice explains, "Because you are standing still and measuring time by your immobility, the others seem to run too fast toward an end. If you were living and running with them, you would cease to be aware of this death that is actually in you because you are watching." Consciousness of the source of her depression is the first step in the cure: Djuna resolves that she will participate in life rather than merely observe it, and the cure is effected.

Djuna walked out into the street . . . she stood in the center of the street eddies, and suddenly she knew the extent of her fear of flowing, of yielding, of depending on another. Suddenly she began walking faster than whoever was walking beside her, to feel the exultation of passing them . . . Moving, moving. Flowing, flowing, flowing. When she was watching, everything that moved seemed to be moving away, but when moving, this was only a tide, and the self turning, rotating, was feeding the rotation of desire (WA, p. 124).

The passage is interesting because it marks the first appearance in Miss Nin's fiction of an image which becomes obsessional in her later work: the flowing of water, which symbolizes active engagement with life and harmonious union between the conscious and unconscious. There was some preparation for this in the opening pages of *House of Incest*, which describe the blissfulness of the prenatal experience, but that experience was a completely passive one. Toward the end of "The Voice" the image, as we shall see, is expanded and made even more explicit.

The incident of Djuna's analysis is followed by two other "case histories." The first concerns a lesbian violinist whose guilt feelings have overwhelmed her to the point that she is no longer able to play. Though her personality is not masculine, she has convinced herself that she cannot enjoy normal sexual intercourse: "I'm sure I wouldn't like it with a man—I tried it once with a toothbrush, and I didn't like it." Nevertheless, she "transfers" onto her analyst the emotion she has previously felt for her lesbian partner, and is enabled finally to resume her work. The second case involves a cellist with a recently paralyzed hand; he also, since birth, has been handicapped by a badly crippled leg. The doctor notices he does not mention the leg, only the hand, and analysis discloses that the latter infirmity is a psychosomatic device for drawing attention away from the former.

The analyst, too, has problems of his own. In a passage which recalls the *Diary* and *The Seduction of the Minotaur*, he confesses to Djuna,

I want to do the things they do. At most I am allowed to watch. I am condemned to see through a perpetual keyhole every intimate scene of their life. But I am left out. Sometimes I want to be taken in. I want to be desired, possessed, tortured too (WA, p. 137).

Djuna reminds him that a woman has committed suicide that very morning by throwing herself from the twenty-fifth floor of the hotel.

You can't stop confessing them, you can't stop. A woman killed herself, right there, under your window; that noise you heard was the fall of her body. She was pregnant. And she was alone. That is why she killed herself (WA, p. 137).

But the analyst (who, it will be seen, has made Djuna his confessor) merely replies:

I listen to them all. They keep coming and coming. I thought at first that only a few of them were sick. I did not know that they were all sick and bursting with secrets. I did not know there was no end to their coming. Did you ever walk through the lobby? I have a feeling that down there they are all waiting to be confessed. They all have more to say than I have time to hear. I could sit here until I die and even then there will be women throwing themselves out of the window on the same floor on which I live (WA, pp. 137–38).

At this point in the narrative the focus shifts rather abruptly from Djuna to Lilith, who is described as meeting her brother on board the ship in which he has returned from India and later as undergoing analysis from the Voice. It is here that the identities of Djuna and Lilith become confused. Speaking of her father, the latter says,

My first feeling was that my father was not tied to anything . . . He was always leaving, forgetting, throwing out, betraying . . . I saw my father leaving and sending postcards from all over the world. The world was immense, it seemed to me, and he was in all of it except the corner where he left us. He not only took himself away, but our faith in the marvelous too. The world of our childhood closed with his departure (WA, p. 143).

And the analyst replies,

All these departures, these upheavals, gave you a hatred of change. You, in your anger and pain, stood in the center and refused to move, decided to make a fixed core within you. You accepted outer change, but fought against it by creating an inner static groove. You would not move. Everything else around you could move, change, but you, because of your mistrust of pain and loss, refused to move. You would be the island, the fixed center (WA, pp. 143–44).

One is forced to conclude either that these experiences of Djuna and Lilith are identical—which, since they are so specific, scarcely seems conceivable—or that the author has for some reason deliberately fused the two characters: what this reason is, however, remains something of a mystery.

In the story of her loveless marriage, Lilith's character is separated from Djuna's, but the fusion recurs when the Voice tells her, "I am not sure that the little girl in you ever died, or her need of a father" and confesses to her his need for an active rather than a vicarious participation in life: "I remain anonymous. I am only allowed to watch the spectacle, but I am not allowed to enter." Again, there is separation when Lilith falls in love with the Voice, but when the latter tells her, "You are seeking for a father," transposition takes place once more.

When Lilith tells Djuna, "I am falling in love with the Voice," the latter warns her, "Don't get any closer to him. If you come closer you will defeat your own salvation . . . You know what happens to a woman when she pursues a mirage, if she has an affair with a mirage?" The tone is maternal, and of course she is merely confirming the analyst's impression; nevertheless, it is hard to resist the suspicion that Djuna's advice is not motivated also by feelings of jealousy—particularly in the light of the scene which immediately follows, a scene of ecstasy blended with pathos: "To lie there, wishing perhaps to be a man for a moment, but as a woman knowing that there is no other way of possessing a woman than as a man." Nevertheless, she does not attempt to deceive Lillian—or herself. "None of this is love," she tells her. "We are the same woman," and continues,

> There is always the moment when all the outlines, the differences between women disappear, and we enter a world where all feelings, yours and mine, seem to issue from the same source. *We lose our separate identities* [italics mine]. What happens to you is the same as what happens to me. Listening to you is not entering a world different from my own, it is a kind of communion (WA, p. 161).

Here, perhaps, is the reason for the author's consistent confusion of the two characters, which may be merely a narrative device for rendering this particular dilemma, but the device is unsuccessful if only because the focus of the story is not on the relationship between Djuna and Lilith: the scene of this "communion" is incidental and comes almost at the end of the narrative.

The relationship between Lilith and the Voice, on the other hand, receives greater emphasis and is depicted with considerable skill. It is unsuccessful because, as he sadly realizes, he wants to be loved as a man rather than as a father, a "symbol of God," but she is interested in loving him only as a symbol.

> What she read in his eyes was the immense pleading of a man, imprisoned inside a seer, calling out for the life in her, and at the very moment when every cell inside her body closed to the desire of the man she saw a mirage before her as clearly as men saw it in the desert, and this mirage was a figure taller than other men, a type of savior, the man nearest to God, whose human face she could no longer see except for the immense hunger in his eyes (WA, p. 163).

The man, in fact, actually repels her.

> While the Voice who was no longer the Seer talked, what she saw was a dark-skinned mythological crab, the cavern-

ous sorrows of the monkey, the agedness of the turtle, the tenderness of the kangaroo, the facile humility of the dog (WA, pp. 163–64).

His insistence that she regard him as a man causes her to think of him with a certain contempt.

> In the Voice she felt the ugliness of tree roots, of the earth, and this terrific dark, mute knowing of the animal, for though he was the one most aware of what happened inside others he was the one least aware of what happened in himself. It was too near. He could read the myths and man's dreams but not his own soul. He did not know that the man in him had been denied. He was begging to be made man. The man had been buried within the sage. He had grown old, withered, without having fulfilled his life on earth. That is what his eyes were begging for: a life on earth. It was a father she was looking for, not a lover (WA, p. 164).

Finally he loses authority for her even as a symbol. It strikes her there is something rather ridiculous about this "little man brusquely deciphering each incident in her life"; his interpretations, she suspects, are arbitrary and merely ingenious.

> What he did not know was that at the same time she was losing her faith in all interpretations, since she saw how they could be manipulated to conceal the truth. She began to feel the illusory quality of all men's interpretations, and to believe only in her feelings (WA, pp. 168–69).

Her disillusionment is now complete, and the extent to which Djuna, consciously or unconsciously, may have been instrumental in the process is an interesting question, and one which the reader must answer for himself.

Though "The Voice" is fragmentary and suffers from lack of narrative unity—it is, as has been said, the least satisfactory of Miss Nin's works—it concludes with a dream description which is as beautiful as anything this author has ever written; it is, indeed, one of the most extraordinary passages in all dream literature. I refer to the last seven pages, printed in italics in all editions. The experience has three stages. In the first, the dream is conceived as a spiral, a labyrinth vertically conceived whose walls are "lined with moist silk"; this has been previously discussed in chapter 1. In the second, the dreamer's identity becomes fused with that of nonhuman forms,[9] the individual human consciousness merging with the primordial unconsciousness of the universe.

> I ceased to be a woman. The secret small pores of the being began to breathe a life of plant and flower. I went to sleep a human being and awakened with the nervous sensibility of a leaf, with the fin-knowledge of fish, with the hardness of coral, with the sulphurous eyes of a mineral. I awakened with eyes at the end of long arms that floated everywhere and with eyes at the soles of my feet. I awakened in strands of angel hair with lungs of cocoon milk . . . All forms became blurred and the woman who was lying there slowly turned into a heavy sea, carrying riches on her breast, or became earth with many fissures of thirst, drinking rain (WA, p. 173).

In the third stage, the concept of flux as harmony, which we noted earlier in our study of "The Voice," is objectified in the symbol of a landlocked boat struggling to reach its native element. The boat was an actual one which Miss Nin once saw in the yard of Maupassant's house at Etretat and about which she had many recurrent dreams.

> The boat I was pushing with all my strength because it could not float, it was passing through land. It was chokingly struggling to pass along the streets, it could not find its way to the ocean. It was pushed along the streets of the city, touching the walls of houses, and I was pushing it against the resistance of earth. So many nights against the obstacles of mud, marshes, garden paths through which the boat labored painfully (WA, p. 173).

The image is merely presented; it is not interpreted for us, and it is probable that when she wrote "The Voice" the author herself was not fully conscious of its significance. In "Houseboat" (*Under a Glass Bell*) and in *Four-Chambered Heart* this symbol receives further development, and in *Seduction of the Minotaur* it is articulated quite explicitly.

HOUSEBOATS, VEILS,
AND LABYRINTHS
*UNDER A GLASS BELL*

WHEN MISS NIN attempted to publish *Winter of Artifice* in this country [1] in 1942, she was unable to receive a single offer; publishers, without exception, labeled it uncommercial. But she was not discouraged. Borrowing a hundred dollars from the Gotham Book Mart, whose proprietress, Frances Steloff, has been for nearly half a century a fixture of the New York literary scene, particularly in its more avant-garde aspects,[2] and another hundred from a group of friends, she bought an antiquated printing press, operated by foot like a bicycle, and ninety pounds of type. She then learned to print, persuaded a stationer and a bookbinder to give her credit, and within two months succeeded in turning out five hundred copies. Illustrated with Ian Hugo's engravings, which she printed directly from his copperplates, this very beautiful edition is now a collector's item. In 1944, with some of the proceeds from *Winter of Artifice*, she printed, by the same method, three hundred copies [3] of her first collection of short stories, and when these were sold printed a second edition of a thousand copies. In 1948, Dutton, her first commercial publisher, reprinted these stories, together with "Hejda," which she had written in the meantime, and the two parts of *Winter of Artifice* with the title *Under a Glass Bell*. A fifth edition was issued by Alan Swallow in 1961.

In her foreword to the first American edition,[4] Miss Nin

wrote, "These stories represent the moment when many like myself had found only one answer to the suffering of the world: to dream, to tell fairy tales, to elaborate and to follow the labyrinth of fantasy." This was in 1944, and she had entered a phase of her career during which she was strongly preoccupied with ideas of social justice; some evidence of this preoccupation may be seen in such stories as "The Mouse" and "The Child Born Out of the Fog." [5] Therefore she added, a little apologetically, "All this, I see now, was the passive poet's only answer to the torments he witnessed . . . I am now in the difficult position of presenting stories which are dreams and of having to say: but now, although I give you these, I am awake!" The taste of the times, as she very well knew, favored a literature of engagement, which perhaps accounts for the tone of self-deprecation. But as Edmund Wilson pointed out in his first review of the book, "This poet has no need to apologize; her dreams reflect the torment, too." [6] The fact is that Miss Nin, at the time, seriously underestimated the importance of her achievement in these stories, which she now prefers above everything else she has written. "When people ask me what book of mine they should begin by reading," she has said, "I invariably reply, 'Under a Glass Bell.' If I had to choose one book by which I would like to be remembered, it is this one." The judgment of authors on their own work is traditionally erratic, yet Under a Glass Bell is certainly one of Miss Nin's best books and one of the most distinguished short story collections published in this country in the forties. It invites comparison with Joyce's Dubliners, and indeed it stands in very much the same relation to the body of her work as that collection does to Joyce's; it contains themes that are later developed more fully in the novels, and the extreme simplicity of the style (as in "Houseboat") as well as the humanitarianism of the attitude (in "The Mouse") reminds one irresistibly of the early Joyce. In Under a Glass Bell Miss Nin achieved a very nearly perfect balance between the realistic and symbolic levels, while some of her longer narratives are uneven in this respect.

The thirteen stories in this collection fall conveniently

into three groups: fantasies, realistic sketches, and portraits whose sources were real-life individuals but who emerge, like the characters in *Winter of Artifice*, as fictional composites. There is some overlapping, to be sure, as in the case of "Houseboat," which combines real and imaginary voyages, and "Ragtime," in which a realistic situation serves as the point of departure for speculation and fantasy; but these two stories belong more properly to the "labyrinth of fantasy" than to the category of realism. Together with "The Labyrinth" and "Through the Streets of My Own Labyrinth" they comprise the first group.

In "Houseboat" the protagonist occupies a dilapidated river boat on the Seine, moored to one of the Paris quays, and from its deck and through its portholes she observes the colorful, swarming life of the river and docks: alcoholic tramps, policemen chatting with prostitutes, fishermen ("The river communicated with them through the bamboo rods of their fishing tackle, transmitting its vibrations"), a sobbing child abandoned by his parents, the bright flags of laundry hung out to dry, the wife of a tugboat captain cooking lunch on deck. One day, because the King of England is coming for a visit, all the houseboat dwellers receive orders to move upstream, and a grand exodus takes place.

Symbolically the boat represents a kind of Noah's Ark, a place of refuge from the life of the city which threatens it, and its appropriateness as an image lies not merely in the fact that it suggests self-containment and independence of external reality (it is identified in the story with the world of dreams) but also in that, being navigable, it can leave and return to the shore at will. From the very first paragraph the author establishes the symbolic equations, with water representing the drug-like serenity of the dream world and land the noisy confusion of everyday life.

> The current of the crowd wanted to sweep me along with it. The green lights on the street corners ordered me to cross the street, the policeman smiled to invite me to walk between the silver-headed nails. Even the autumn leaves obeyed the current. But I broke away from it like a fallen

piece. I swerved out and stood at the top of the stairs leading down to the Quays. Below me flowed the river. Not like the current I had just broken from, made of dissonant pieces colliding rustily, driven by hunger and desire (*UGB*, p. 11).

A little later the narcotic function of the houseboat is made quite clear.

The noises of the city receded completely on the gangplank . . . As soon as I was inside the houseboat, I no longer knew the name of the river or the city. Once inside the walls of old wood, I might be inside a Norwegian sailing ship traversing fjords, in a Dutch boyer sailing to Bali, a jute boat on the Brahmaputra. At night the lights on the shore were those of Constantinople or the Neva. The giant bells ringing the hours were those of the sunken Cathedral. Every time I inserted the key in the lock, I felt this snapping of cords, this lifting of anchor, this fever of departure. Once inside the houseboat, all the voyages began. Even at night with its shutters closed, no smoke coming out of its chimney, asleep and secret, it had an air of mysteriously sailing somewhere (*UGB*, p. 13).

It is the same kind of escape that is afforded by dreams—or by drugs.

Technically the story is remarkable for the skill with which it alternates between incidents in the inside and outside world, the imaginary voyages and the real. Occasionally the two are fused, as in the following passage which combines a description of the mass journey upstream with a description of a dream journey.

The dream rolled on again. We passed a second bridge with the tugboat bowing down like a salute, passed all the houses I had lived in. From so many of these windows I had looked with envy and sadness at the flowing river and passing barges.[7] Today I was free, and traveling with my bed and my books. I was dreaming and flowing along with the river, pouring water out with pails, but this was a dream and I was free (*UGB*, pp. 23–24).

Fusions of this type occur in much of modern poetry,[8] and indeed this story, like many of those in the collection, is a kind of prose poem.

The source of the houseboat image was the wrecked fishing boat referred to in the last chapter, which Miss Nin saw in Maupassant's garden at Etretat, where it had been washed ashore in a storm, and which also inspired the boat passage in the final dream section of "The Voice." The memory of this boat prompted her to write an allegorical story concerning a ship which lost its anchor and drifted about for twenty years. She was dissatisfied with the allegory, however, and reworked it, giving it a literal as well as a symbolic dimension: the present story, one of the best in the collection, is the result. In "The Voice," where it figured as part of a dream experience, the boat image was presented as such, without any symbolic significance; here it becomes a means of transportation to the world of dreams and the unconscious, and this use of it prepares for the more elaborate treatment which it receives in *Four-Chambered Heart* and *Seduction of the Minotaur.* The water symbol, of course, occurs as early as *House of Incest,* and here, as in that book, there is a suggestion that the voyages are journeys not merely to random areas of the imagination but atavistic returns to the collective unconscious, journeys to shores which are therefore strangely familiar ("passed all the houses I had lived in"). But its principal function here, as in Miss Nin's fiction generally, is to suggest the freedom of the unconscious in contrast to the static quality of the land, which symbolizes ordinary reality. Furthermore, as we have seen, in "Houseboat" the land is identified with frustration and chaos, and the water with peace and fulfillment, albeit the fulfillment of illusion.[9]

"Ragtime" is a haunting, enigmatic story whose setting is the ragpickers' village near the Paris Flea Market. It begins realistically, with a description of the scene and its somewhat sinister occupants, but when the ragpicker reveals to the protagonist the blue dress in which she had danced when she was seventeen, and presents her with her former wisdom tooth and the discarded tresses of her hair, it is clear that we have entered the world of fantasy and symbol. The theme of the story is transmutation, and the idea which it dramatizes is that nothing is ever lost: we cannot, even if we wish to and however hard we may try, completely free ourselves from the past. Long-discarded objects keep turning up and are put to new and different uses.

> The ragpicker worked in silence and never looked at anything that was whole. His eyes sought the broken, the worn, the fragmented. A complete object made him sad. What could one do with a complete object? Put it in a museum. Not touch it. But a torn paper, a shoelace without its double, a cup without saucer, that was stirring. They could be transformed, melted into something else . . . Fragments, incompleted worlds, rags, detritus, the end of objects, and the beginnings of transmutations (*UGB*, pp. 58–59).

The beginnings of transmutations. When the protagonist asks the ragpicker, almost despairingly, "Can't one throw anything away forever?" he laughs, and sings a "serpentine song":

> *Nothing is lost but it changes*
> *Into the new string old string*
> *in the new bag old bag*
> *in the new pan old tin*
> *in the new shoe old leather*
> *in the new silk old hair*
> *in the new hat old straw*
> *in the new man the child*
> *in the new not new*
> *the new not new*
> *the new not new* (*UGB*, pp. 61–62).

It is an imaginative statement of the physical law that matter can neither be created nor destroyed, but of course the ragpicker's song has reference not merely to objects in the physical world; he means that for better or worse nothing, absolutely nothing, is ever lost in the universe—an idea, an emotion, a phrase (spoken or unspoken), a human relationship, anything at all. And in a sense, of course, this is perfectly true.

The remaining two stories of fantasy, "The Labyrinth"

and "Through the Streets of My Own Labyrinth," have a more personal quality. We noted in our study of the Diary that it served the author as a refuge from, and a substitute for, reality, and this accounts for the metaphor of which the first story is an extension, "I was eleven years old when I walked into the labyrinth of my diary." The story is really a double metaphor, in which diary equals dream, and dream as elsewhere in this author's work equals labyrinth. It makes use of actual dream experiences, and contains some of the most beautiful surrealist passages in all Miss Nin's work. Of particular interest, because of its affinity with surrealist painting, in which animal, mineral and vegetable forms frequently fuse and overlap, is the following:

> I moved my lips to remember the words I had formed, but I felt they no longer articulated words. My lips moved like the sea anemone, with infinite slowness, opening and closing, rolling under the exterior pressure, to breathe, forming nothing but a design in water. Or they moved like the noses of animals quivering at the passing wind, to detect, to feel, forming no word but recognition of an odor. Or they moved as flowers close for the night, or against the invasion of an insect. They breathed with fin slowness, with the cadence of a bulb flowering (*UGB*, pp. 63–64).

It will be remembered that a similar fusion of human with nonhuman forms occurs in the dream passage toward the end of "The Voice," where the individual identity dissolves, during sleep, to assume a variety of primordial conditions.

The fragmentary "Through the Streets of My Own Labyrinth" begins by describing a visit to Cadiz, which the author had first seen as a child of eleven. The city has not changed, but she has: "When I landed in Cadiz I found the palm tree, the Cathedral, but not the child I was." The scene then shifts to Fez, where she has lived in the meantime ("The last vestiges of my past were lost in the ancient city of Fez, which was so much like my own life, with its tortuous streets, its silences, secrecies, its labyrinths and its covered faces"), and the remainder of the sketch fancifully develops this comparison. This is the slightest of the stories in the collection, as it is also the briefest; it is interesting chiefly for biographical reasons and for its connection with the Diary, which describes in greater detail the trip Miss Nin made to Morocco in 1936, after which date the image of the labyrinth and the veil occur with increasing frequency.

In the second category (realistic sketches) belong "The Mouse," "Birth," and "The Child Born Out of the Fog." The first two are masterpieces, and the third is a wistful, poetic study of miscegenation. "The Mouse" is the pathetic story of a pregnant maidservant who, abandoned by her soldier sweetheart, attempts a clumsy abortion upon herself and who, because of the circumstances, is unable to secure proper medical attention.

> There was an infection, and no doctor would come to the houseboat. As soon as they heard what it was about they refused to come. Especially for a servant. That happened too often. They must learn, they said, not to get into trouble (*UGB*, p. 32).

At last a doctor is persuaded to examine her. He is, as he pompously explains, a *grand blessé de guerre*, unaccustomed to treating patients who live in houseboats, and, grumbling because he must traverse the shaky gangplank with his wooden leg, he ends by recommending that she go to a hospital. Our final glimpse of her, seated in the admitting room of a great public institution and answering endless questions, is unforgettable.

> The woman bleeding there on the bench meant nothing to them. The little round moist eyes, the tiny worn piece of fur around her neck, the panic in her. The brand-new Sunday hat and the torn valise with a string for a handle. The oily pocketbook, and the soldier's letters pressed between the pages of a Child's Reader. Even this pregnancy, accomplished in the dark, out of fear. A gesture of panic, that of a mouse falling into a trap (*UGB*, p. 34).

This is Miss Nin at her very best. The super-simple style, as has been said, is strongly reminiscent of the early Joyce, as is also the humanitarian note, and is there not a strong similarity between the protagonist of "The Mouse" and Maria, in "Clay," and Eveline in the story of the same name in Joyce's *Dubliners?* [10]

The second story in this group, "Birth," is perhaps the best known of Miss Nin's shorter works. It originally appeared in *Twice a Year*,[11] and was later included in the Honor Roll of Edward J. O'Brien's collection, *Best American Short Stories* of 1937. It is perhaps the most extraordinary description in English of the traumatic experience of a woman's giving birth, after prolonged labor, to a stillborn child. In spite of the pain, she feels a curious reluctance to cooperate with the doctor and nurses.

> A part of me did not want to push out the child. The doctor knew it. That is why he was angry, mysteriously angry. He knew. A part of me lay passive, did not want to push out anyone, not even this dead fragment of myself, out in the cold, outside of me. All in me which chose to keep, to lull, to embrace, to love, all in me which carried, preserved and protected, all in me which imprisoned the whole world in its passionate tenderness, this part of me would not thrust out the child, even though it had died in me. Even if it threatened my life. I could not break, tear out, separate, surrender open and dilate and yield up a fragment of a life like a fragment of the past, this part of me rebelled against pushing out the child, or anyone, out in the cold, to be picked up by strange hands, to be buried in strange places, to be lost, lost, lost . . . (*UGB*, p. 96).

Rarely has physical and psychological anguish been communicated with such intensity as in this story, which reproduces with almost unbearable accuracy the drug-laden atmosphere of the delivery room: the baffled, impatient doctor, who "would like to take a knife"; the impersonally interested nurses (one of whom remarks, "Mine passed through me like an envelope through a letter box"); the white glare of the lamps; the gleaming surgical instruments; the repeated thrusts of the needle as the anaesthetic wears off and has to be readministered. And the climax, when the patient, delivered at last, sits up and demands, "Show it to me."

> The doctor holds it up. It looks dark and small, like a diminutive man. But it is a little girl. It has long eyelashes on its closed eyes, is perfectly made, and all glistening with the waters of the womb (*UGB*, p. 101).

If "The Child Born Out of the Fog" is less successful than these, it is partly because they set such a high standard of excellence—partly, too, because "The Mouse" and "Birth" are simpler in scope; in each of them the situation is almost perfectly suited to the length. In this story, on the other hand, a fairly involved situation is treated perhaps too sketchily; the characters are not sufficiently explored except in terms of their racial difference, which is an inadequate basis for sympathy in fiction as in life; and a considerable period of time has been telescoped to fit the length of the story (a mere three and a half pages). It concerns a Negro singer, Don; his wife, Sarah; and their little girl, Pony.[12] Sarah is the only character about whom we are told very much. Her first lover had been a blond boy who had not loved her deeply.

> Everyone who is hurt takes a long voyage. You travel as far as you can from the place of the hurt. Sarah traveled far from gold hair to black hair as men of old traveled into virgin forests to heal a wound, as they traveled to foreign lands to forget a face (*UGB*, p. 83).

She meets Don at a political rally, and suffers ostracism as a result of their union: "They never walked together and she could not carry Pony safely through the streets." The story, which would perhaps be more plausible nowadays if we were told that its scene was a Southern city—for it is obviously a city of some size—ends on a note of pathos.

> He left the house with his guitar, walking proudly and not proud, walking nobly and smoothly, and yet hurt and bowed.
> She sat in the bus alone.
> At one moment the bus passed her.

They were not allowed to wave to each other (*UGB*, p. 85).

It will be seen that this is really the material for a novel, and it is curiously untypical of the author's usual method, which is to take very simple materials and elaborate them, sometimes at considerable length. In its concern with social justice this story somewhat resembles "The Mouse," but is generally inferior to it.

Of the remaining six stories, which are portraits, the most outstanding are probably "Hejda" and the title story, "Under a Glass Bell," in that order. It is odd that "Hejda" should succeed, and succeed so well (it is one of Miss Nin's most effective stories) where "The Child Born Out of the Fog" does not—or rather, succeeds less well. For "Hejda," like the other story, encompasses a considerable period of time and treats of relationships which are by no means simple. Here again the material might have served for a novel, yet the story runs to only ten pages. The difference lies mainly in the technique, about which two things must be observed. First, it is uniformly rather than intermittently abstract. (It opens: "The unveiling of women is a delicate matter. It will not happen overnight. We are all afraid of what we shall find." [13]) Second, the basic image of the veil about which the narrative is constructed and which, as we have seen, is introduced in the very first sentence, is developed with greater consistency and in greater detail than was the fog image in the other story; it is also less ambiguous.

When we first meet her, Hejda is a little Arab girl, a primitive "whose greatest pleasure consisted in inserting her finger inside pregnant hens and breaking the eggs, or filling frogs with gasoline and setting a lighted match to them." At seventeen she goes to study art in Paris, where she meets Molnar, a Roumanian painter, and marries him. She soon discovers, however, that he will not accept her as she is; he must remake her so that she will conform to his image of her (one is reminded here of the situation in *Winter of Artifice*, where both the father and the daughter have difficulty in reconciling their idealized images of each other with the truth). Her naturalness—she is still something of a primitive—and her generous feminine charms, which in public she conceals beneath her veils, repel him.

> He is critical of her heaviness. He dislikes her breasts and will not let her show them. They overwhelm him. He confesses he would like her better without them . . . At every turn nature must be subjugated. Very soon, with his coldness, he represses her violence. Very soon he polishes her language, her manners, her impulses. He reduces and limits her hospitality, her friendliness, her desire for expansion (*UGB*, p. 90).

Molnar even goes so far as to design her dresses, and imposes his identity upon her so strongly that she soon loses interest in her own painting and becomes absorbed in his.

> He paints a world of stage settings, static ships, frozen trees, crystal fairs, the skeletons of pleasure and color, from which nature is entirely shut off. He proceeds to make Hejda one of the objects in this painting; his nature is more and more castrated by this abstraction of her, the obtrusive breasts more severely veiled. In his painting there is no motion, no nature, and certainly not the Hejda who liked to run about without underwear, to eat herbs and raw vegetables out of the garden [14] (*UGB*, p. 91).

Cunningly, with an almost surgical economy, the exact nature of the relationship is laid bare for us.

> Her breasts are the only intrusion in their exquisite life. Without them she could be the twin he wanted, and they could accomplish this strange marriage of his feminine qualities and her masculine ones. For it is already clear that he likes to be protected and she likes to protect, and that she has more power in facing the world of reality, more power to sell pictures, to interest the galleries in his work, more courage too. It is she who assumes the active role in contact with the world. Molnar can never earn a living, Hejda can. Molnar cannot give orders (except to her) and she can. Molnar cannot execute, realize, concretize as well

as she can, for in execution and in action she is not timid (*UGB*, p. 91).

The relationship, obviously, is doomed, and for the same reason that, in *House of Incest*, the relationship between the narrator and Sabina is also doomed. Molnar, who will not allow Hejda to have a separate existence, is not really in love with his wife but with himself; the union is ultimately incestuous. We have seen this pattern at work also in *Winter of Artifice*, where the daughter's love for her father was also, ultimately, narcissistic.

When Molnar will no longer allow her to sell his pictures, and even stops painting, poverty sets in. Now, she thinks, perhaps the roles will reverse themselves, and Molnar will turn about and protect her.

> It is the dream of every maternal love: I have filled him with my strength. I have nourished his painting. My painting has passed into his painting. I am broken and weak. Perhaps now he will be strong (*UGB*, p. 93).

But no, Molnar is powerless to change, and Hejda at last leaves him, whereupon the process of her unveiling begins.

> Several people help her to unwind the binding wrapped around her personality first by her family life, then by her husband. Someone falls in love with her ample breasts, and removes the taboo that Molnar had placed upon them. Hejda buys herself a sheer blouse which will reveal her possessions (*UGB*, p. 94).

She begins to paint again, and her paintings become larger and more assertive. There is, the author tells us simply, "more of her."

> Her voice grows louder, her language, freed of Molnar's decadent refinement, grows coarser. Her dresses grow shorter. Her blouses looser . . . There is more food on her table. She becomes proud of her appetite (*UGB*, pp. 94–95).

Hejda's behavior and personality finally swing full circle.

> She is back in the garden of her childhood, back to the native original Hejda, child of nature and succulence and

sweets, of pillows and erotic literature. The frogs leap away in fear of her again (*UGB*, p. 95).

Perhaps nowhere else in Miss Nin's work is she more successful at achieving the essence of a character by a deliberate flatness, an abstraction of statement that can be peculiarly effective. Thus, in describing her protagonist's dilemma, she writes,

> A part of her wants to expand. A part of her wants to stay with Molnar. This conflict tears her asunder. The pulling and tearing brings on illness.
> Hejda falls.
> Hejda is ill.
> She cannot move forward because Molnar is tied, and she cannot break with him.
> Because he will not move, his being is stagnant and filled with poison. He injects her every day with this poison (*UGB*, p. 93).

The passage violates what was, at least until the example of some of the newer writers, one of the most elementary rules of "modern" fiction: it *reports* rather than *renders* and is abstract rather than concrete. It is "undramatic" in the usual sense of that word, as any instructor in a narrative writing course would be sure to point out unless he happened to be aware that in writing thus simply and thus directly (not an easy thing to do, incidentally) and in deliberately ignoring the rules of so-called "good writing" Miss Nin has actually arrived at a high degree of sophistication. If it seems contrived it is precisely because, paradoxically, it is not. Another reason "Hejda" is noteworthy is that it represents a firm step in the direction of what was to become one of this author's chief ambitions as a novelist: to depict the complex influences which individuals, consciously or unconsciously, exert upon one another—the delicate nuances and mutations of human relationships.

"Under a Glass Bell" is a reworking and an expansion of the same brother-sister situation which was treated earlier in *House of Incest*, and, as we have seen, in the

*Diary.* It is a story of psychological incest, and the chief differences between it and the earlier version in *House of Incest* are that Jeanne has two brothers instead of one, so that the relationship is further complicated and the quality of interdependency heightened; and she attempts an abortive romance with a Persian prince which the narrator tries to fan by sending her a series of ingenious gifts, ostensibly from her admirer (Jeanne has complained of his lack of imagination). Like "Hejda," this story has been given formal unity by means of a basic image, in this case a glass bell of the kind which, covering china birds or flowers, used to be a fixture of Victorian parlors.

> The light from the icicle bushes threw a patina over all objects, and turned them into bouquets of still flowers kept under a glass bell. The glass bell covered the flowers, the chairs, the whole room, the panoplied beds, the statues, the butlers, all the people living in the house. The glass bell covered the entire house (*UGB*, p. 36).

It is a peculiarly apt image, suggesting as it does the artificiality and sterility of the world inhabited by Jeanne and her brothers—as well as its isolation, its immunity from the contamination of ordinary life.

From the point of view of style, "Under a Glass Bell" is quite possibly the finest of all Miss Nin's narratives: the first three paragraphs are breathtakingly beautiful, as beautiful, perhaps, and as perfectly suited to their subject, as anything in modern fiction. And the character of Jeanne, a noble woman trapped in an impossible situation, has greater reality than in *House of Incest*, where she was used more as a symbol than as a character. The long monologue in which she speaks directly is extraordinary.

> My own children do not mean as much to me as my brothers. I am devoted to my children only because I have given my word, I owe them that, but what I do for my brothers is a great joy. We cannot live without each other. If I am sick they get sick, if they are sick I get sick. All joys and anxieties are tripled. Their opinion of me and mine of them is our only standard. It forces me into a kind of heroic living. If I should ever say to Jean: 'You have done a petty

thing,' he would kill himself. We three belong to the Middle Ages. We have this need of heroism, and there is no place for such feelings in modern life. That is our tragedy (*UGB*, pp. 36–37).

She continues,

I am not living on earth. Neither are my brothers. We are dead. We reached such heights in love that it made us want to die altogether with the loved one, and so we died. We are living in another world. Our having bodies is a farce, an anachronism . . . I can't bear to see them as bodies, to see them growing old. Once I sat writing letters and the two of them were playing cards. I looked at them and thought what a crime it was our being alive: it was a simulacrum, everything was really finished long ago (*UGB*, pp. 37–38).

People, it may be objected, do not talk like this in real life—to which the obvious reply is that Jeanne is no ordinary person, and she is not, by her own admission, in real life.[15]

Modeled somewhat more obviously on a real-life individual is "The Mohican"—or perhaps, being a less stylized story than "Hejda" or "Under a Glass Bell," it may merely seem to be. And of course it too is a composite, for the "real" subject was not an American Indian but a Swiss aristocrat living in Paris with whom both Miss Nin and Henry Miller were well acquainted—the black sheep of a wealthy family. It is interesting, incidentally, to compare this story with Miller's less sympathetic portrait of the same person in *Devil in Paradise*. "The Mohican" is a skillful exercise in characterization, whose subject is an astrologer who, ironically, is unable to interpret his own horoscope: "Because the ultimate statement depended on the interpretation of the facts he could not trust his objectivity." He is, not surprisingly, a fatalist, and though he is extraordinarily gifted as a conversationalist, he keeps his listeners at a certain distance, for the essence of his character is secrecy.

His talk was like the enormous wheel at the Fair, carrying little cages filled with people, the slow movement of the wheel, the little cages traveling spherically—the illusion of a vast circular voyage which never took one any nearer to the hub. One was picked up on the edge of the wheel, whirled in space, and deposited again without for an instant feeling nearer to its pulse. He carried people up and around him always at the same mathematical distance, breaking all the laws of human life which demand collisions and intermarriages (*UGB*, p. 43).

The story has a fanciful ending:

> When the Germans came, because of his charts, maps, calculations, and predictions of the death of Hitler, he was arrested as a celestial saboteur [16] (*UGB*, p. 47).

The extraordinary character whom we met in "Je Suis le Plus Malade des Surréalistes" was modeled after Antonin Artaud, the man who is now acknowledged to have been the founder of the Theater of the Absurd, who was partly responsible for the development of theater-in-the-round, and who has exercised such a profound influence upon the career of Jean Louis Barrault. Like the modern Christ in *House of Incest*, whom he very obviously resembles, his eyes are deep-set, he wears an agonized expression, and his lips are scummed with veronal. He suffers from hallucinations, and is in fact a kind of inspired madman. What he says about his theatrical ambitions ought to have interest for students of modern drama.

> I am starting a Theater of Cruelty. I am against the objectivity of the theater. The drama should not take place on a stage separated from the audience, but right in the center of it, so near to them that they will feel it happening inside of themselves. The place will be round like an arena, the people sitting close to the actors. There will be no talking. Gestures, cries, music. I want scenes like the ancient rituals, which will transport people with ecstasy and terror. I want to enact such violence and cruelty that people will feel the blood in them. I want them to be so affected that they will participate. They will cry out and shout and feel with me, with all of us, the actors (*UGB*, pp. 48–49).

In this story too we encounter that fusion and overlapping of natural kingdoms (in this case animal and mineral) which is one of the favorite devices of surrealism, in painting as well as in literature.[17]

> In the face of stone I saw the face of Pierre. I saw the face of Pierre when he retired behind life, behind the flesh world, into the mineral, everything drawn inward and petrified. I saw the face of Pierre in which nothing moved except the eyes, and the eyes moved like a terrified ocean, seeking wildly to withdraw also, but unable to, still liquid, still foaming and smoking, and this effort of the water in his body against the invasion and petrification of the stone, made the bitter sweat break out all over his body (*UGB*, pp. 50–51).

The first part of the story is prevented by touches of melodrama from being first-rate; the stylized nature of the dialogue does not quite prevent it from descending into occasional bathos. But the second part, which describes the narrator's visit to the poet-madman, who has been confined in a straitjacket,[18] is beautifully written. The white phoenix with which he identifies in his paranoia is the artist type, which is persecuted by the black eagles (philistines), and this is the source of his psychosis. When he says, "I have no friends," and the doctor asks, "Why?" he replies,

> Because when one is white like the white phoenix and the others are black one has enemies. It is always the same. It is the white phoenix that you want to take away from me (*UGB*, p. 57).

Another disquieting study of paranoia is "The Eye's Journey," the slight but sensitively written story of a painter who signs his canvases with the design of a small human eye in the corner and whose favorite pastime is watching mice being devoured by a snake at the zoo. He suffers from a strong sense of impending doom, which alcoholism has served to intensify, and identifies imaginatively with the victim.[19] His feelings of persecution reach such a point that he will not leave his room for fear his paintings will be stolen, whereupon he is confined to an asylum.[20] The model for this story, which combines biographical truth with fantasy, was another friend of Miss Nin's and Miller's in Paris during the thirties.

The last of the stories in this group, "The All Seeing," concerns a dreamer who, when his mother discourages him from studying the violin as a child, becomes the "archaeologist of his own soul, searching and looking blindly for the source of that music killed by the mother." He becomes a wanderer over the face of the earth.

> He feared to look backward and see the shadow of this that had been killed in him but he also feared to stay where he was and lose it altogether, so he pursued it blindly to the farthest corners of the world, returning each time to the violin which hung on his wall crucified and muted (*UGB,* p. 72).

When his loneliness becomes unendurable, he chooses a dream lover rather than a live, flesh-and-blood one.

> He fell in love with the Unknown Woman of the Seine, who had drowned herself many years ago and who was so beautiful that at the Morgue they made a plaster cast of her face. It was this picture he carried about. Around her he embroidered the most luxurious enchantments which she could not destroy, as other women destroyed the enchantments around them. Her silence permitted the unfolding of all his inventions. In death alone could love grow to such an absolute. One of the lovers must be dead for the absolute to flourish, the impossible, unattainable flower of the infinite. In death alone there is no betrayal and no loss. So Jean gave his infinite love to the drowned Unknown Woman of the Seine. His spiritually aristocratic love found no rival in death (*UGB,* pp. 74–75).

Though slight, "The All Seeing" contains some of Miss Nin's most beautiful writing.

> The music that was in him was never silenced, it flooded his place and every object vibrated with it. Wherever he went the place was filled with resonances like the inside of an instrument. The harmonies of his being lay concealed in the very shell of his misery as the echo of the sea inside the sea shells, and while he talked about the loss of music, one could place one's ear against any object in his room, against

his walls, against his rugs, against his pillows, and hear distinctly the music his mother had not been able to kill (*UGB*, pp. 72–73).

This character suffers from the same hypersensitivity, the same exacerbation of nerves, of which the father in *Winter of Artifice* was a victim—and, to a greater extent, the protagonist of "Je Suis le Plus Malade des Surréalistes" and the modern Christ in *House of Incest*. It is also, as we have noted, a characteristic of Roderick Usher, and indeed of many protagonists in romantic fiction. Together with "Je Suis le Plus Malade des Surréalistes" and "The Eye's Journey," this story presents the theme of the artist as victim of society.

*Under a Glass Bell* met with a mixed reception from the critics. The highest praise came from Edmund Wilson, whose knowledge of the literature of French Symbolism qualified him uniquely for the task of reviewing it (*The New Yorker*, April 1, 1944). He singled out "The Mouse," "Ragtime," and "Birth," calling them "beautiful little pieces," and said of the book generally:

> The pieces in this collection belong to a peculiar genre sometimes cultivated by the late Virginia Woolf. They are half short stories, half dreams, and they mix a sometimes exquisite poetry with a homely realistic observation. They take place in a special world, a world of feminine perception and fancy, which is all the more curious and charming for being innocently international.

He added, a little uneasily,

> There are passages in her prose which may perhaps suffer a little from an hallucinatory vein of writing which the Surrealists have overdone: a mere reeling out of images, each of which is designed to be surprising but which, strung together, simply fatigue.

But he added, "In Miss Nin's work, however, the imagery does convey something and is always appropriate."

Isaac Rosenfeld, in *The New Republic* (April 17, 1944) was rather less enthusiastic. While praising the quality of the writing, he was obviously inclined to view it as that of a minor talent which did not justify the claims made for it by Henry Miller and William Carlos Williams that it was the work of "a pioneer among women writers, striking out a new area in the experience and repression of her sex." The feminine equivalent of a literary Daniel Boone or Natty Bumppo, he prophesied, will never be found, and he also had reservations about what he regarded as the excessive subjectivity of the writing, "It is the sort of writing which conveys more about the author in a general sense than it does, specifically, about itself." But if this be true of Miss Nin's work, it is even more true, say, of Lawrence's, and is not Lawrence now regarded as a kind of pioneer? Actually this kind of subjectivity is a characteristic of romantic writing generally, both good and bad; it is dangerous to introduce it as a criterion, either positive or negative, of literary value, and it is absurd to say that it prevents one from being a literary pioneer. In a period of prevailing classicism, for instance, to write subjectively would obviously be to make a pioneering gesture, and the more intense the subjectivity the more emphatic the gesture.

One of the most interesting reviews was that of Vernon Young, in *The Hudson Review* (Autumn, 1948), who at least did Miss Nin the justice of examining the book thoroughly, thoughtfully, and at some length. I think he somewhat misplaces the focus of her work, which he claims is mainly dedicated to defending the feminine sex against what he believes Miss Nin thinks is its eternal enemy, the male.

> Better than anyone writing today, she can reveal the psychic essence of the feminine polarity and her revelation, as a consequence of being acutely implicated, arrives at the anxiety proportional to obsessive neurosis. The Female as Female is embraced with such tenderness, such solicitation of her particularity, such a ferocity of defense that man is necessarily, to the morbid guardian of the woman veiled, the natural enemy—man's inhumanity toward woman is, therefore, the special injustice in the world of Nin.

He continued,

Reading outward from this center, however, one discovers that the agonized privacy of the Nin heroine is endemic and does not indisputably follow upon the violation, by incomprehension, of the male. The objective honesty of "Hejda" and "Djuna" . . . is cancelled . . . by the confessional in "The Voice" and by various passages in the other stories, many of which emit a distinctly Sapphic odor. Nin's woman does not want man; again and again this decision is ratified by Nin's inability to set in believable motion any male who is not pompous, vain, ill or mad.

Though the idea that woman has been obliged by man to create a false image of herself is, as we noted in the first chapter, one of Miss Nin's favorite themes, it is by no means her only one: the problem of multiple identity, to which it does bear some relation, is another one; the alienation of the artist, quite independently of sex, is yet another; and the problem of objective versus subjective reality is still a third. Even if we concede his terms, the "obsessive neurosis" which Young claims dominates the collection is apparent in only a few of the stories therein, and he does not always read those with sufficient care. In "Hejda," for instance, no *blame* attaches to Molnar, and certainly not because he is a male; he is simply bad for Hejda. Young also apparently forgets that, after her experience with Molnar, Hejda does find a lover— presumably a *bona fide* male—who appreciates her "ample breasts." Another instance of careless reading is his labeling of Jean, the wanderer in "The All Seeing," as homosexual; there is not the slightest evidence for this in the story, and he is probably confusing it with "The Mohican," where it is *suggested* that the protagonist has a penchant for boys.

It is also an oversimplification of Miss Nin's position on the subject of the sexes to argue, as does Young, that her women do not really *want* men; most of them, perhaps, do not want *half* men—and Molnar, though Miss Nin is not so naive as to suggest it is a *fault* in him, is only half a man in contrast to the lover who later appreciates what is feminine in Hejda. Miss Nin never makes the mistake of implying that a woman can *substitute* for a man in a man-woman relationship; she does believe (as Lawrence did) that a human being *of either sex* requires for his total well-being an emotional relationship with a member of his own sex as well as an emotional *and* physical relationship with someone of the opposite. The "Sapphic overtones" which so disturbed Young have nothing more for their source than this conviction. His on the whole discerning review has little in common with the hysterical editorial in *John Bull* which denounced Lawrence's *Women in Love*, yet he has been guilty of the same kind of misreading. He does, however, give credit where it is obviously due.

> I believe there is little question that when Anaïs Nin is writing on her master subject, the interior stresses of the female personality, she has no equal in minute analysis, in conveying the nuances of expectation and withdrawal, the delicacies and gaucheries of contact.

Oddly enough, the severest censure came from women critics.[21] Diana Trilling, in *The Nation*, objected to "Hejda" on the ground that the child's "youthful sadism" was not "traced to its psychic causes," the assumption apparently being that in small children cruelty toward animals is a pathological manifestation. The assumption is false; it is a *natural* manifestation, which is precisely why it is so shocking, and in any case Miss Nin's purpose is not to explain how Hejda "got that way" but rather to show what happens when a woman who has retained her naturalness forms a mésalliance with a man who is her psychological opposite. Mrs. Trilling further stated that this "sensational activity" was not "connected with later manifestations of Hejda's character," which is patently false, since this is the personality, the "basic self," to which, atavistically, the mature woman reverts by a symbolic unveiling after her recoil from Molnar; the story, as I have shown, has a pattern which is perfectly symmetrical. With Mrs. Trilling's dislike of "Hejda" there is no point in quarreling; it is an error of taste. But to claim that the story is structureless is an error of intelligence.

Most merciless of all the critics was Elizabeth Hardwick, who declared in *Partisan Review*,[22]

> Anaïs Nin, one of our most self-consciously uncompromis-
> ing writers, seems old-fashioned. She is vague,[23] dreamy,
> mercilessly pretentious; the sickly child of distinguished
> parents—the avant-garde of the twenties—and unfortu-
> nately a great bore . . . She shuns the real world as if it had
> a bad reputation. This elegant snobbishness seems not
> designed to get her on in good society, but to allow her to
> sneak away to the psychological underworld . . .

Even without the puritanical bias of the last phrase, the
highly personal tone of this comment would render it
suspect. She continued,

> A few of the stories in *Under a Glass Bell* are quite
> effective, but in all of them there is too much straining for
> the exotic and a pathological appetite for mystification . . .
> No writer I can think of has more passionately embraced
> thin air. Still, she has nerve and goes on her way with a fine
> foolishness that is not without beauty as an art, though it is
> too bad her performance is never equal to her intentions.

It seems a curious judgment from someone who is herself
an author of some distinction—though perhaps it is not so
curious when one considers that Miss Hardwick, as a
traditionalist and a classicist, writes from a completely
different set of assumptions and is obviously intolerant of
literary experiments. On the whole her review is an object
lesson in the folly of that kind of criticism which attempts
to judge, by the standards of one school of writing, the
work of another school with completely different standards.

In *Under a Glass Bell* Anaïs Nin freed herself from
many of the obscurities of her early period (*House of
Incest*) and also from her dependency upon autobiography and biography (*Winter of Artifice*) to achieve maturity as a literary artist of unusual originality and distinction.
In this book the symbolism which is such an important
part of her literary method is less ambiguous, more firmly
controlled, and combines more easily with the realistic

elements of her fiction. The humorlessness, also, that some critics remarked in *Winter of Artifice* has here given way to an attitude which is often gently whimsical, as in such stories as "Houseboat" and "The All Seeing," though it is seldom this writer's purpose to make us laugh out-right. A story such as "Hejda" functions in a dimension and on a level which, at least in American fiction, are quite new. As Lawrence Durrell wrote: [24]

What I think you are doing (possibly have done) is creat-ing a new art . . . You are the novelty and your work through you achieves a status, a totality, which no longer concerns me as a man meeting a woman—but as a man meeting his maker. This is very good because it spells an emotional freedom we have all got waiting for us: a new IS.

LADDERS TO FIRE, the first of the five novels [1] comprising the series, *Cities of the Interior,* was published by Dutton in 1946 [2] and again by Alan Swallow in 1966. The first section, "This Hunger," had been printed personally by Miss Nin in 1945 by the same method which she used for *Winter of Artifice* and *Under a Glass Bell* [3] and which has been described in the last chapter; the book is illustrated with five woodblocks by Ian Hugo.

In her Foreword to the early editions (it does not appear in the Swallow printing) the author explains that her subject is "destruction in woman," and, more specifically, "woman's struggle to understand her own nature." Here we are reminded of the *Diary,* in which she records her conviction derived partly from Otto Rank that women have been prevented throughout history from knowing their true selves because they have been obliged by men to play a false role, the role in which men wish to see them: "Women are still occupied in making the world as man wants it, and then trying as best they can to create the one they can breathe in." Today, a few exceptional women have succeeded in triumphing over this obstacle, but the majority, she feels, still fail to realize their own nature.

Today marvelous women speak for themselves in terms of heroic action, integrating the woman, mother, wife, in harmonious relation to history, to larger worlds of art and science. But many more, when entering action or creation, followed man's patterns and could not carry along or integrate within them the feminine part of themselves. Action and creation, for woman, was man—or an imitation of man. In this imitation of man she lost contact with her nature and her relation to man.

In *Ladders to Fire*, she goes on to say, her concern is with this latter group, "the negative pole, the pole of confused and twisted nature." And so the characters we encounter in this novel are chiefly women: "Man appears only partially in this first volume, because for the woman at war with herself, he can only appear thus, not as an entity." And these women represent varying cases and degrees of frustration which has this essential conflict for its source.

Since this is Miss Nin's first full-scale novel, some explanation of her general theory of fiction and the techniques by which she attempts to practice it is obviously in order. Such explanation is the more necessary since this theory and these techniques are, to say the least, untraditional, and Miss Nin has suffered considerable injustice from critics who were unaware of her intentions. To say, as has sometimes been said,[4] that she does not write about life is absurd; she does, but she writes about it on a level to which very few novelists aspire: in her work, the motivation and characterization are enormously complicated, for what interests her is the ultimate motive behind the apparent ones, the genuine self beneath the many false ones. "Man," she has written, "is his own most elusive impersonator . . . we are all Walter Mittys as described by Thurber, going about our daily living while living a secondary, a third, a fourth life simultaneously as heroes of amazing adventures." It should be obvious that, where several characters are involved, the fictional possibilities become very nearly infinite, and this is the reason why in a typical Nin novel a single character or two, or perhaps at the most three, is explored in very great detail and the others are defined in relation to this character: it is her way of limiting material that would otherwise be inexhaustible. I think it can be said that Miss Nin conceives of fiction primarily as characterization; theoretically, she requires only a single character, for the others, though they have dimensions of their own, exist primarily for the purpose of defining the protagonist's—they are fictional satellites.

The comparison with astronomy is inevitable, and this is the kind of astronomy that interests Miss Nin: the relation of the central self to the satellite selves, the relation of the central character (with his satellite selves) to the satellite characters (with *their* separate selves). It is a kind of space fiction, but it is inner rather than outer space, and the spheres are psychological rather than physical. "They sat rotating around each other like nearsighted planets," she writes of the café habitués in *Children of the Albatross*, "mutating, exchanging personalities." [5] Elsewhere she has said, "It is necessary to travel *inwardly*, to find the levels at which we carry on, in a free-flowing, immensely rich vein, the uninhibited inner monologue in distinction to the controlled manner in which we converse with others." There is nothing, to be sure, that is very new or startling about any of this: one thinks of Joyce, of Woolf, even of Faulkner, who, since he is interested in physical, frequently violent action involving a wide variety of characters, does not sustain the theory to such extremes.

Miss Nin's originality is less a matter of her intentions than of the means by which she seeks to realize them. Since she conceives of fiction mainly as characterization, her technique concentrates necessarily on a solution of the problem of character, and she solves this problem in two ways: by directly presenting the reader with the symbols encountered in the characters' dreams, daydreams, and fantasies; [6] and by analyzing and interpreting these symbols through the methods of psychoanalysis. However, Miss Nin does not herself play the psychoanalyst; she is too subtle a writer for that. The revelation of character that results from such analysis is achieved either independently, through a series of experiences leading to self-knowledge, or through the assistance of other characters.

Concerning the symbolist technique in fiction, the author has written,

> The meaning of a symbol can penetrate our unconscious before revealing itself to our conscious intelligence, achieving direct communication as music does, by way of the feelings and the senses. The flexibility of interpretation is an invitation to participate in creation exactly as music demands of us response rather than a rational dissection. It is by this very mobility of interpretation that the living quality is preserved, so that one can *feel* and *experience* a novel rather than merely read it as one would a detective story, without feeling, as another pastime of the intelligence.[7]

Her technique has for its object, therefore, not so much the telling of a story as the direct revelation of experience, and her use of rhythmical language has the same object, as a kind of catalyst which (like the drumming at a primitive ceremony) induces in the hearer a state of proper receptivity. This is exactly the effect that her style, through a frequently monotonous accumulation of carefully parallel constructions, produces: a trance-like state of mind that is in fact a kind of hypnosis, aurally induced. A number of critics have commented that the uncompromising symmetry of her rhetorical constructions suggests the movement in certain dances which, like classical ballet or those Oriental dances that are really elaborate exercises in symbolism, are highly stylized.

While symbolism and psychoanalysis are the author's favorite devices for characterization, she also occasionally resorts to a deliberate flatness of statement of the kind that we noted in our discussion of "Hejda." An even more striking example of this method, at once the most elementary and the most sophisticated of all techniques for characterization, occurs in *Ladders to Fire*, where, in the description of Lillian at the beginning of the section entitled "Lillian and Djuna," it is sustained for the length of three full pages. So far as I know, there is nothing quite like this passage in modern fiction, and had Miss Nin written not another word about her character she would have remained forever fixed in the reader's mind. But of course this is exactly what she wishes to avoid: characters, if they are to be real (and not merely realistic) [8] cannot be static identities, and so Miss Nin finds it necessary to continue from there. Moreover, skillful as it is, this is merely a description of the external Lillian, the Lillian that others see, the self that lies nearest the surface; it is not the self with whom, in *Seduction of the Minotaur*, Lillian finally comes face to face.

Curiously enough, the practice of defining a character thus flatly and thus directly, in abstract terms, has more in common with that of certain nineteenth-century novelists who did not hesitate to tell the reader, in so many words, what their characters were like—to *judge* them, so to speak—than with the practice of most modern novelists who, in the tradition of Flaubert and Conrad, struggle desperately to maintain a *technical* objectivity toward them, allowing the reader, at least theoretically, to form his own opinions. Miss Nin's is, I think, a more honest method, for the "modern" writer, no less than the nineteenth-century one, wants the reader to accept the writer's own evaluation of his characters. There is thus a kind of hypocrisy—a kind of *coyness*, even—in his method of carefully scattering clues and innuendoes that will influence the reader's opinion of the characters in the direction that the author wishes.

But the tendency to focus almost exclusively, and in such detail, on the *essence* of an individual character at a given moment in his development and to ignore many of his more random and nonsymbolic activities entails a definite sacrifice, and results in a certain vagueness where the ordinary materials of narrative are concerned—setting, exterior action, apparent motivation. And indeed it is possible to push this kind of selectivity to a point beyond which even a sympathetic reader may feel that he is being cheated of something—something for which no amount of close and sensitive scrutiny can compensate. There is an obvious analogy with close-range photography: one is grateful for the power of the lens, but the proximity causes a sacrifice of scope, a blurring of background and accessory objects which, if artistically exploited, could add interest and variety as well as a surface coherence to the view. More than the later novels—certainly more than *Seduction of the Minotaur*—*Ladders to Fire*, in spite of its brilliance, suffers, I think, from this tendency. Or perhaps the difficulty is that the author does not employ the technique throughout with sufficient consistency or discretion—one of the reasons, possibly, why the novel seems somehow lacking in unity. I cannot for this reason agree with those critics who have acclaimed it her best book and who have objected, on that basis, to her more recent work.

*Ladders to Fire* is divided into two parts: "This Hunger," which consists of the two stories "Stella" and "Lillian and Djuna"; and "Bread and the Wafer." The connection between the first two stories is extremely tenuous; they are both studies in feminine frustration, but the source of the frustration is quite different, and if we are to accept the author's statement in the Foreword that *Ladders to Fire* is concerned with woman's struggle to free her true self from the self which has been man-imposed, then it is difficult to see how "Stella" fits into the design of the book. It is really a sort of sequel to *Winter of Artifice*, for Stella has much more in common with Djuna in that novel than with Lillian in *Ladders to Fire*. Thus, "Stella" should probably have been published either as a sequel to *Winter of Artifice* or as a separate story.[9]

As in *Winter of Artifice*, the father (who is here an actor instead of a musician—and this is the only essential difference between the two characters) deserts the family, and this proves traumatic experience for Stella (as it did for Djuna) because it permanently destroys her faith in love. Again as in *Winter of Artifice*, the daughter, when she grows up, attempts to recover this lost faith through further association with the father, but to no avail: his selfishness makes a genuine reconciliation impossible. All of this is presented as background in the framework of the story, whose direct concern is with depicting two abortive romances in which Stella attempts to free herself from the burden of her past.

The grown-up Stella is a famous movie star who envies

her own public image: on the screen she appears free and self-confident, whereas in reality she is filled with doubts and hesitations. Her dilemma is that she wishes to be loved for her true self, while it is with her false self that people have fallen in love. Her love affairs with her public are smashing successes; her private love affairs are failures. There is a fine scene in which she goes to a theater and watches her own image on the screen.

> Sitting next to her, they did not see her, intent on loving the woman on the screen . . . They courted the face on the screen, the face of translucence, the face of wax on which men found it possible to imprint the image of their fantasy (WA, pp. 8–9).

Even when she has a real flesh-and-blood lover, he does not love her true self but the image of her which he has manufactured.

> He saw her in reality, yet he did not see Stella but the dream of Stella. He loved instantly a woman without fear, without doubt, and his nature, which had never taken flight, could now do so with her. He saw her in flight. He did not sense that a nature such as hers could be paralyzed, frozen with fear, could retreat, could regress, negate, and then in extreme fear, could also turn about and destroy.

This is the only thread which connects the story to the overall theme of *Ladders to Fire,* but it is a tenuous one, for the source of Stella's unhappiness is not that she attempts to live up to this false image which her lover has formed of her, but rather the doubt that has been implanted in her nature through the experience involving her father.

With this first lover, a married man whose name is Bruno, her doubt requires that she demand endless assurances from him. She herself is willing to sacrifice everything for love.

> No matter how exigent was the demand made upon Stella by her screen work, she always overthrew every obstacle in favor of love. She broke contracts easily, sailed at a mo-

ment's notice, and no pursuit of fame could interfere with the course of love (WA, p. 16).

Her mistake consists in expecting that he shall do likewise.

> But he was a person who could only swim in the ocean of love if his moorings were maintained, the long established moorings of marriage and children. The stately house of permanency and continuity that was his home, built around his role in the world, built on peace and faith, with the smile of his wife which had become for him the smile of his mother—this edifice made out of the other components of his nature, his need for a haven, for children who were as his brothers had been, for a wife who was that which his mother had been. He could not throw over all these creations and possessions of his day for a night's dream, and Stella was that night's dream, all impermanency, vanishing and returning only with the night (WA, pp. 16–17).

Bruno demands no assurances from Stella; he is confident—too confident, in view of the outcome—of her love. The two characters are masterfully contrasted: he lives by faith; she by doubt. And like Tolstoy's Anna Karenina, whom in this respect she resembles, nothing will satisfy her: "She had reached the exaggeration, known to the emotionally unstable, of considering every small act as an absolute proof of love or hatred, and demanding of the faithful an absolute surrender." She is jealous of all his other interests and commitments: "If a telephone call or some emergency at home tore him away from her, for her it was abandon, the end of love." And she becomes fiercely possessive, with the kind of smothering, devouring possessiveness which we find in Lawrence's women characters—it was the trait in women he most despised.[10]

> To have touched the point of fire in him was not enough. To be his secret dream, his secret passion. She must ravage and conquer the absolute, for the sake of love. Not knowing that she was at this moment the enemy of love, its executioner (WA, p. 22).

Like the armless dancer in *House of Incest,* who has been punished for clinging, Stella is the victim of a false philosophy of love; she has made the fatal error of not respecting the privacy of her partner. When she has punished herself to the limits of her endurance in a daydream, one of those moments of self-realization which Miss Nin's heroines frequently experience, her lips form the word *masochism,* and she asks herself, "Am I a masochist?" She then abandons the relationship. It is not easy to do, and there is a superb scene in which, anticipating Bruno's telephone call, she puts a long-playing concerto on the record-player: "Stella allowed the music to produce its counter-witchcraft. Against the mechanical demand of the telephone, the music spiralled upward like a mystical skyscraper, and triumphed."

Her next attempt at romance is with a professional philanderer, a Don Juan type whose attitude toward women resembles that of her father, as she realizes one day when she waits for him in his apartment, which is filled with the souvenirs of his conquests: "Her fingers recognized objects made for or given by women." Among these is a set of toilet articles almost identical to the one her father had owned; she sees in it a symbol of his selfishness, and foresees the outcome of the relationship: "In this love Philip will receive bouquets from women, and Stella will find again the familiar pain her father had given her, which she did not want." There are limits to her masochism, and once more she retreats, this time into the shelter of the self.

> Human beings have a million little doorways of communication. When they feel threatened they close them, barricade themselves. Stella closed them all. Suffocation set in. Asphyxiation of the feelings (WA, p. 54).

Instead of throwing herself, like Tolstoy's heroine, under the wheeels of a train, Stella takes another part in a film and scores another public triumph: people send her enormous bouquets of rare flowers, and when she receives them she murmurs, "Flowers for the dead." [11] It is a form of suicide.

"Stella," however, does not remind us of Tolstoy so much as of Lawrence. It is probably the most Lawrentian of all Miss Nin's narratives, not merely in its subject, but also in the rendering of particular scenes. Take the following, for instance, which might easily have been written by Lawrence.

> She remembered a day spent in full freedom with Bruno. He had fallen asleep late and she had slipped away for a swim. All through the swimming she had the impression of swimming into an ocean of feeling—because of Bruno she would no longer move separately from this great moving body of feeling undulating with her which made of her emotions an illimitable symphonic joy. She had the marvelous sensation of being a part of a vaster world and moving with it because of moving in rhythm with another being.
>
> The joy of this was so intense that when she saw him approaching she ran towards him wildly, joyously. Coming near him like a ballet dancer she took a leap towards him, and he, frightened by her vehemence, and fearing that she would crash against him, instinctively became absolutely rigid, and she felt herself embracing a statue. Without hurt to her body, but with immeasurable hurt to her feelings (WA, p. 13).

There is the same emotional exaggeration, the same tendency toward melodrama, which we find in Lawrence. Or take this, which might almost have come from *Lady Chatterley's Lover.*

> There was always this mingling of hairs, which later in the bath she would tenderly separate from hers, laying the tendrils before her like the signs of the calendar of their love, the unwitherable flames of their caresses (WA, p. 21).

Not the best of Miss Nin, certainly, any more than similar passages are the best of Lawrence, but even here it is interesting to note that she has not been content with making a merely realistic observation but has, through the use of the metaphor "calendar of their love," lifted it out of the category of the purely physical—something that Lawrence does not always do. Nevertheless, the affinity is unmistakable. Such passages, it may be remarked in passing, are rare in Miss Nin's later work.

"Stella," in spite of occasional slips, remains one of this author's most thoroughly realized performances. She has taken the timeworn theme of the possessive female and examined it with her microscopic lens from new and interesting angles, and the result is an achievement which, though only indirectly supporting the general thesis of *Ladders to Fire*, is nevertheless of a very high order.

The section entitled "Lillian and Djuna" is the most substantial in the novel, the one which most pertinently and most dramatically presents its theme of woman's search for completion. We are introduced first to Lillian, a concert pianist, who is to become the central figure of *Cities of the Interior* [12] —a woman of unbounded, restless vitality and voracious appetites.

> Lillian was always in a state of fermentation. Her eyes rent the air and left phosphorescent streaks. Her large teeth were lustful. One thought of a Negress who had found a secret potion to turn her skin white and her hair red (*LF*, p. 7).

She is married and has two children but takes no interest in her family, resigning her responsibility to an affectionate nanny. In her defense it should be said that her husband makes the mistake of thinking of her as she was rather than as she is.

> When they sat together, alone, in the evenings, Larry did not appear to see her. When he talked about her he always talked about the Lillian of ten years ago. How she looked then, how she was, what she said. He delighted in reviving scenes out of the past, her behavior, her high temper and the troubles she got herself into. He often repeated these stories. And Lillian felt that she had known only one Larry, a Larry who had courted her and then remained as she had first known him. When she heard about the Lillian of ten years ago she felt no connection with her. But Larry was living with her, delighting in her presence. He reconstructed her out of his memory and sat her there every evening they had together (*LF*, pp. 26–27).

Larry will not acknowledge the basic principle of life, the fact of change and growth. For Lillian the atmosphere of the house becomes laden with death, and the situation is symbolized by the incident which happens next door, where a young doctor whose wife has died six months previously continues to sleep beside her decaying body—the neighbors investigate, exactly as in Faulkner's "A Rose for Emily," because of the odor. But whereas the situation in Faulkner's story is merely sensational and Gothic, here it serves, and very successfully, a symbolic purpose, since Larry is living with the Lillian who has died. Finally she takes a lover, Gerard, a mother-fixated individual who is her psychological opposite, but the affair quickly miscarries; Lillian's aggressiveness frightens him, "He feared the new invasion which endangered the pale little flame of his life." Observe how skillfully the author shows us their relationship.

> 'Do you want to come . . . Do you?'
> 'I never know what I want,' he smiled because of her emphasis on the 'want,' 'I do not go out very much.' From the first, in this void created by his not wanting, she was to throw her own desires, but not meet an answer, merely a pliability which was to leave her in doubt forever as to whether she had substituted her desire for his. From the first she was to play the lover alone, giving the questions and the answers too (*LF*, p. 10).

The situation affords Miss Nin an opportunity to make one of her favorite observations, "When man imposes his will on woman, she knows how to give him the pleasure of assuming his power was greater and his will became her pleasure but when the woman accomplished this,[13] no man ever gave her a feeling of any pleasure, only of guilt for having spoken first and reversed the roles." [14]

Recoiling from this experience, Lillian takes another lover, who visits her when her husband is out of town. The story of their lovemaking is told in a scene that might have come straight from the *Decameron*.

> A cricket had lodged itself in one of the beams of her room. Perfectly silent until the young man came to visit

> her, until he caressed her. Then it burst into frenzied
> cricket song.
> They laughed.
> He came again the next night, and at the same moment
> the cricket sang again.
> Always at the moment a cricket should sing.
> The young man went away. Larry returned. Larry was
> happy to be with his wife.
> But the cricket did not sing. Lillian wept. Lillian moved
> into a room of her own (*LF*, p. 26).

Then she meets Djuna, a woman fragile in appearance but
with an inner strength that is born partially of her ability
to ignore reality when she wishes and live in the world of
dreams. Djuna becomes her confidante; her composure
acts as ballast to Lillian's instability. What the two
women have in common is "this hunger"—in Lillian's
case, a hunger for life; in the case of Djuna, who was
reared in an orphanage and semistarved emotionally as
well as physically (the dreams were her only escape) a
hunger for warmth and affection. Djuna's desire is not so
much to love a particular individual; it is all-embracing in
a mystical, Whitmanesque sort of way.[15]

> While wearing the costume of utter femininity, the veils
> and the combs, the gloves and the perfumes, the muffs and
> the heels of femininity, she nevertheless disguised in herself
> an active lover of the world, the one who was actively
> roused by the object of his love, the one who was made
> strong as man is made strong in the center of his being by
> the softness of his love. Loving in men and women not
> their strength but their softness, not their fullness but their
> hunger, not their plenitude but their needs (*LF*, p. 36).

She will love, in other words, the spiritual orphans of the
world, and Lillian is such an orphan.

The friendship between the two women is complicated
when Lillian meets Jay, a casual and irresponsible bohemian, whose personality (he too is mother-fixated) qualifies him for the kind of maternal love which is as yet the
only kind of which Lillian is capable. "His helplessness,"
we are told, "made him the 'homme fatal' for such a

woman." An extraordinary passage, commented upon by many reviewers of *Ladders to Fire,* demonstrates the peculiar nature of their relationship.

> The windows of the taxi had frosted, so they seemed completely shut off from the rest of the world. It was small and dark and warm. Jay buried his face in her fur. He made himself small. He had a way of becoming so passive and soft that he seemed to lose his height and weight. He did this now, his face in her fur, and she felt as if she were the darkness, the smallness of the taxi, and were hiding him, protecting him from the elements. Here the cold could not reach him, the snow, the wind, the daylight. He sheltered himself, she carried his head on her breast, she carried his body become limp, his hands nestling in her pocket. She was the fur, the pocket, the warmth that sheltered him. She felt immense, and strong, and illimitable, the boundless mother opening her arms and her wings flying to carry him somewhere, she his shelter and refuge, his secret hiding place, his tent, his sky, his blanket (*LF,* pp. 54–55).

And again:

> It was in her frenzy to shelter, cover him, defend him that she laid her strength over his head like an enormous starry roof, and the stretching immensity of the boundless mother was substituted for the normal image of the man covering the woman (*LF,* p. 59).

But unlike Larry, Jay does not merely take; he has something to give as well. It is true that, like Molnar in "Hejda," he will not work, but he is a master of the art of living without working. His zest for life is contagious, and through him Lillian learns how to enjoy the swarming, colorful life of Paris, which is the scene of the book—though only remotely so, since the story is not at all realistic in this sense. But he is also heartless, often consciously cruel, and enjoys telling her about his other conquests. Nevertheless, she is powerless to judge or punish him.

> At times Lillian asked herself: what will he make of me someday, when will he hurt me? And what if he does? I will try to love him gaily, more easily and loosely. To endure space and distance and betrayals. My courage is

born today. Here lies Jay, breathing into my hair, over my neck. No hurt will come from me. No judgment. No woman ever judged the life stirring within her womb. I am too close to you. I will laugh with you even if it is against me (*LF*, p. 63).

"No woman ever judged the life stirring within her womb." The justice of this sentiment lies not merely in the fact that Lillian's relation to Jay is that of a mother toward her child but also in the fact that, since she is beginning to live vicariously through Jay, he is in this sense the source of her own life. The unremitting nature of her devotion is beautifully revealed in the following passage, which at the same time displays the consummate artistry with which this author makes symbolic use of the most commonplace activities to depict, in the form of an extended conceit, a human relationship.

When she sewed on buttons for him she was not only sewing buttons but sewing together the sparse, disconnected fragments of his ideas, of his inventions, of his unfinished dreams. She was weaving and sewing and mending because he carried in himself no thread of connection, no knowledge of mending, no thread of continuity or repair . . . She was sewing on a button and the broken pieces of his waywardness, sewing a button and his words too loosely strung, she was sewing their days together to make a tapestry, their words together, their moods together which he dispersed and tore . . . She was sewing together the little proofs of his devotion out of which to make a garment for her tattered love and faith. He cut into the faith with negligent scissors, and she mended and sewed and rewove and patched . . . She sewed his pockets, that he might keep some of their days together, hold the key to the house, to their room, to their bed together. She sewed the sleeve so he would reach out his arm and hold her, when loneliness dissolved her. She sewed the lining so that the warmth would not seep out of their days together, the soft inner skin of their relationship (*LF*, pp. 57–58).

Jay's feeling for Djuna is one of friendship, uncomplicated by sexual passion. "Christ," he exclaims (with D. H. Lawrence), "have a man and woman ever been friends, beyond love and beyond desire, and beyond everything, friends?" Their relationship is similar, at this stage, to that which Djuna enjoys with Lillian. But Lillian is fiercely possessive, and ingenious in her possessiveness. When Jay introduces her to Helen, a potential rival, she disposes of her with a ruse that borders on genius: she makes Helen *her* friend, thus substituting herself for Jay in Helen's affections, and the latter, not realizing what is happening, becomes virtually enamored of her—thus presenting another problem for Lillian, who again, however, proves that she is equal to the occasion by persuading Helen (who is almost too suggestible for credence) that she needs a change of scene, whereupon Helen drops out of their lives.[16] Another incident that might have come from the *Decameron!* When Lillian confesses to Jay that she is pregnant, his annoyance causes her to pray for the child's death, and in fact she loses it through a miscarriage.[17]

Jay is Miss Nin's best male character, and his relationship to Lillian is the most successfully portrayed of the four which comprise the bulk of this section (the others being Lillian-Larry, Lillian-Gerard, Lillian-Djuna). This is as it should be, for what it demonstrates is the thesis, stated in the Foreword, that "woman at war with herself has not yet been related to the man, only to the child in man, being capable only of maternity." The theme of rebellion and incompletion in women is poetically restated in the final section, where we see Lillian giving a performance on a grand piano at a society gathering: she attacks the keyboard as if it were an enemy, with the same fierce energy that she attacks life itself. But her aggressiveness masks a secret unrest, for beneath the violence of the surface lies the masochistic yearning to be herself used passively: "She pounded the coffer of the piano as she wanted her own body pounded and shattered . . . storming against her piano, using the music to tell all how she wanted to be stormed with equal strength and fervor." She is still a woman "at war with herself," without the poise that characterizes maturity and completeness. Djuna, listening to the concert, notices through the open doors that three large mirrors have been placed in the garden, reflecting the plants and the flowers; and this surrealist scene signifies, the author tells us in her Foreword, the reluctance with which women are willing to regard their natural selves: fearful of looking at the nudity of exposed nature, they content themselves with artificial reflections. In this passage the Proustian, overcivilized interior—the women "candied in perfume, covered in cosmetics," the men "preserved in their elegance"—contrasts with the naturalness of the garden outside, but by placing the mirror in the garden the people of the salon have brought it outdoors and imposed its atmosphere upon the natural scene.

> The eyes of the people had needed the mirrors, delighted in the fragility of reflections. All the truth of the garden, the moisture, and the worms, the insects and the roots, the running sap and the rotting bark, had all to be reflected in the mirrors (*LF*, p. 81).

In a stylized, artificial society such as this, Miss Nin is telling us, women are denied direct contact with their natures.[18] The section closes on an ominous note, with the warning that this society is doomed, that nature will not always suffer itself thus to be denied.

> Under the house and under the garden there were subterranean passages and if no one heard the premonitory rumblings before the explosion, it would all erupt in the form of war and revolutions.
> The humiliated, the defeated, the oppressed, the enslaved. Woman's misused and twisted strength . . . (*LF*, p. 81).

"Bread and the Wafer," the second part of *Ladders to Fire*, continues the exploration of Jay's character by means of two traditional devices: flashbacks into his childhood, and contrast with a minor character, Faustin. We learn that when Jay was a small boy he suffered a betrayal from which he has never recovered: his father, on the pretext of taking him to visit a battleship, takes him instead to the doctor's office, and his hedonism, his insatiable thirst for excitement, is his attempt to compensate for this deception—a lifelong visit to the battleship. This throws additional light on his relationship to Lillian: "Strong direction was given to her activity . . . as the provider of innumerable battleships in compensation for the one he had been cheated of . . . It was the paying off of a debt to the cheated child." But Lillian is attempting the impossible.

> Lillian did not know then that the one who believes he can pay off the early debt meets a bottomless well. Because the first denial has set off a fatality of revenge which no amount of giving can placate. Present in every child and criminal is this conviction that no retribution will repair the injury done. The man who was once starved may revenge himself upon the world not by stealing just once, or by stealing only what he needs, but by taking from the world an endless toll in payment of something irreplaceable, which is the lost faith (*LF*, p. 95).

This is sound analysis, and Jay, who is the type of alienated artist at war with respectable society, feels a strong affinity with criminals.

> Perhaps I should not be allowed to go free, perhaps I should be jailed with the criminals. I feel in sympathy with them. My murders are committed with paint. Every act of murder might awaken people to the state of things that produced it, but soon they fall asleep again, and when the artist awakens them then they are quick to take revenge. Very good that they refuse me money and honors, for thus they keep me in these streets and exposing what they do not wish me to expose. My jungle is not the innocent one of Rousseau. In my jungle everyone meets his enemy. In the underworld of nature debts must be paid in the same specie: no false money accepted. Hunger with hunger, pain with pain, destruction with destruction.
> The artist is there to keep accounts (*LF*, pp. 107–8).

By contrast with Jay, Faustin personifies the rational principle. "You must care," he tells Jay, "you must hold on to something." And Jay replies, "I never hold on. Why hold on? Whatever you hold on to dies." As always in Miss

Nin's fiction, rationalism is associated with stasis and death: Faustin's face, we are told, is "completely static, and one was surprised that the words could come through the closed mouth." Jay's mouth, by contrast, is "always a little open." And when Lillian asks, "Why did you paint Faustin without a head? That's what he's proudest of—his head," Jay answers, "Because that's what he should lose, to come alive."

Jay has much in common with the type of "holy tramp" with which we have recently become so familiar in the work of Kerouac and other writers of the Beat persuasion. He loves the Paris hoboes, the "smiling old men who sat on benches beautifully drunk," because, the author tells us, "they were his father." "He had so many fathers," she says, "because he was one to see the many." And like Kerouac's hero-tramps (and Walt Whitman) he is capable of loving simultaneously in all directions.

> I believe we have a hundred fathers and mothers and lovers all interchangeable, and that's the flaw in Lillian; for her there is only one mother, one father, one husband, one lover, one son, one daughter, irreplaceable, unique—her world is too small. The young girl who just passed me with lightning in her eyes is my daughter. I could take her home as my daughter in place of the one I lost. The world is full of fathers, whenever I need one I only need to stop and talk to one (*LF*, pp. 104–5).

Sabina, who is one of the most interesting characters in *Ladders to Fire* and who is destined to play an important part in the series, makes her appearance very late in the book, and this is perhaps the place to say that because of their freedom from conventional structure it is sometimes less convenient to consider Miss Nin's novels as independent organizations than as continuing units in a series.[19] This Sabina receives fuller development than the one we meet in *House of Incest*, and is introduced to us in images that suggest the excitement—and the danger—of a big-city fair.

> All dressed in red and silver, the tearing red and silver cutting a pathway through the flesh. The first time one

looked at Sabina one felt: Everything will burn! (*LF*, p. 108).

For poets, who like children enjoy fires, she is a true *femme fatale*, and her command to them, when she arrives with her ladders is "Climb." But Sabina's ladders, we are told, lead to fire. Sabina's natural destructiveness has been analyzed in our study of *House of Incest*. Here it is sufficient to say that she is a primitive, predatory woman who refuses to acknowledge any ties, and it is this quality which accounts for her lies and labyrinthian evasions, for she will not be cornered, captured, or tamed. In some respects she is very similar to Jay, and though we gather she later becomes his mistress, their first meeting is disastrous: "From the very first Jay hated her, hated her as Don Juan hated Doña Juana, as the free man hates the free woman, as man hates in woman this freedom in passion which he solely grants to himself." Lillian, on the other hand, is attracted to her at once, and the two women actually have an affair which, as soon as it is consummated, proves disappointing.

> Their bodies touched and then fell away, as if both of them had touched a mirror, their own image upon a mirror. They had felt the cold wall, they had felt the mirror that never appeared when they were taken by a man (*LF*, p. 125).

This, Lillian realizes, is not the road to completion; on the contrary, the affair has the unexpected consequence of making her more possessive of Jay than ever. For it occurs to her to wonder, "If she had wanted so much to be Sabina so that Jay might love in her what he admired in Sabina, could it be that Sabina wanted of Lillian this that made Jay love her?" Furiously she tells Sabina, "It's Jay you love, not me. Get up. I don't want him to find us here together."

*Ladders to Fire* ends with a fanciful surrealistic description of a party at Jay and Lillian's studio in Montparnasse. As in so much of Miss Nin's work, this fantasy had its source in a real party, and the guests whom she describes, though they have been abstracted to serve as symbols for ways of life and principles of being, were all real-life individuals. Moving adroitly among them is the Chess Player, who knows instinctively who should meet whom, and who conceives of the floor as a chess board and of the party as an exercise in strategy. He introduces Djuna, the woman of many moods, to an Irish architect who plans for her a house capable of matching each of them, but his attempt to introduce the Zombie-like Faustin to Sabina is a failure: "She merely turned her face away; she was too richly nourished with pollen, seeds and sap to wither before any man, even a dead one." Rango, the guitar player whom we shall meet later in *Four-Chambered Heart*, charms the guests with his playing, and Jay comes staggering in with five of his drinking companions. Stella, "susurrating in a taffeta skirt and eating fried potatoes out of a paper bag," is accompanied by an artist "known for his compulsion to exhibit himself unreservedly," but leaves him to speak to a formidable art critic, the arbiter of modern taste to whom is entrusted the delicate matter of answering the question, "Is it tomorrow's art?" In Stella's case, the answer is a polite "No": "To look at her in this ironic manner while scrupulously adhering to medieval salutations this man must know that she was one to keep faded flowers." Lillian, overcome by her own self-doubts and monumental lack of poise, sinks to the floor in a kind of symbolic suicide. Of all these guests, Djuna is perhaps the most difficult because of her habit of retreating into her cities of the interior, whence she views them all with a kind of clairvoyance, seeing what it is in them that has caused them to be as they are—the concealed humiliations, the forgotten lesions.

> She no longer saw the Chess Player as made of wood directed by a delicate geometric inner apparatus, as everyone saw him. She saw him before his crystallization, saw the incident which alchemized him into wood, into a chess player of geometric patterns. There, where a blighted love had made its first incision and the blood had turned to tree sap to become wood and move with geometric carefulness, there she placed her words calling to his warmth before it had congealed (*LF*, p. 151).

She sees them, in other words, with the eye of an analyst, and since this is also the author's purpose in her fiction, the tendency to identify her here with Djuna is irresistible. Not surprisingly, the guests resent the accuracy of this vision.

> From the glass bastions of her city of the interior she could see all the excrescences, deformities, disguises, but as she moved among them she incurred great anger.
> "You demand we shed our greatest protections!"
> "I demand nothing. I wanted to attend a Party. But the Party has dissolved in this strange acid of awareness which only dissolves the calluses, and I see the beginning" (*LF*, p. 151).

The symbolism of the party is thus made clear. Djuna wants to live by truth at the moments of heightened awareness ("I wanted to attend a Party"), but the guests, who are unwilling or unable to attain these heights—who will not or cannot live in their own cities of the interior—have a quite different notion of what a successful party ought to be, and they remove her forcibly from the gathering.

*Ladders to Fire* caused a storm of controversy, effectively —and in some cases permanently—dividing Miss Nin's critics into irreconcilable camps. Edmund Wilson continued loyal, noting that "Bread and the Wafer," in particular, represented a "distinct advance" over the earlier work; and the book was praised in some of the "little" magazines. But the popular reviews were for the most part distinctly unfavorable. The reception accorded to *Ladders to Fire*, more than any of her other books, seemed to make it clear that Miss Nin was not a writer for the general reading public, and the fact that her work had been praised by so many writers of distinction was taken to mean that she was a "writer's writer," doomed to permanent exile on a planet whose atmosphere was too rarefied for ordinary lungs.

In *The New York Times* (October 20, 1946), Herbert Lyons, conceding that Miss Nin "is a natural storyteller, and, try as she will, she cannot succeed in preventing the reader from recognizing the tale," added,

> Inasmuch as the "avant garde" may not listen to the radio, it is perhaps worth noting that numerous daytime serials are almost exclusively devoted to less fancy variations on this same theme of woman's struggle to understand her own nature . . . As in much of modern music, there is little originality. The novel contains traces of Djuna Barnes, Henry Miller and Edmund Wilson and a large deposit of French surrealism. These days many things get by under the banner of complexity and super-sensitivity; artiness and obscurantism, as always, are sometimes disguises for second-rate talents. But Miss Nin's novel has a certain interest as a pastiche of contemporary preciousness.

And Harrison Smith, in a facetious article in *The Saturday Review of Literature* (November 30, 1946), declared,

> A few critics have been misled by the line drawings which obfuscate the book into stating that Miss Nin is of the advanced guard of writers, the holy few who can only appeal endlessly to a limited and long-haired audience. Actually, after serious critical appraisal, this novel seems no more surrealist, imagist, or "modern," than any woman in a permanent tantrum, from the Middle Ages, or from the Renaissance, or any other period; any woman in fact who had grown up and had lived too long in the art colonies of the world, and had too little to do with children, cooking, and the garden in the backyard. As for its ancestry, *Ladders to Fire* might be considered as the illegitimate child of Marie Corelli's *Sorrows of Satan* and Edmund Wilson's *Memoirs of Hecate County*.

But if we overlook the reactions of those "middlebrow" critics who objected to the book on the general, frequently vague principle that it was too "experimental" or too "avant garde," and also of those who disliked it for extra-literary reasons because they rejected its assumptions about the relations of the sexes, we find that specific objections centered around two tendencies in this author's work: first, overabstraction, that is, failure to provide sufficient "factual" information which would enable the reader to participate in the story on a realistic level; and, second, an overlapping and apparently deliberate confusion of characters, particularly women characters. Today, after twenty years of further exposure to abstractness in fiction, the first charge does not seem as valid as the second: the modern reader may receive a temporary jolt to learn, after watching Lillian unsuccessfully struggle to achieve a harmonious relationship with Gerard, her lover, that she is married and lives at home with her husband and two children, but he will not be permanently disaffected, as was Mrs. Trilling,[20] nor does he necessarily assume an error on the part of the author, who may have had her reasons for delaying this information, and for imparting it so casually. The truth is, in this case at least, that Larry and the children are not, as we have seen, really important in Lillian's life; they mean less to her than her lovers—even less than Gerard, which may well be the reason we meet him first.

It is true that Anaïs Nin tends to compress and to telescope to an extreme degree, particularly in those matters where a novelist writing in the realistic manner would often choose to dilate and to sustain, but it is also true that in areas which such a novelist would overlook—areas of the most delicate sensibility—she is capable of expanding at great length and achieving that effect of "gold to airy thinness beat" described by John Donne in his famous image. Expansion of this type obviously involves a sacrifice somewhere, and the only legitimate quarrel would be with the area which the artist has chosen. Similarly with the matter of motivation: some actions are elaborately prepared for, while in others motivation may appear to be almost nonexistent. Miss Nin does not always, in *Ladders to Fire*, exercise the discretion in these respects which she does in some of her later work.

The other objection, to the overlapping of identities in the various characters, is less easily refuted. We noted this tendency in *Winter of Artifice*, where it loomed larger and constituted a definite flaw in the book, and it continues in *Ladders to Fire*: more than one reviewer commented on the

characteristics that Stella, Lillian and Sabina have in common and that make it difficult for the reader to keep them
separated as he follows them in their various adventures.
This tendency is related to the other—the reluctance
to place the characters in a context that is sufficiently
realistic. The advantage of providing such a context
is that it serves to define the characters more sharply.
This is the reason why Lawrence's characters have reality
both as essences and as flesh-and-blood personages, for
Lawrence is very skillful at inventing circumstances which
create the essence of his characters, as is also Joyce. In this
aspect of her technique Miss Nin is closer to Kafka than
to either of these, but Kafka's characters, for all their
abstractness, do not blur and overlap. To a large extent
the separation of identity is a requirement for dramatic
interest; moreover, Miss Nin's women are all archetypes,
and if archetypes overlap they tend to lose their symbolic
force.

The source of this difficulty in Miss Nin's work may
well be the *Diary*, for reading therein we find experiences
which in the fiction are ascribed to the several women, but
it is possible to be confused even without having read the
*Diary*. What happens is that the author, rather than
identifying with a single character, projects aspects of her
own personality into several, and the result is sometimes
baffling. Djuna is the character in *Cities of the Interior*
with whom Miss Nin chiefly identifies, but she is not the
only one. The resemblances among the various characters
are not always psychological, nor are they limited to the
women: Sabina's mouth is "always a little open, pouring
forth that eddying voice that gave one vertigo," and so is
Jay's; he is, we are told, "like the south wind blowing,
melting and softening with his purring voice and mouth."
For all these faults, *Ladders to Fire* is a book of considerable beauty, a worthy inaugurator of the series which Miss
Nin has aptly called *Cities of the Interior*.

THE PHOSPHORESCENCE
OF FAITH
*CHILDREN OF THE ALBATROSS*

ABANDONING TEMPORARILY the theme of incompleteness in
women, Anaïs Nin, in *Children of the Albatross*, the second novel of *Cities of the Interior*,¹ writes about a group
of young bohemians in Paris; the book is a kind of epiph-
any, a celebration of *jeunesse dorée*, the idyllic period
before the lack of faith, that mysterious substance that
"shines from the body like phosphorescence from the
albatross." It is one of her most beautiful works, and
perhaps the one in which she is most successful in suiting
the style to the subject. It consists of two parts, "The
Sealed Room" and "The Café." The protagonist of Part
One is Djuna, whose character is further explored for us
by methods similar to those by which Jay was presented in
"Bread and the Wafer": by flashbacks, and by analysis of
her relationship with a group of young men—Michael,
Donald, Paul, and Lawrence.

The flashbacks establish that by becoming a professional dancer Djuna has raised herself above the poverty
of her background: her dancing is a form of compensation
for the experience in the orphanage, and the glamor of her
present profession contrasts with the drabness of her childhood. In a reverie she recalls an adolescent infatuation for
a boy who used to pass beneath her window, and how, in
order to meet him, she would bribe the watchman by
allowing him to take liberties with her: "There was the

man who demanded, and outside was the gentle boy who demanded nothing, and to whom she wanted to give everything." This early experience forces her attitude toward the opposite sex into the pattern by which she will always be ruled, for it causes her to mistrust men of power and to give her love instead to those who are gentle and undemanding.

From another reverie we learn that when Djuna was in dancing school, her teacher begged her to accompany him as his partner, promising that he would make their names famous all over Europe. It is the dream of every romantic young girl, but because she lacks the necessary confidence she refuses. Her teacher is nothing if not impulsive; this is how he shows his admiration.

> She had not yet taken off the voluminous skirt of the dance, the full-blown petticoat, the tight-fitting panties, so that when he entered the dressing room it seemed like a continuation of the dance. A continuation of the dance when he approached her and bent one knee in gallant salutation, and put his arms around her skirt that swelled like a huge flower. She laid her hand on his head like a queen acknowledging his worship. He remained on one knee while the skirt like a full-blown flower opened to allow a kiss to be placed at the core. A kiss enclosed in the corolla of the skirt and hidden away (CA, pp. 12–13).

Here, as in the bathtub scene in *Ladders to Fire*, the sensuality of the passage is modulated by means of metaphor.

We are returned from the flashbacks to the level of present time, which discovers Djuna living in an old house with a garden on the edge of Paris—a house with twelve windows, one of which, because of some transformation which the building has undergone in its long history, corresponds to no room. The reader will recognize this at once as the house at Louveciennes described in the *Diary* and referred to also in *House of Incest*. It is this window that has caused Djuna to buy the place: "Djuna had taken the house because of this window which led to no room, because of this impenetrable room, thinking that someday she would discover an entrance to it." The rooms of the house correspond to the compartments of the self, as we are told quite explicitly, and we are told also that "in herself was one shuttered window." There is a part of herself, that is, which remains a "sealed room." What this room contains we shall learn later.

Djuna is restless and dissatisfied in this house which she has always longed for. She feels strangely remote from the world. She has many friends, many visitors, but none of them comes "near enough." There is always a barrier, and this barrier, she realizes, is of her own making. In the beautiful Surrealist image on page 33 she feels herself walking through a "desert of snow," her body muffled in furs, carrying always Ariadne's thread of caution, fearful that if she loses it she will be at the mercy of the people she mistrusts. In another image she is described as having made of herself a veritable fortress.

> The only words which opened her being were the muffled words of poets so rarely uttered by human beings. They alone penetrated her without awakening the bristling guards on watch at the gateways, costumed like the silver porcupines armed with mistrust, barring the way to the secret recesses of thought and feelings (CA, p. 34).

In Michael she meets a young man capable of uttering such words, and allows him to share with her "the peaceful fields of her interior landscape, where white flowers placed themselves against green backgrounds as in Botticelli paintings of spring." The description of this relationship, done in terms of dance images, is very skillful.

> Because of their youth, and their moving still outside of the center of their own desires blindly, what they danced together was not a dance in which either took possession of the other, but a kind of minuet, where the aim consisted in *not* appropriating, *not* grasping, *not* touching, but allowing the maximum space and distance to flow between the two figures. To move in accord without collision, without merging. To encircle, to bow in worship, to laugh at the same absurdities, to mock their own movements, to throw upon

the walls twin shadows which will never become one. To dance around this danger: the danger of becoming one! . . . A deft dance of unpossession (CA, pp. 38–39).

Djuna can arouse Michael's jealousy (we are reminded here of the situation between Lillian and Gerard in *Ladders to Fire*) but not his desire. Michael idealizes her, calling her his Yseult; like so many of Miss Nin's lovers, he cannot see the real Djuna because of the romantic image he imposes upon her. But there is another reason for his indifference, a reason which she is too young to understand and assumes therefore that it is she who is to blame. Eventually she forgets him.

> With time, her marriage to another, her dancing which took her to many countries, the image of Michael was effaced.
> But she continued to relate to other Michaels in the world. Some part of her being continued to recognize the same gentleness, the same elusiveness, the same mystery (CA, p. 46).

Years later, when she meets him with his lover, Donald, the mystery is dissipated. Donald is vain, coquettish; he has a horror of permanency, of "anything resembling marriage," and does not reciprocate the genuine love which Michael has for him: "In his flight from women, it seemed to Djuna, Michael had merely fled to one containing all the minor flaws of women." Donald has conceived a unique plan for revenging himself upon normal society: "This society which condemns me . . . do you know how I am revenging myself? I am seducing each one of its members, one by one." Observe how beautifully, and with what economy, the author analyzes this strange friendship which develops among the three.

> Warmth in the air. The spring foliage shivering out of pure coquetry. Love flowing now between the three, shared, transmitted, contagious, as if Michael were at last free to love Djuna in the form of a boy, through the body of Donald to reach Djuna whom he could never touch directly, and Djuna through the body of Donald reached Michael—and the missing dimension of their love accomplished in space like an algebra of imperfection, an abstract

drama of incompleteness at last resolved for one moment by this trinity of woman sitting between two incomplete men (*CA*, p. 52).

The young man with whom this section is chiefly concerned, however, is neither Michael nor Donald but Paul, a seventeen-year-old boy in flight from his parents. In his gentleness he somewhat resembles the Michael whom Djuna knew years ago, before he took the step which changed so radically the direction of his life. "When," Djuna meditates, "will I stop loving these airy young men who move in a realm like the realm of birds, always a little quicker than most human beings, always a little above, or beyond humanity, always in flight, out of some great fear of human beings, always seeking the open space, weary of enclosures, anxious for their freedom, vibrating with a multitude of alarms, always sensing danger all around them?" Paul is such an "airy young man," as Lawrence, another androgynous youth to whom Djuna introduces him, quickly senses, declaring, "*C'est une jeune fille en fleur*," but through Djuna—who initiates Paul into the mysteries of love and sex—he achieves a certain stability and independence. Djuna is ten years his senior, and the story of their romance bears not a little resemblance to Radiguet's *Devil in the Flesh*. In the timid, unsure adolescent she sees the man whom he is capable of becoming.

> Others would see a young man experiencing his first drunkenness, taking his first steps in the world, oscillating or contradicting himself. But she felt herself living with a Paul no one had seen yet, the man of the future, willful, and with a power in him which appeared in him intermittently (*CA*, p. 80).

The feeling is obviously maternal, and reminds us somewhat of Lillian's for Jay, with the important difference that Jay is a finished product rather than a man in the making: his personality has crystallized, and Lillian is powerless to shape and give it direction. Djuna's maternalism, moreover, is compounded with nostalgia.

> In his presence she did not feel herself a mature woman, but again a girl of seventeen at the beginning of her own

life. As if the girl of seventeen had remained undestroyed by experience—like some deeper layer in a geological structure which had pressed but not obliterated the new layers (CA, p. 72).

It is a response which Paul has the (totally unconscious) ability to evoke in older people generally.

> He did not know himself to be the possessor of anything they might want, not knowing that in his presence they were violently carried back to their first dream. Because he stood at the beginning of the labyrinth—not in the heart of it—he made everyone aware of the turn where they had lost themselves. With Paul standing at the entrance of the maze, they recaptured the beginning of their voyage, they remembered their first intent, their first image, their first desires (CA, p. 100).

One of the things Djuna and Paul have in common is their distrust of the father figure, and it is implied that this is one of her motives in maintaining the relationship, for in so doing she makes herself an ally in his rebellion against his parents, who insist that he leave her and return home. When he consents to spend his eighteenth birthday in the family circle, the conventional observances of that occasion—the cake and the candles, the former "iced and sprinkled with warnings against expansion, cautions against any new friends . . . the cake of caution" and the latter lighted "as if to say, 'Only within the radius lighted by these birthday candles are you truly safe,' "—are contrasted with the spiritual ceremony at which Djuna has officiated.

> They had not attended the birthday of his manhood, the birthday of his roguish humorous self, of his first drunkenness, his first success at a party; or the birthday of his eloquent self on the theme of poetry, painting, or music. Or the birthday of his imagination, his fantasy, of his new knowledge of people, of his new assertions and his discoveries of unknown powers in himself (CA, p. 101).

Another quality the two lovers have in common is their ability to shut out the external world, with its repellent power figures, and live in the world of the dream. The "sealed room," it now becomes apparent, is the locale of this world, a place of extreme privacy from which have been excluded all the violence and cruelty of ordinary reality, and in the beautiful final pages of this section Djuna and Paul are seated together in this room without physical dimension listening to César Franck's *Symphony in D Minor*.

Paul is one of Miss Nin's best characters. His white scarf is the symbol of his peculiar innocence; it is the "appropriate flag of his voyages," whose purity is proof against all that is ugly and sordid, "The white scarf asserted the innumerable things which did not touch him: choked trees, broken windows, cripples, obscenities penciled on the walls, the lascivious speeches of the drunks, the corrosions and miasmas of the city." Like some of the other young men—children of the albatross—in the story, he is surrounded by an aura whose evanescent source is youthful idealism and innocence.

> There is a phosphorescence which comes from the magic world of childhood.
> Where does this illumination go later? Is it the substance of faith which shines from their bodies like phosphorescence from the albatross, and what kills it? (CA, pp. 68–69).

There is one point in the story at which Djuna feels compunction at having forced the bloom of Paul's maturity. In a scene that Lawrence might well have written, she opens a bowl of tulip buds one by one, and when Paul cries sharply, "Don't do that!" she knows a moment of fear and guilt.

> She looked at the flowers. She looked at Paul's face lying on the pillow, clouded with anxiety, and she was struck with fear. Too soon. She had opened him to love too soon. He was not ready (WA, p. 85).

This scene might have been more effective if the symbolism had not been spelled out quite so literally.

The reader will remember that in her Foreword to the

first American edition of *Under a Glass Bell* Anaïs Nin referred somewhat apologetically to her tendency to follow the "labyrinth of fantasy," declaring "Now I am awake" and implying that in the future she would concern herself less with the personal and the subjective and more with external reality and, specifically, with "the suffering of the world." We noted that this resolution coincided, a little tardily (1944), with the literary taste of the time, which showed a preference for broad social themes, movements, and causes.[2] But *Children of the Albatross*, so far from confirming this intention, shows instead a decided deepening and narrowing of interest in the personal, and the fact is that during the three years which separated the publication of the two books Miss Nin came to feel that her original impulse had been wiser: she became convinced—and remains so—that self-knowledge is primary, that an understanding of the self is essential to an understanding of the outside world and ought therefore to have priority over it. Now that the first volumes of the *Diary* have been published, readers will have little difficulty in tracing the process of this change. Throughout *Cities of the Interior*, it is the men who personify the objective principle, who function primarily on the level of the abstract, the universal, and the impersonal; and the women who interest themselves in what is personal, particular, and concrete. Thus, in *Children of the Albatross*, Paul takes refuge from the complexities of the personal into the relative simplicity of the impersonal.

> It was then that he practiced as deftly as older men the great objectivity, the long-range view by which men eluded all personal difficulties: he removed himself from the present and the personal by entering into the most abstruse intricacies of a chess game, by explaining to her what Darwin had written when comparing the eye to a microscope, by dissertating on the pleuronectidae or flat fish, so remarkable for their asymmetrical bodies (*CA*, p. 96).

For Djuna, however, such escape is neither necessary nor desirable.

And Djuna followed this safari into his worlds of science, chemistry, geology with an awkwardness which was not due to any laziness of mind, but to the fact that the large wave of passion which had been roused in her at the prolonged sight of Paul's little finger was so difficult to dam, because the feeling of wonder before this spectacle was as great as that of the explorers before a new mountain peak, of the scientists before a new discovery (CA, p. 96).

With her genius for investing the trivial with fictional significance, Miss Nin makes of Paul's finger a symbol of the microcosm.

She knew what excitement enfevered men at such moments of their lives, but she did not see any difference between the beauty of a high flight above the clouds and the subtly colored and charming landscapes of adolescence she traversed through the contemplation of Paul's little finger (CA, pp. 96–97).

The contrast between macrocosm and microcosm is extended, by the method of conceit, to extremes that would perhaps surprise a seventeenth-century reader less than a modern one.

A study of anthropological excavations made in Peru was no more wonderful to her than the half-formed dreams unearthed with patience from Paul's vague words . . . and no forest of precious woods could be more varied than the oscillations of his extreme vulnerability which forced him to take cover, to disguise his feelings, to swing so movingly between great courage and a secret fear of pain. The birth of his awareness was to her no lesser miracle than the discoveries of chemistry; the variations in his temperature, the mysterious energy, the sudden serenities, no less valuable than the studies of remote climates (CA, p. 97).

It is passages of this type, perhaps, that have given Miss Nin her reputation for preciousness. Let it be said at once (for the benefit of those who prefer less radical flights of the imagination) that they do not occur very often in "The Sealed Room," which is one of the most controlled of all this author's fictions.

The second part of *Children of the Albatross*, "The Café," drops the romance of Djuna and Paul, who has gone away to war, and resumes the adventures of the characters whom we met in *Ladders to Fire*. Sabina, Lillian, and Djuna are reintroduced in that order, and redefined for us both in their own right and in relation to Jay, who dominates this section. Faustin, Michael, and Donald are also present, and there is a new character, a mysterious personage whom everyone calls Uncle Philip.

Sabina, as we learned in *Ladders to Fire*, has a passion for secrecy. She cannot bear to have a permanent address, dislikes giving out her telephone number, has a fondness for wearing disguises, hates being registered in official books, changes her name constantly "as criminals efface their tracks." Her greatest pleasure is to go to an out-of-the-way café, or to "a little known hotel, if possible a room from which the number had been scratched off." She is perpetually engaged in building up a false image of herself—why, we do not know, nor does Sabina ("She herself did not know what she was preserving from detection, what mystery she was defending"),[3] but it is connected somehow with the habit which many women have of fitting themselves to the image of them which men have invented, and thus with the theme of *Ladders to Fire*. "As soon as a man appeared," Miss Nin writes, "the game began."

> She must keep silent. She must let him look at her face and let his dream take form. She must allow time and silence for his invention to develop.
> She let him build an image. She saw the image take form in his eyes. If she said what she wanted to say he might think her an ordinary woman! . . . Nothing more difficult to live up to than man's dreams. . . .
> She wanted desperately to answer man's most impossible wishes. If the man said: you seem perverse to me, then she would set about gathering all her knowledge of perversity to become what he had called her (*CA*, p. 116).

Sabina's numerous affairs do not satisfy her, but her anguish is of a different kind from that of Lillian, who wants from Jay proof of devotion which he is temperamentally incapable of supplying: he uses her body, she feels, as he would that of a prostitute. To revenge herself, she borrows Sabina's cape (a symbolic gesture, for in it she is going to enact a false role) and has a casual sexual relationship with a stranger in a hotel room. But the experiment is a failure.

> No sooner had she shed her cape . . . than she recognized the room, the man, the scene, and the feelings as not belonging to her, not having been selected by her, but as having been borrowed from Sabina's reportoire of stories and adventures (CA, p. 132).

Djuna's relationship with Jay, which is that of a sympathetic friend, is more comfortable. He feels at ease with her, and though Sabina—to Lillian's intense annoyance—is the only one of the three women he wants to paint, he paints better when Djuna is present.

> She merely sat there and the colors began to organize themselves, to deepen, as if he took the violet from her eyes when she was angry, the blue when she was at peace, the gray when she was detached, the gold when she was melted and warm, and painted with them. Using her eyes as a color chart (CA, p. 124).

Jay is useful to Djuna too, for his acceptance of ordinary life is a corrective to her tendency to dwell almost exclusively in her cities of the interior. Hitherto her participation in life has been symbolic, secondhand.

> Somewhere, in the labyrinth of her life, bread had been transformed into a wafer,[4] with the imponderability of symbols. Communion had been the actual way she experienced life—as communion, not as bread and wine (CA, p. 144).

The three women are in fact archetypes: Sabina is the *femme fatale*, restless, devious, and predatory; Lillian is the Earth Mother, substantial, nourishing, and direct; and Djuna is the feminine friend, serene, understanding, and undemanding. They are defined in terms of their appropriate elements: fire, bread, and light. In the scene in Jay's studio, where he is painting Sabina while the other women are present, his eyes pass from one to the other.

> In this way he passed from the eyes of Lillian which said: "I am here to warm you." Eyes of devotion.
> To the eyes of Sabina which said: "I am here to consume you."
> To the eyes of Djuna which said: "I am here to reflect your painter's dream, like a crystal ball."
> Bread and fire and light, he needed them all (*CA*, pp. 124–25).

When one of the three quarrels with another, he feels distressed, almost as if one part of himself were at war with another.

Faustin, the Zombie-like character whom we met in *Ladders to Fire*, in this book is shown in the symbolic situation of overhearing a dialogue between a couple who are lying in bed in an adjoining room. The two are arguing the subject of faithfulness in love, and Faustin, who takes the woman's side, cannot resist the temptation to shout his opinion through the thin wall which separates the rooms. "All living," we are told, "had taken place for him in the other room, and he had always been the witness. He had always been the commentator."

Michael and Donald also reappear in a scene that reveals the gulf that is widening them. Discussing a new weasel at the Zoo, who cries when she is left alone, Michael asks Donald (who has been singing the same song which the ragpicker sang in *Under a Glass Bell*, "Nothing is lost but it changes," etc.), "Would you cry like that?" and Donald replies, "Not at all. I wouldn't mind at all. I like to be left alone." He sings another verse of the song and adds, "Anyhow, what I like best in the Zoo is not the weasel, it's the rhinoceros with his wonderful tough hide."

> Michael felt inexplicably angry that Donald should like the rhinoceros and not the weasel. That he should admire the toughness of the rhinoceros' skin, as if he were betraying

him, expressing the wish that Michael should be less vulnerable (CA, p. 161).

The song, which suggests Donald's conviction that nothing is permanent, including their relationship—that a new lover might do as well as the one he now has—adds to Michael's annoyance. They go to the Flea Market, where Michael buys Donald a music box and is hurt once more: "Donald did not offer it to Michael's ear, as if he were listening to a music not made for him." For himself, Michael buys a book on astronomy which Donald does not even glance at.

The new character is Uncle Philip, a man obsessed by family allegiances—the Eternal Relative. He has family connections all over the world, and never misses a function involving any one of them—a wedding, a funeral, or a christening. He is the very image of propriety, always correctly if colorlessly dressed, with "the solicitous walk of an undertaker, the unctuous voice of a floor-walker." He is a strange addition to the motley group which swarms in and out of the café, and of course this is the reason for including him, for his loyalty to the blood tie is intended to contrast with the loyalty which these bohemians (refugees for the most part from the kind of family to which he is devoted) feel for the family of their own choosing.

> He thought they were rootless, and yet he felt they were bound to each other, and related to each other as if they had founded new ties, a new kind of family, a new country.
> There was one kind of family, and Uncle Philip wished he could discover the secret of their genealogy (CA, p. 153).

*Children of the Albatross* received mixed reviews. Robert Gorham Davis, in a generally favorable article (*New York Times*, November 23, 1947), made the surprising comment that "Miss Nin's preoccupation with dreams is not surrealist." He added,

> She does not transcribe the grotesquely credible illogic, the vivid and symbolic particularity of night dreams. Instead she is fascinated in a simplifically psychoanalytic way with

waking fantasies, with ego-ideals, and our pictures of ourselves as they affect our relations with others.

It is true that "night dreams" do not figure in *Children
of the Albatross* as they do in the earlier fiction, where, as
we have seen, many of the images had their source in
dreams of this type, but it is a narrow view of surrealism
which conceives it as involving exclusively the kind of
dreams that occur in sleep. Fantasies, daydreams, trance
states, hallucinations (with or without the stimulus of
drugs), even profound reveries—all of these have traditionally provided legitimate material for artists employing
the surrealist method. He is closer to the truth when he
observes,

> Except for occasional flashes into the past, she does not
> work out articulated case histories. She omits what can be
> directly observed and objectively reported.[5] She does not
> look at scenes and faces like a photographer or even a
> painter. Of her principal characters, physically we catch
> only the color of hair or the texture of skin or some
> characteristic movement. There is no dramatic develop-
> ment of incident.

In her best work Miss Nin is well aware of the difference
between a psychiatric report and a work of art, and this is
one of the reasons why, I think, "The Voice" must be
counted among her lesser fictions, for there she does not
always seem sufficiently aware of this difference. In our
study of *Ladders to Fire*, we noted that her usual technique consists in having her characters arrive at self-
knowledge either independently, through a series of revelations, or through the assistance of other characters, who
are not professional analysts like The Voice. Mr. Davis
ended his review on a note of praise that was not without
qualification.

> What Miss Nin records are subjective states, configurations
> of character, the fields of electric tension, movement and
> resistance in human relationships. She defines these with
> elegance and insight in apothegmatic general statements of
> a sometimes pretentious sort with their carefully designed

series of parallel constructions. Her words are often abstractions: "separateness," "freedom," "possession," "dissolution," "wholeness," "fulfillment," "obstruction"; or simple conventional metaphoric images: "fire," "river," "seeds," "roots," "blood," "light," "womb," "wine," "bread." The result is an abstract, psychic music, a dance of generalities and types, charming and suggestive in a narrowly romantic way. But the outer realities from which it derives its meaning are so incompletely seen—beyond the mirror-like windows of brightly lighted and barely furnished inner rooms.

In one of the most perceptive comments ever made by a critic of Anaïs Nin's work, Violet A. Lang wrote in the *Chicago Review* (Spring, 1948):

> It may be we have grown able, in this country, to recognize and accept this specialized and deeply private kind of experience—the kind of experience that a Surrealist painting commands and evaluates—without our old reaction of scorn or of indignation at the baffling in art: the past decade has forced us into the recognition of the internal drama. I think some part of the hostility with which Anaïs Nin has been dismissed by some readers may be attributed to this betrayal of objectivity; she is *embarrassing*. She has discredited the importance of environment of place and time; her streets are alike in New York or in Paris; she has returned to the natural city. Her emphasis is upon emotional interdependence, upon creation and destruction, upon the familial situation. Because these written lives are not lived in the language or seen from the perspective we are accustomed to assume, in the act of recognition, we are caught unawares. This is unsettling, and we are not used to it. We have not the conventions to do so. We look for a careful balance between reality and poised mentality in our novels; we look for a habit of intelligence, an intellectual capacity, which we identify readily as insight, character, typical behavior of family type. Anaïs Nin upsets all this; she dismays the balance; the vivid discord of this painful inner reality must rise to create its own balance, demand its own perspective.

Some of these points, in a negative context, had been made previously, as we have seen, by other critics. But Mrs. Lang's context is positive.

It is possible, on the other hand, to deny that the adjustment must be made, or that participation is required of the reader; it is possible to condemn the whole discomfiting assumption of experience by unquestionable critical principles. She can be condemned for indiscretions of plot-manipulation (which have little importance for her), for repetitions and exaggerations, too rich characterizations, or even for her overwhelming use of emotional and connotative language—but this condemnation is pointless. She is not an objective writer; she is not trying to tell a good story; she is above all not attempting to manipulate social action. What she is trying to do, and does very well, is to interpret deep personal relationships by writing of them in those circumstances which interpret them, the moments of change, the moments of revelation, the time of terrible intensity. She does this with deep sincerity, and with humility.

The sense of "inner reality" which, as this critic correctly perceived, is what more than anything else interests Anaïs Nin as an artist, has, in *Children of the Albatross*, been created and sustained to a degree that is more than usually successful. Her technique here is under firmer control and is employed more consistently than in any of her previous novels. The characters who are to figure prominently throughout the series are explored with a depth and an intensity of observation that enables us to watch them henceforth with the interest and concern that are indispensable to the novel of character.

## 7    THE DROWNING OF THE DOLL
*THE FOUR-CHAMBERED HEART*

IN *The Four-Chambered Heart*, third volume of *Cities of the Interior*,[1] Miss Nin achieves greater unity than in any of her preceding work. There are only three main characters: Djuna; Rango, a Guatemalan musician who has exchanged the colorful past of wandering over Europe with a tribe of gypsies for a shabby domesticity in a prison-like house in Paris; and Zora, Rango's wife, who is a nagging invalid. The first few paragraphs, which describe Rango playing his guitar in the Paris night clubs, tend to be disappointing in that they repeat, word for word, the scene wherein Rango makes his first appearance in *Ladders to Fire*. But once this minor defect (visible in any case only to readers familiar with the other book) has been accepted and forgotten, the story gathers force and the tensions that exist among the three characters accumulate toward a climax that is as effective as anything this author has written.

Djuna and Rango fall in love almost from the moment of their meeting, and Djuna rents an abandoned houseboat on the Seine which had been used as a theater by a group of itinerant actors; now it is to serve as the theater of her and Rango's passions. Here as in Miss Nin's earlier work the river symbolizes life itself, and more particularly the life of the unconscious, so that adjustment to its flow signifies not merely an acceptance of life on a literal level but also the act of living in harmony with the rhythms of one's true nature (which this author always identifies with the unconscious mind), an obedience to the laws of the basic self. The houseboat, whose natural element is water or life, thus contrasts with the sordid dwelling which is the scene of Rango and Zora's union—a union which, we are told, has for some years been without physical consummation, a fact which might be offered in extenuation, if extenuation were required, for Djuna's action, for she is not seeking to break up a marriage which has meaning. (Zora is also childless.) Here is Rango's legal residence:

> The windows of the house were long and narrow. They seemed barred . . . The black forest of his bewilderment as he stood about to enter a house too gray, too shabby, too cramped for his big, powerful body (*FCH*, pp. 8–9).

And here is the dwelling to which Djuna introduces him, thereby inviting him to participate actively in life and in love.

> The walls of the barge curved like the inside of a whale's belly . . . They descended the turning stairway and Rango smelled the tar with delight. When he saw the room, the shadows, the beams, he exclaimed: "It's like the Tales of Hoffman. It's a dream. It's a fairy tale" (*FCH*, pp. 16, 9).

A passing ship causes the houseboat to heave; Rango lies down and says, "We're navigating." It is, of course, an illusion, but they are idyllically happy and Djuna forgets what a policeman has told her, that the barge is leaky and "unsafe for long voyages."

On the houseboat they attempt to create a world of their own—a world which did not exist until the moment of their meeting. "And now they were content," writes the author, "having attained all lovers' dream of a desert island, a cell, a cocoon, in which to create a world together from the beginning." Instinctively they avoid all references to that period of their lives which immediately preceded their union.

> In the dark they gave each other their many selves, avoiding only the more recent ones, the story of the years before they

met as a dangerous realm from which might spring dissensions, doubts, and jealousies. In the dark they sought rather to give each other their earlier, their innocent, unpossessed selves.

This was the paradise to which every lover liked to return with his beloved, recapturing a virgin self to give one another (*FCH*, p. 32).

The paradise, however, is short-lived. The first problem is created by Rango's jealousy of Jay and Paul, particularly the latter, whom he has never met. For in spite of all her best intentions Djuna makes the mistake of telling Rango about her affair with Paul, and she does so in order to destroy the false image which he has of her as an angel. Vainly thereafter does she try to convince him that no rivalry is involved, that her love for Paul was a unique thing, very different from what she now feels for Rango. Why, she wonders, must he use the past to destroy the present? "No two caresses ever resemble each other," she meditates. "Every lover holds a new body until he fills it with his essence, and no two essences are the same, and no flavor is ever repeated." Elsewhere she cries, "Your jealousy is necrophilic! You're opening tombs!" The tenses of love are separate, and to confuse them is, for the lover, the most fatal of all errors. For paradoxically, by his jealousy Rango is constantly reminding Djuna of the lover with whom, in Rango's jealous state, she cannot help comparing him unfavorably.

He was driving the image of Paul into another chamber of her heart, an isolated chamber without communicating passage into the one inhabited by Rango. A place in some obscure recess, where flows eternal love, in a realm so different from the one inhabited by Rango that they would never meet or collide, in these vast cities of the interior (*FCH*, p. 54).

In a medical book, or an encyclopaedia, she discovers the metaphor which applies to the situation and which, incidentally, gives the novel its title: "The heart . . . is an organ . . . consisting of four chambers . . . A wall separates the chambers on the left from those on the right and no direct communication is possible between them."

Rango's jealousy leads him to hate the books she had discussed with Paul, and there is a painful scene in which he insists on burning them. So far from protesting, however, Djuna assists at the holocaust.

> To her this was not only an offering of peace to his tormenting jealousy, but a sudden anger at this pile of books whose contents had not prepared her for moments such as this one. All these novels so carefully concealing the truth about character, about the obscurities, the tangles, the mysteries. Words words words words words and no revelation of the pitfalls, the abysms in which human beings found themselves. Let him burn them all; they deserved their fate (FCH, pp. 52–53).

The situation provides the author with an opportunity for a tirade against the literature of realism, novels which pretend to tell the truth about life but which cheat the reader of genuine emotional experience, novels whose authors concerned themselves with peripheral material and did not face squarely the problem of depicting human relationships, novels whose action is on the surface and which are therefore of only superficial interest. We are perhaps justified here in identifying Djuna's thoughts with those of Anaïs Nin.

> Rango thinks he is burning moments of my life with Paul. He is only burning words, words which eluded all truths, eluded essentials, eluded the bare demon in human beings, and added to the blindness, added to the errors. Novels promising experience, and then remaining on the periphery, reporting only the semblance, the illusions, the costumes, and the falsities, opening no wells, preparing no one for the crises, the pitfalls, the wars, and the traps of human life. Teaching nothing, revealing nothing, cheating us of truth, of immediacy, of reality. Let him burn them, all the books of the world which have avoided the naked knowledge of the cruelties that take place between men and women in the pit of solitary nights. Their abstractions and evasions were no armor against moments of despair (FCH, p. 53).

But Djuna realizes the real threat to their love does not lie in externals; unlike Rango, who "believed the seed of destruction lay in the world around them, as for example in those books which revealed to Rango too blatantly the difference between their two minds." The destruction of love, she knows, comes from within, not without, and from this danger not even the "cocoon" they have woven about themselves, not even the "desert island" to which they have retreated, is entirely safe. "Love never dies of a natural death," Djuna meditates. "It dies because we don't know how to replenish its source, it dies of blindness and errors and betrayals. It dies of illnesses and wounds, it dies of weariness, of witherings, of tarnishings, but never of natural death. Every lover could be brought to death as the murderer of his own love."

Rango's jealousy, unfortunately, is not the only obstacle to their happiness. He is determined that Djuna shall be friends with his wife, saying, "She is very ill and you might help her." The appeal is directed to her "good" self, and here, because of her childhood, when she had been constantly admonished by her parents, "Be good or you will not be loved," Djuna is particularly vulnerable. Through a sense of *noblesse oblige* she decides she will make the effort, though she feels little sympathy for Zora—and indeed there is very little about Rango's shrewish spouse to arouse sympathy in anyone, for her illnesses, as Djuna soon discovers, are largely imaginary. But Rango believes in them, and the mixture of pity and duty which he feels for Zora makes of him her slave—and Djuna, when she enters the scene, soon becomes enslaved also.

For Zora is shrewd. At their first meeting she tells Djuna, "I knew that sooner or later he would love another woman, and I am glad it's you because you are kind, and you will not take him away from me. I need him." It is another appeal to her "good" self, and though her natural self rebels, Djuna once more obeys the former. Zora also says, "The other day I went to church and prayed desperately that someone should save us, and now you are here." When Djuna and Rango return to the barge after this painful session, the author tells us that they are no longer a couple but "a trinity, with Zora's inexorable needs conducting all their movements, directing their time together, dictating the hours of separation."

It is not merely goodness, or *noblesse oblige*, that enables Djuna to play this difficult part. As in Carson McCullers' *Ballad of the Sad Café* (where Miss Amelia, because of her love for Cousin Lymon, consents to take in Marvin Macy, whom she loathes),[2] Djuna discovers that her love for Rango is large enough that it can include his concern for his wife: "Rango had placed Zora under Djuna's protection and her love for Rango had to extend in magnitude to include Zora." And there is another, less obvious reason for Djuna's acceptance of the situation. Rango is a man of nature, violent and impulsive; and through him the natural self in Djuna, which she has suppressed and controlled, finds vicarious expression: he acts out this self which she has buried in her childhood.

> For this complicity in the dark she must share the consequences with him.
> The realm she had tried to skip: darkness, confusion, violence, destruction, erupted secretly through relationship with Rango. The burden was placed on his shoulders. She must therefore share the torments, too. She had not annihilated her natural self; it reasserted itself in Rango. And she was his accomplice (*FCH*, p. 87).

Rango reminds us of one of Lawrence's primitives. His body, we are told, had not been "chiseled like a city man's," but "modeled in clay more massive, more formless, too, cruder in outline, closer to primitive sculpture, as if he had kept a little of the heavier contours of the Indian, of animals, of rocks, earth, and plants." He is in constant rebellion against the urban environment, asserting his own rhythm against that of the city.

> Clock time, machines, auto horns, whistles, congestion caught man in their cogs, deafened, stupefied him. The city's rhythm dedicated to man; the imperious order to remain alive actually meant to become an abstraction. Ran-

go's protest was to set out to deny and destroy the enemy. He set out to deny clock time and he would miss, first of all, all that he reached for. He would make such detours to obey his own rhythm and not the city's that the simplest act of shaving and buying a steak would take hours, and the vitally important letter would never be written (*FCH, pp.* 39–40).

He is a simple man, easily taken in by Zora's hypo-chondria, and Djuna shrinks from disillusioning him for fear he will mistake her motives. He is a poor provider, and it is Djuna who must buy the medicines, the warm clothes and the special foods. Like the elderly aunt in *Swann's Way*, Zora dislikes nothing so much as being told she looks better. And her character, like that of Aunt Léonie, is not without its humorous side. Concerning a book lying at the foot of her bed she tells Djuna,

> "It's a book about illness. I love to read about illness. I go to the library and look up descriptions of the symptoms I have. I've marked all the pages which apply to me. Just look at all these markings! Sometimes I think I have all the sicknesses one can have!" She laughed. Then looking at Djuna plaintively, almost pleadingly, she said: "All my hair is falling out" (*FCH*, p. 92).

The situation becomes increasingly difficult as Zora's imaginary needs and real demands begin to multiply. At first Rango spent every other night at the barge, but as his wife's condition, as he thinks, worsens, he spends two nights a week there, and finally only one. As the unac-knowledged struggle of the two women for possession of Rango mounts, it is clear that we are dealing once more with archetypes: Zora personifies the destructive principle (her favorite pastime is ripping seams) and Djuna the constructive. Djuna makes halfhearted attempts to per-suade her to take better care of herself, and this is what happens:

> When she got a new room in the sun, she kept the blinds down and shut out air and light. When they went to the beach together up the river, her bathing suit, given to her

by Djuna, was not ready. She had ripped it apart to improve its shape. When they went to the park she wore too light a dress and caught cold. When they went to a restaurant she ate the food she knew would harm her, and predicted that the next day she would be in bed all day (*FCH*, p. 112).

To escape from this situation, Djuna falls into the habit of going out of town for two and three days at a time, and notices that during her absence Zora makes a mysterious improvement, but invariably suffers a relapse on her return: "Whenever Djuna returned there would be an aggravation, and thus Djuna and Rango could not meet that evening." Rango is blind to this coincidence, and Djuna does not dare to point it out: "Any departure from what he believed he considered a betrayal of her love." But the tensions between the two women disturb him—his intuition tells him that a battle is in progress—and he has his own method for escaping, which is to identify himself with a political cause, the cause of assisting a revolution in his native Guatemala. Incapable of solving the personal problem, he turns his attention, like other male characters in Miss Nin's fiction, to the impersonal one, and this decision (which the author regards as characteristically masculine) provides her with yet another opportunity for expounding one of her favorite convictions:

> It saddened Djuna that Rango was so eager to go to war, to fight for his ideas, to die for them. It seemed to her that he was ready to live and die for emotional errors as women did, but that like most men he did not call them emotional errors; he called them history, philosophy, metaphysics, science. Her feminine self was sad and smiled, too, at this game of endowing personal and emotional beliefs with the dignity of impersonal names. She smiled at this as men smile at women's enlargement of personal tragedies to a status men do not believe applicable to personal lives (*FCH*, p. 72).

It is a simplistic view of life and the world, requiring (as in the case of Lawrence) a sharp polarization—sharper than is perhaps consistent with reality—between the sexes.

But Djuna in any case is determined to put first things first, and for her, as for Lawrence, first things are those involving human relationships in a universe that is anthropocentrically conceived.

> Parties changed every day, philosophies and science changed, but for Djuna human love alone continued. Great changes in the maps of the world, but none in this need of human love, this tragedy of human love swinging between illusion and human life, sometimes breaking at the dangerous passageway between illusion and human life, sometimes breaking altogether. . . .
>
> She smiled at man's great need to build cities when it was so much harder to build relationships, his need to conquer countries when it was so much harder to conquer one heart, to satisfy a child, to create a perfect human life. Man's need to invent, to circumnavigate space when it is so much harder to overcome space between human beings, man's need to organize systems of philosophy when it is so much harder to understand one human being, and when the greatest depths of human character lay but half explored . . . Man turned his telescope outward and far, not seeing character emerging at the opposite end of the telescope by subtle accumulations, fragments, accretions, and encrustations.
>
> Woman turned her telescope to the near, and the warm (*FCH*, pp. 72, 73, 164–65).

In the hope of lessening the tension, Djuna persuades Rango and Zora to accompany her on a vacation to the Riviera. Here, while Rango is busy nursing his wife, she encounters some of the airy young men, "other extensions of Paul," who satisfy the peace-loving side of her nature to which Rango has no access. With one of them, whom the author refers to as "Paul the second," she forms a particularly close friendship, thereby infuriating Rango: "The black sun of his jealousy eclipsed the Mediterranean sun, churned the sea's turquoise gentleness." Now thoroughly disillusioned, Djuna returns with the pair to Paris, and she is more than ever convinced that the tenses of love are separate.

> It was clear to Djuna now that the four-chambered heart was no act of betrayal, but that there were regions necessary to life to which Rango had no access. It was not that Djuna wanted to house the image of Paul in one chamber and Rango in another, nor that to love Rango she must destroy the chamber inhabited by Paul—it was that in Djuna there was a hunger for a haven which Rango was utterly incapable of giving to her, or attaining with her (FCH, p. 130).

Djuna's position is that of the modern woman who demands for herself the same kind of independence in love that men traditionally enjoy, yet she is far from corresponding to the stereotype of the militant feminist; neither does she resemble Sabina, another "modern" woman, whose ambition to enslave her partners may perhaps be construed as a secret hatred of them. Djuna is unique, and she is possessed of considerable insight: "She knew that we love in others some repressed self. In consoling Rango, reassuring him, was she consoling some secret Djuna, who had once been jealous and not dared to reveal it?" Djuna, in fact, is constantly aware of the several selves which comprise her personality, and this awareness increases in direct ratio to the discomfort of the situation.

> Not one but many Djunas descended the staircase of the barge, one layer formed by the parents, the childhood, another molded by her profession and her friends, still another born of history, geology, climate, race, economics, and all the backgrounds and backdrops, the sky and nature of the earth, the pure sources of birth, the influence of a tree, a word dropped carelessly, an image seen, and all the corrupted sources: books, art, dogmas, tainted friendships, and all the places where a human being is wounded, defeated, crippled, and which fester . . . (FCH, pp. 163–64).

The sense of division is conveyed by means of an image which recurs in A Spy in the House of Love (where it applies to Sabina).

> The movement of the many layers of the self described by Duchamp's Nude Descending a Staircase, the multiple selves growing in various proportions, not singly, not evenly

developed, not moving in one direction, but composed of multiple juxtapositions revealing endless spirals of character as the earth revealed its strata, an infinite constellation of feelings expanding as mysteriously as space and light in the realm of the planets (*FCH*, p. 164).

Through Rango, the barge becomes a meeting place for revolutionists plotting to overthrow the Guatemalan government. Rango attempts to interest Djuna in this cause, but she replies characteristically, "You know what I believe. The world today is rootless: it's like a forest with all the trees with their heads in the ground and their roots gesticulating wildly in the air, withering. The only remedy is to begin a world of two; in two there is hope of perfection, and that in turn may spread to all . . . But it must begin at the base, in relationship of man and woman." Rango's zeal, for all its intermittent intensity, lacks a genuine center, and his commitment to the revolution is essentially theoretical. His laziness, his indifference to time, and his inability to discipline himself in even the smallest matters make him ineffective as a party member, and when he receives a reprimand from their leaders he is crushed.

Depressed by Rango's failures and by a harrowing incident in which Zora, whose jealousy has rendered her temporarily insane, attempts to stab her with a hatpin, Djuna decides the time has come to end the relationship: "The barge was sailing nowhere, moored to the port of despair." In a symbolic gesture, she tears a board from the bottom of the boat and lies down to await death beside the sleeping Rango. She enters the world of the dream, where, in a series of water images that recall *House of Incest*, she surrenders her individual identity to the cosmic unconscious.

Below the level of identity lay an ocean, an ocean of which human beings carry only a drop in their veins; but some sink below cognizance and the drop becomes a huge wave, the tide of memory, the undertows of sensation (*FCH*, p. 177).

Upon reunion with this profoundest part of her self, the lowest common denominator of the psyche, she perceives that her error has consisted in thinking that a perfect union is possible in an imperfect world: the real obstacle is not Zora, nor Rango, but the romantic idealism which has led her to expect the impossible. On the threshold of her self-willed death, she realizes that "exaggeration is the cause of despair," and now, with the clarity born of great distance, "the barge was smaller, Rango did not loom so immense, Zora had shrunk." From this perspective, she sees all their maneuverings as games, and understands that, because of her own illusions, she has falsely invested them with the importance of high tragedy. So purified, she awakens and decides that she will accept whatever destiny the imperfections of human beings—including her own—may require of her. "Rango!," she calls, "wake up! There's a leak!" And they set about repairing it.

Later they stroll on the quay, and notice that a fisherman has made an unusual catch.

> It was a doll.
> It was a doll who had committed suicide during the night.
> The water had washed off its features. Her hair aureoled her face with crystalline glow (*FCH*, p. 187).

The doll who had "committed suicide during the night" is the childish part of herself, the part which delighted in playing games, which persisted in fantasy and illusions, which expected the impossible, which refused to make any compromises in the face of reality—the child whom all the books that she and Paul read together had not prepared to accept the shortcomings either in herself or in others.

*The Four-Chambered Heart*, in the opinion of a number of critics, is the best of Miss Nin's longer narratives. It has greater unity, both technically and thematically, than any of her other novels, and is able to stand by itself in a way that none of the other items in the series can do. Yet it clearly belongs in the series—and in a way that *Children of the Albatross*, for all its haunting beauty does not—for the theme of feminine completion underlies the more obvious one, to which it is related, of the fallibility of human love: Djuna realizes that she will achieve fulfill-ment only when she has learned to accept the fact of human weakness and adjust to it. *The Four-Chambered Heart* may also be this author's most dramatic work; cer-tainly the pattern of its action is more inevitable at the same time that it is more obvious, and the suspense is skillfully maintained to the very end. Of all her books it is probably the one which corresponds most closely to the conventional idea of the "well-made novel," and those critics who welcome the familiar were correspondingly grateful. An example is James Korges, who, in a curious essay (*Critique*, Spring-Summer, 1965) in which he com-pares Miss Nin's novels of character unfavorably with James's *Turn of the Screw* and Ford Madox Ford's *The Good Soldier* (as if there were any value in such com-parisons,[3] it being almost impossible to think of two novelists whose assumptions are more unlike Miss Nin's) noted:

> For the first time, I think, Nin was close to rendering the relationship between two people, rather than reporting monologues and actions, notations copied from a diary set down for psychoanalysis. Nin does not discuss this ro-mance, but instead presents it in some richly romantic images: the apparent stability of the romantic love of Rango and Djuna is not discussed but embodied in the houseboat, tied to the stone shore but floating on the flux and change of the Seine, on the symbol itself.

The distinction which Korges makes in his first sentence between *rendering* and *reporting* suggests his commitment to the Impressionist theories of Ford Madox Ford (whose terminology this is) and Conrad, as do also the frequent admiring references to Ford throughout his essay. It is true that the Impressionist technique, when employed by a master, can accomplish masterpieces. But like any other fictional technique it involves a sacrifice, and the tech-nique of Impressionism, which makes a fetish of invisible authorship and point of view, calls for sacrifices that few major novelists in the history of world literature have been willing to make: it subsumes a particularly narrow view of fiction, and to invoke the Impressionist standard in the general service of literary criticism is manifestly absurd. (A particularly notorious example of such invocation is Ford's own *March of Literature*.)

After discussing *The Four-Chambered Heart* in some detail, Mr. Korges concluded:

> I am not prepared to argue that this is a great novel; but it is a fine achievement by a minor, flawed novelist. The virtue of Miss Nin's writing has always been her intense feminine insights (as in some short stories, such as "Birth"); and in this book I think she comes as close as she ever did to a balance of intensity and control, of insight and art. I wish Swallow had reissued only *Four-Chambered Heart*, for now this best of Nin's fiction is buried in the 700 pages of the repetitious, incoherently structured *Cities of the Interior*.

The depth of the academic bias from which this grudging praise proceeds may be judged by the fact that, in the same essay, he seriously takes to task Allan Seager for having used a dangling modifier in *A Frieze of Girls!*

Rather more pertinently, Lloyd Morris observed (*New York Herald-Tribune*, March 12, 1950):

> Wishing to exact from readers an intense participation in the experience of her heroine, Miss Nin has developed a narrative method very unlike any to which traditional fiction has accustomed us . . . The elements of time and scene are casually treated. For Miss Nin is not, in the usual sense, trying to tell a story. Her object is to reveal experience directly. She wishes to immerse readers in that flow of sensibility and reflection from which human beings distillate significance of what they do and suffer.

And René Fülop-Miller noted in the *New York Times* (January 29, 1950),

> A maturer artist now, Miss Nin has been able in her new book to give form to psychic tensions and to translate inner events into narration . . . To describe the course of its

action is to convey only a part of *The Four-Chambered Heart*. For to Miss Nin external events form only one side of true reality, in which two realms—the inward and the outward, the world of dream and of waking—are united. Miss Nin has the gift of communicating this unity directly. External action is deepened by being converted to inward experience; the visionary and hallucinatory become integral parts of reality.

Concerning the theme of *The Four-Chambered Heart*, poet Hayden Carruth believed it to be the struggle between the human ego and the dehumanizing, repressive forces of modern society.

> This is a story about Djuna's terrifying struggle to find within herself some answer to two related problems: encroaching, absorbing modern society on one hand; indomitable, but escaping individuality on the other. This is truly the central drama of today, and here it is set down clearly and humanly, with none of the fuzzy sociological overtones that so often confuse the ambitious writer.[4]

This was, of course, one of Lawrence's major themes, as it is also a favorite theme of the so-called Beat writers of the present decade; it is certainly present in *The Four-Chambered Heart*, but I believe that Carruth overstates the case when he says that this is what the book is "about." [5] More than anything else, Anaïs Nin is writing in this novel about the fallibility of human love, and Morris, in the review from which I have already quoted, is closer to the truth when he declares,

> She [Djuna] exalts love as the exclusive goal of living, and she can be fulfilled only by that absolute and total union with a lover which, intellectually, she knows to be beyond the reach of human nature. This is the predicament that constitutes the matrix of her experience, and the essential subject of the novel.

He continues, "It is, of course, one of the oldest subjects of literature, for it springs from an awareness of the ultimate isolation of every individual, against which the human spirit permanently rebels." This would suggest that, insofar as its theme is concerned, *The Four-Chambered Heart* is closer to the novels of Carson McCullers than to those of Lawrence; and indeed, except for the note of despair on which McCullers' novels almost invariably close—and which never finally triumphs in Miss Nin's—there is a very close resemblance between *The Four-Chambered Heart* and such works as *The Heart Is a Lonely Hunter* and *The Ballad of the Sad Café*. "She was fully, painfully aware," writes Miss Nin of Djuna, "that very rarely did midnight strike in two hearts at once, very rarely did midnight arouse two equal desires, and that any dislocation in this, any indifference, was an indication of disunity, of the difficulties, the impossibilities of fusion between two human beings." This is the same bitter knowledge which McCullers' lonely lovers share, and which motivates the tramp in "A Tree, a Rock, a Cloud" to search for a "science of love" which will enable him to master this most difficult of all arts.[6]

JUST AS *The Four-Chambered Heart* was concerned primarily with Djuna, A *Spy in the House of Love* is an
in-depth study of Sabina, the third in the gallery of Miss
Nin's feminine archetypes—or fourth, if we include Stella.
And the pattern of the two books is similar in that their
climax (which is in both cases an interior climax, having
little to do with the level of surface action) occurs when
the protagonist, after a series of frustrations, arrives at a
state of self-awareness. But A *Spy in the House of Love,*
which is a novella rather than a full-scale novel, differs
radically in technique from its predecessor; in this respect
it is the most ambitious of all the author's longer narratives, the most "experimental," the one which relies least
upon the conventions of the realistic novel. Its arrangement is spatial rather than chronological, consisting of a
series of episodes which are not related by any causal
connection—so that it does not greatly matter which pre-
cedes which—but which have the common purpose of
dramatizing the plight of the protagonist, of depicting the
spiritual anguish that is born of self-division. One critic
was reminded of "harmonized tableaux such as one sees
on the unfolding panels of old Japanese screens, of figures
presented in revealing poses."

Readers of the first three volumes of *Cities of the
Interior* will recall the frantic efforts which Sabina made

to surround herself with secrecy. "It made life difficult," Miss Nin wrote in *Children of the Albatross,* "she lived the tense, strained life of an international spy"—thereby anticipating the title of the present book, in which we learn the source of Sabina's unrest, the reasons for her obsessive secrecy. But before we can understand this, a few words in explanation of Sabina's general character are in order, for it will not do to think of her as a mere nymphomaniac in the way some reviewers have done. She is a woman of considerable dignity, even a certain nobility, and she possesses a very keen ethical sense which causes her to experience powerful feelings of guilt. More than anything else, she is a woman of enormous, almost unbounded vitality. She has a zest for life, a thirst for experience, which are of almost Whitmanesque proportions, and this is the real root of her difficulty, for she is reluctant to lead a single life; she wants to live in all directions at once. This means, where her love life is concerned, that she is unwilling to make a permanent emotional investment in any one man, for that man, she feels, will satisfy only one of the several selves of which she is composed. But when she attempts simultaneous relationships, she discovers that the selves will not coexist harmoniously, that they conflict and quarrel with one another; and this tension is aggravated by a sense of guilt which, as we have noted, is her constant burden.

A *Spy in the House of Love* combines fantasy with reality in a way that is disconcerting to the type of reader who would prefer for it to be one or the other or to alternate between the two at regular and easily recognizable intervals. For example, there is an early scene in a Greenwich Village night club (the setting of this story is New York instead of Paris) at which we discover Sabina talking with a group of friends. The scene recurs toward the end of the novella (pages 112–25), and if the reader has been thinking along temporal lines he naturally assumes a passage of time between the two, but it soon becomes apparent that it is the same scene rendered from another point of view, so that the same impressions registered by one character in the early scene are registered by another in the later one, and the author increases the effect of hallucination, of *déja vu*, by deliberately, in certain passages, using the same words to describe both scenes. Though an element of fantasy is present in the first scene, it is largely realistic; the second scene is entirely so. But there is yet a third night-club scene, this one obviously involving a lapse of time and therefore different from the other two, which, except for the presence in it of Djuna, is pure fantasy. There is no denying that the peculiar and unpredictable blending of fantasy with reality in this story makes for considerable difficulty, and it is not always clear for what purpose it has been accomplished.

Notwithstanding the complication of its technique, which somewhat resembles that of Marguerite Duras, *A Spy in the House of Love* has an essentially simple situation, that of a woman torn between the love she feels for her husband, a love which is closer to filial piety than to passion, and the love (different in each case) that she feels for a series of other men. The guilt inspired by the necessity of concealing these illicit relationships from her husband is personified in the form of an imaginary character, the Lie Detector, who follows her about making entries in a notebook. It is clear from the first that this character is Sabina's own invention: in the telephone conversation which takes place in the first chapter he tells her, "You wouldn't have called me if you were innocent. Guilt is the one burden human beings can't bear alone. As soon as a crime is committed, there is a telephone call, or a confession to strangers." True to his name, he ignores her rejoinder, "There was no crime," and continues,

> There is only one relief: to confess, to be caught, tried, punished. But it's not quite so simple. Only half of the self wants to atone, to be freed of the torments of guilt. The other half of man wants to be free. So only half of the self surrenders, calling "Catch me," while the other half creates obstacles, difficulties, seeks to escape. It's a flirtation with justice. If justice is nimble, it will follow the clue with the criminal's help. If not, the criminal will take care of his own atonement (*SHL*, p. 6).

When Sabina asks, "Is that worse?," he replies: "I think

so. I think we are more severe judges of our own acts than professional judges. We judge our thoughts, our intents, our secret curses, our secret hates, not only our acts." Sabina acknowledges the truth of this observation by hanging up. She then goes to a bar, where she seeks comfort in alcohol and in a series of feverish conversations. But the Lie Detector, who has traced her call, follows her, and when she gets up the next morning she sees him standing on the corner pretending to read a newspaper: "It was not a surprise, because it was a materialization of a feeling she had known for many years: that of an Eye watching and following her throughout her life." Thereafter he shadows all her actions.

In the next chapter Sabina checks out of the hotel in which she has been staying with a lover and returns to Alan, her husband, a man who is the very essence of stability and devotion and who trusts her implicitly—fortunately, since he has never been tempted to check on her movements. She accounts for her periodic absences by saying she has been touring with a theatrical company. She has developed a real proficiency for telling lies; this time she says,

> The trip was tiring, but the play went well. I hated the role at first, as you know. But I began to feel for Madame Bovary, and the second night I played it well, I even understood her particular kind of voice and gestures. I changed myself completely. You know, how tension makes the voice higher and thinner, and nervousness increases the number of gestures? (SHL, p. 19).

There is irony, of course, in the part she pretends to have been playing, and the irony is multiplied when Alan answers,

> "What an actress you are! You've entered into this woman's part so thoroughly you can't get out of it! You're actually making so many more gestures than you ever did, and your voice has changed" (SHL, pp. 19–20).

Were Alan less gullible, the irony would have been intentional, and the situation—interesting though it is—might have been even more so because of this added dimension.

One is tempted to wonder, incidentally, if Alan is really the innocent that he appears to be—he would probably have forgiven her anything, docile as he seems to be, and might even have closed his eyes to her infidelities, betraying his consciousness of them only in ironic remarks of this sort—but there is no evidence for this in the text. In any case Sabina would never be the one to disillusion him, and this not so much because of self-interest, for fear she might lose him, but because, being a kind person, she cannot bear to hurt Alan; she remembers the one time she has seen him lose his self-composure, when his father died, and his hoarse sobs on that occasion, testimony to the depth of his suffering, made an indelible impression: "This image wakened her with horror, with compassion, and again her feeling was, I must always be on guard, to protect his happiness, always on guard to protect my guardian angel." But the strain is almost unbearable. Following her return to Alan, in an interior monologue which is one of the finest passages in the book, she meditates thus:

> Why am I loved by him? Will he continue to love me? His love is for something I am not. I am not beautiful enough, I am not good, I am not good for him, he should not love me shame shame shame for not being beautiful enough, there are other women so much more beautiful, with radiant faces and clear eyes. Alan says my eyes are beautiful, but I cannot see them, to me they are lying eyes, my mouth lies, only a few hours ago it was kissed by another. He is kissing the mouth kissed by another, he is kissing eyes which adored another . . . shame . . . shame . . . shame . . . the lies, the lies . . . (*SHL*, p. 21).

In this monologue, the author's genius for investing particulars with imaginary significance, and for entering so completely into the point of view of her women characters, are both apparent.

> The clothes he is hanging up for me with such care were caressed and crushed by another, the other was so impatient he crushed and tore at my dress. I had no time to undress. It is this dress he is hanging up lovingly . . . can I forget yesterday, forget the vertigo, this wildness, can I

come home and stay home? Sometimes I cannot bear the
quick change of scene, the quick transitions, I cannot make
the changes smoothly, from one relationship to another.
Some parts of me tear off like fragments, fly here and there.
I lose vital parts of myself, some part of me stays in that
hotel room, a part of me is walking away from this place of
haven, a part of me is following another as he walks down
the street alone or perhaps not alone: someone may take
my place at his side while I am here, that will be my
punishment, and someone will take my place here when I
leave. I feel guilty for leaving each one alone, I feel responsible for their being alone, and I feel guilty twice over,
towards both men (SHL, pp. 21–22).

In no other of her works has Miss Nin been so successful
at depicting the anxieties of self-division, the peculiar
anguish and pathos attendant upon the attempt to lead a
multiple existence.

Wherever I am, I am in many pieces, not daring to bring
them all together, anymore than I would dare to bring the
two men together. Now I am here where I will not be hurt,
for a few days at least I will not be hurt in any way . . . but
I am not all of me here, only half of me is being sheltered.
Well, Sabina, you failed as an actress. You rejected the
discipline, the routine, the monotony, the repetitions, any
sustained effort, and now you have a role which must be
changed every day, to protect one human being from sor-
row. Wash your lying eyes and lying face, wear the clothes
which stayed in the house, which are his, baptized by his
hands, play the role of a whole woman, at least you have
always wished to be that, it is not altogether a lie . . .
(SHL, p. 22).

That night, rendered sleepless by guilt, she reconstructs
one of her affairs, an eight-day idyl with a handsome opera
singer whom she met on the beach at Provincetown, a
professional Don Juan named Philip. Her only rival is a
woman who stands in the same relation to Philip as Alan
to Sabina—a plain, self-effacing person to whom Philip
has given singing lessons: "For this other woman Philip
had the sympathy Alan had for Sabina. He spoke tenderly
of her health not being good, to Sabina who had kept so

fiercely the secret of being cold when they swam, or tired when they walked too long, or feverish in too much sun." But they have a comfortable, passionless relationship of which Sabina is not jealous, knowing that when Philip "would want fever he would call her." For her part, Sabina thinks of him romantically as a kind of Tristan — when he meets her on the beach he is singing an aria from *Tristan und Isolde*.

At this point the level of reverie is interrupted by another flashback, actually a flashback within a flashback, which takes Sabina back to the period of her adolescence, when she was in the habit of taking "moon baths" — "first of all because everyone else took sun baths, and second, she admitted, because she had been told it was dangerous," an allusion to the common superstition. "She had always," we are told, "preferred the night to the day," and she feels an affinity with the mysterious planet which, like herself, likes to shroud itself in secrecy.

> It accentuated her love of mystery. She meditated on this planet which kept a half of itself in darkness. She felt related to it because it was the planet of lovers. Her attraction for it, her desire to bathe in its rays, explained her repulsion for home, husband and children. She began to imagine she knew the life which took place on the moon. Homeless, childless, free lovers, not even tied to each other (*SHL*, p. 43).

The reader will remember that as early as *House of Incest* Sabina was defined in terms of a moon image, in contrast to the narrator, who was identified with sunlight and warmth. The associations are not quite the same, however, for the Sabina with whom we are here concerned lacks the coldness and invulnerability of her prototype. The moon imagery here has another context, provided by Sabina's obsession for leading a multiple life; "day people," it is suggested, are content to live a single life: "They spoke of one birth, one childhood, one adolescence, one romance, one marriage, one maturity, one aging, one death, and then transmitted the monotonous cycle to their children." "Night people" are different.

But Sabina, activated by the moonrays, felt germinating in her the power to extend time in the ramification of a myriad lives and loves, to expand the journey to infinity, taking immense and luxurious detours as the courtesan depositor of multiple desires. The seeds of many lives, places, of many women in herself were fecundated by the moon-rays because they came from that limitless night life which we usually perceive only in our dreams, containing roots reaching for all the magnificence of the past, transmitting the rich sediments into the present, projecting them into the future (*SHL*, p. 44).

Even the sleep into which she finally falls (and which ends the two flashbacks) is "the restless sleep of the night watchman continuously aware of danger and of the treacheries of time seeking to cheat her by permitting clocks to strike the passing hours when she was not awake to grasp their contents."

After a week with Alan, she is impelled to renew her affair with Philip, who has returned to the city and whom she still continues to think of as Tristan. This time, however, the romantic illusion is dispelled: after their lovemaking she realizes that she has been in love with an image of her own making and feels curiously free, "free as man was, to enjoy without love." "How good not to love," she reflects. "I remember the eyes of the woman who met Philip at the beach. Her eyes were in a panic as she looked at me. She wondered if I were the one who would take him away." One afternoon,[1] while Philip is asleep, she slips away and returns to Alan feeling like the spy she is—a spy in the house of love. Shortly thereafter, walking along a street in Greenwich Village, she hears the sound of drums coming from a basement night club, enters, and strikes up an acquaintance with a *café au lait* musician named Mambo: "Among the dark faces there was a pale one. A grandmother from France or Spain, and a stream of shell-white had been added to the cauldron of ebony." And just as she had been lured by Philip's singing, she allows herself now to be captivated by Mambo's more primitive rhythms.

His singing was offered to her in this cup of his mouth, and she drank it intently, without spilling a drop of this incantation of desire. Each note was the brush of his mouth upon her. His singing grew exalted and the drumming deeper and deeper and it showered upon her heart and body. Drum-drum-drum-drum-drum upon her heart, she was the drum, her skin was taut under his hands, and the drumming vibrated through the rest of her body. Wherever he rested his eyes, she felt the drumming of his fingers upon her stomach, her breasts, her hips. His eyes rested on her naked feet in sandals and they beat an answering rhythm. His eyes rested on the indented waist where the hips began to swell out, and she felt possessed by his song. When he stopped drumming he left his hands spread on the drumskin, as if he did not want to remove his hands from her body, and they continued to look at each other and then away as if fearing everyone had seen the desire flowing between them (*SHL*, pp. 58–59).

Sabina and Mambo dance, and then she goes with him to his studio on Patchen Place, thus beginning the second of the furtive liaisons described in the story. It is complicated by three factors: Sabina's sense of guilt (symbolized by the ubiquitous Lie Detector); the necessity for concealment which requires that she avoid the places where Alan might see her with her new lover; and by Mambo's increasing suspicion that she does not love him for himself but for the quality of exoticism which—again romantically—he personifies for her. At one point he tells her fiercely, "It's desire, but not for *me. You don't know me.* It's for my race, for the sensual power we have." As for Sabina, we are told that she "did not feel guilty for drinking of the tropics through Mambo's body: she felt a more subtle shame, that of bringing him a fabricated Sabina, feigning a single love." But she continues to alternate between the two men, feeling more like a spy than ever.

It was when she saw the lives of spies that she realized fully the tension with which she lived every moment, equal to theirs. The fear of committing themselves, of sleeping too soundly, of talking in their sleep, of carelessness of accent or behavior, the need for continuous pretending, quick improvisations of motivation, quick justifications of their presence here or there (*SHL*, p. 72).

"I am," she reflects, "an international spy in the house of love," and recalls that the traditional fate of a spy is an ignominious death.

The scene then shifts abruptly to a beach town on Long Island, where Sabina is expecting Alan to join her. He telephones that he will be delayed overnight, and she takes advantage of his absence to seduce a young aviator, John, who has been grounded from combat duty and who tortures himself with the thought that while he is free to enjoy himself his comrades are risking their lives. The victim of a Puritan background, John is convinced that sex is evil, and Sabina cannot escape the feeling that he thinks of her as a "bad woman." Even his tenderness cannot compensate for this feeling.

> He tucked her in gently and with all the neatness of a flyer's training, using the deftness of long experience with camping. She lay back accepting this, but what he tucked in so gently was not a night of pleasure, a body satiated, but a body in which he had injected the poison which was killing him, the madness of hunger, guilt and death by proxy which tormented him. He had injected into her body his own venomous guilt for living and desiring. He had mingled poison with every drop of pleasure, a drop of poison in every kiss, every thrust of sensual pleasure the thrust of a knife killing what he desired, killing with guilt (*SHL*, pp. 85–86).

When the aviator's father comes to stay with him, Sabina abandons this unsatisfactory affair and becomes interested in a youth who reminds her of John: "When she saw the slender body of Donald, the same small nose, and head carried on a long-stemmed neck, the echo of the old violent emotions was strong enough to appear like a new desire." But this Donald, like his namesake in *Children of the Albatross*, is an androgynous character, and here it should be pointed out that among women writers in English Miss Nin has few equals in the skill with which she can create such types.[2] Donald's personality, again like that of his namesake, is chameleon-like, and he has an almost uncanny insight into the ways of women; in certain respects he is more feminine than Sabina herself.

> He ridiculed women in their cycles of periodic irrationality with an exact reproduction of whims, contrariness and commented on the foibles of fashion with a minute expertness Sabina lacked. He made her doubt her femininity by the greater miniature precision of his miniature interests. His love of small roses, of delicate jewelry seemed more feminine than her barbaric heavy necklaces, and her dislike of small flowers and nursery pastel blues (*SHL*, p. 94).

But his empathy takes a malicious turn.

> Above all he possessed a most elaborate encyclopedia of women's flaws. In this gallery he had most carefully avoided Joan of Arc and other women heroines, Madame Curie and other women of science, the Florence Nightingales, the Amelia Earharts, the women surgeons, the therapists, the artists, the collaborative wives. His wax figures of women were an endless concentrate of puerilities and treacheries (*SHL*, p. 95).

Finally she discovers the source of this malice.

> "Where did you find all these repulsive women?" she asked one day, and then suddenly she could no longer laugh: caricature was a form of hatred (*SHL*, p. 95).

Like other of this author's mother-dominated males, Donald accomplishes an unconscious revenge.

> In his gentleness lay his greatest treachery. His submission and gentleness lulled one while he collected material for future satires. His glance always came from below as if he were still looking up at the monumental figures of the parents from a child's vantage point. These immense tyrants could only be undermined with the subtlest parody: the mother, his mother, with her flurry of feathers and furs, always preoccupied with people of no importance, while he wept with loneliness and fought the incubus of nightmares alone (*SHL*, p. 95).

This curious relationship, which may or may not have been consummated physically (we are never told this definitely), is terminated suddenly when Sabina, climbing the stairs with a heavy market bag, sees herself in the mirror and is shocked to discover how she has come to resemble her own mother—"wearing the neutral-toned clothes of self-effacement, the external uniform of goodness."

Alan, on the occasions when she accompanies him to the theater, is puzzled by her tears; he thinks they are caused by envy of other actresses' success, but in reality they have another source.

> To whom could she explain that what she envied them was the ease with which they would step out of their roles, wash themselves of it after the play and return to their true selves? She would have wanted these metamorphoses of her personality to take place on the stage so that at a given signal she would know for certain they were ended and she might return to a permanent immutable Sabina (SHL, p. 107).

In real life, on the other hand, it is not quite so simple: "When she wished to end a role, to become herself again, the other felt immensely betrayed, and not only fought the alteration but became angered at her. Once a role was established in a relationship it was almost impossible to alter." And it even occurs to her to wonder if she has a self to which return is possible, if the spy has a country which he can call his own.

> Even if she succeeded, when the time came to return to the original Sabina, where was she? . . . She was afraid because there was no Sabina, not ONE, but a multitude of Sabinas lying down yielding and being dismembered, constellating in all directions and breaking (SHL, pp. 107, 109).

Oppressed by such feelings as these, she goes to Mambo's night club, where she sees Jay, who has just returned from Paris and introduces her to a character named Cold Cuts, who works in a morgue and who, when drunk, can sing in sixteen languages "including alcoholic Esperanto," imitating, in quick succession, "a French street-singer, a

German opera singer, a Viennese organ grinder singer,"
etc. His affinity with Sabina is obvious, but beyond this
there seems no reason for including Cold Cuts in the
story, for he does not figure importantly therein and never
reappears. It is at this point that the two night club scenes
fuse, and the impressions we receive of Sabina, mainly
from a series of rambling, incoherent monologues, are
registered through the consciousness of Jay rather than
that of the Lie Detector, as in the first scene. When dawn
arrives she goes to a hotel room, takes a sleeping pill, and
returns that evening to the night club (third scene),
where she finds Djuna and the Lie Detector. In a burst of
confessional fervor, thinking that the latter is planning to
arrest her, she makes a rather extraordinary speech. It was
in her childhood, she says, that she developed her capacity
for playing roles; the multiple lives which she lived then
were imaginary, involving no one but herself, and therefore no sense of guilt.

> I could step out of my ordinary self or my ordinary life into
> multiple selves and lives without attracting attention. I
> mean that my first crime as you may be surprised to hear
> was committed against myself. I was then a corrupter of
> minors, and this minor was myself. What I corrupted was
> what is called the truth in favor of a more marvelous world.
> I would always improve on the facts. I was arrested for this
> (*SHL*, p. 132).

Sabina has sufficient insight to realize that the reason her
affairs with Philip and Mambo miscarried is that she was
guilty of creating a romantic image of them which did not
fit their true selves, and, in a passage which reminds us of
the book-burning scene in *The Four-Chambered Heart*,
she traces this weakness to its proper source.

> As an investigator you may be more interested to know that
> in self defense, I accuse the writers of fairy tales. Not
> hunger, not cruelty, not my parents, but these tales which
> promise that sleeping in the snow never caused pneumonia,
> that bread never turned stale, that trees blossomed out of
> season, that dragons could be killed with courage, that
> intense wishing would be followed immediately by fulfill-

ment of the wish. Intrepid wishing, said the fairy tales, was more effective than labor. The smoke issuing from Aladdin's lamp was my first smokescreen, and the lies learned from fairy tales were my first perjuries. Let us say I had perverted tendencies: I believed everything I read (*SHL*, p. 133).

Awareness, in analysis, is the first step toward cure, and Sabina's speech proves that she has at least taken this step. The Lie Detector, abandoning the policeman's authority with which her guilt has invested him, now assumes the authority of a psychoanalyst. He tells her she is her own prisoner, and that she will never be free until she learns to love: "You've only been trying to love, beginning to love." Some early shock, he suggests, made her distrustful of a single love; fearful of making a large emotional investment, she thereafter, as a safety measure, has attempted to divide her emotion. "Trust alone is not love," he says, "desire alone is not love, illusion is not love, dreaming is not love."

All these were paths leading you out of yourself, and so you thought they led to another, but you never reached the other. You were only on the way. Could you go out now and find the other faces of Alan, which you never struggled to see, or accept? Would you find the other face of Mambo, which he so delicately hid from you? Would you struggle to find the other face of Philip? (*SHL*, p. 136).

The final chapter is ambiguous. Accompanied by Djuna and the Lie Detector, Sabina goes to Djuna's apartment, and there they listen to a recording of a Beethoven quartet. Sabina bursts into tears, and the Lie Detector holds out his hands "as if to reassure her" and says cryptically, "In homeopathy there is a remedy called pulsatile for those who weep at music." This last scene has the formal beauty of a tableau, yet many readers will find it oddly unsatisfying. We may speculate, considering the part that music plays in the story, as a symbol of the kind of perfection that is unattainable in human relations ("You sought your wholeness in music," the Lie Detector has told her), that Sabina's tears are caused by her awareness of the discrepancy that exists between the ideal world of art, the world of dreams where all is possible, and the world in which she is compelled to live; and by regret that she cannot unite the two. If this interpretation is correct, I believe the ending can be defended against the charge of inconclusiveness: if there is no resolution in the ordinary sense there *is* culmination; and the very nature of the *roman fleuve* makes resolution, at the end of individual works, of dubious value, for continuity, in such novels, is of the essence. We cannot tell what Sabina will do with her new-found awareness, for the author's purpose has been merely to accompany her protagonist to the moment of illumination, the moment of truth, and this moment is the culmination and the climax of the book. Were Miss Nin writing a novel of action rather than a psychological novel, the reader would be justified in expecting a more decisive conclusion, but *A Spy in the House of Love* is a novel of character in which the level of action is negligible; and to object to its ending on this score is to be guilty of an irrelevance.

*A Spy in the House of Love* has a curiously international publishing history. Part of it originally appeared (Spring, 1954) in an Australian literary magazine, *Meanjin Papers*, and the manuscript was first printed in book form in Amsterdam by an English house (British Book Center) whose headquarters was New York! Four versions, each different from the other, are owned by Northwestern University's Deering Library, and each of these, in turn, differs slightly from the text of the book, the reason for this being that the Dutch printers, who mailed the galleys to Miss Nin, forgot to enclose the original manuscript, and the author, pressed for time, had to proofread without it.[3]

In the opinion of most critics, this novella does not do full justice to Miss Nin's very considerable talents. A typical reaction is that of Jerome Stone, who wrote (*The Saturday Review of Literature*, May 15, 1954), "This is not among Miss Nin's best work, being neither as poetically imaginative nor as psychologically profound; but it does suggest her ability to illuminate the subcellars of the female psyche." An exception is Jean Fanchette, who in his preface to the French translation of the book acclaims it her best; and here it may be pertinent to remark that French critics—through familiarity, perhaps, with the work of such innovators as Jouve, Beckett, Robbe-Grillet and Duras—are generally more receptive to literary experiment than their Anglo-American colleagues. But it is probably true on both sides of the Atlantic that tricks of technique, even when brilliantly performed (perhaps especially then!) can distract the reader's attention from the essential subject of the narrative, and that when the subject is serious and the attitude sincere, as is the case here, they can present a real obstacle. The chief danger of an artist's preoccupying himself so exclusively with matters of technique is that he is likely to end by regarding it as an end in itself: for this, in the vocabulary of literary criticism, there is a name, and that name is decadence.

The book is marred, moreover, by certain repetitions that, unlike the repetitions in Proust or even Gertrude Stein, which have a thematic *raison d'être*, seem to serve no strategic purpose. For example, the fine passage wherein Sabina sees in Duchamp's *Nude Descending a Staircase* an image of her own fractured self is greatly weakened by the fact that it has previously been used, word for word, to apply to Djuna in *The Four-Chambered Heart*—almost as if the author, conscious of its effectiveness, had not been able to resist the temptation to use it a second time, even at the risk of causing the two characters to blur and overlap in the reader's mind.[4] This tendency, as we have noted previously, is one from which her work suffers generally. Similarly, the fire-engine image with which Sabina is introduced has previously been used not once but twice—in both *Ladders to Fire* and *Children of the Albatross*—and the same is true of certain accessory images which describe her various compulsions. Again, the passage on page 124 beginning "How right he [Jay] had been to paint Sabina as a mandrake with fleshy roots" occurs also, with very few changes, in *Children of the*

*Albatross*, page 123, and readers familiar with the earlier novel will not see the need for its being repeated here. Were the passages in question less striking, their repetition would not seem so obvious nor so offensive.

Nor does the repetition always involve different books; thus, we are told no fewer than three times, and in very rapid order, that, because of the luxuriance of Mambo's body, his bones do not show on it! There is also a certain staginess, a theatricality about certain scenes which is in dubious taste. Consider for example the following:

> He reached for her wrists and spoke close to her face: "It destroys me. Everywhere desire, and in the ultimate giving, withdrawal. Because I am African. What do you know of me? I sing and drum and you desire me. But I'm not an entertainer, I'm a mathematician, a composer, a writer." He looked at her severely, the fullness of his mouth difficult to compress but his eyes lashing. "You wouldn't come to Ile Joyeuse and be my wife and bear me black children and wait patiently upon my Negro grandmother!" (*SHL*, p. 60).

On the positive side, *A Spy in the House of Love* has a charm which is undeniable—a charm which, ironically, might have been sacrificed, or at least compromised, had its technique been less untraditional, for it is achieved through a kind of stylization. As *The Atlantic Monthly* commented (August, 1954), "The story's structure and rhythms are somehow suggestive of a ballet in which the heroine acts out her relationships with five very different men." We have already noted (in our study of *House of Incest*) the analogy between the action of Miss Nin's novels and the movements of a dance, an analogy which has also been suggested by Robert Gorham Davis in his review (*op. cit.*) of *Children of the Albatross*. Furthermore, *A Spy in the House of Love* contains, in individual scenes—particularly scenes of passion—some of this author's best writing. And her ability to give symbolic significance to seemingly trivial objects is nowhere more in evidence—as, for example, in the scene wherein Sabina searches Chinatown for a tiny paper umbrella to replace the one she wore in her hair and which has been torn by the wind. A shopkeeper cries, "It's made in Japan, throw it in the gutter."

> Sabina had looked at the parasol, innocent and fragile, made in a moment of peace by a workman dreaming of peace, made like a flower, lighter than war and hatred. She left the shop and looked down at the gutter and could not bring herself to throw it. She folded it quietly, folded tender gardens, the fragile structure of dream, a workman's dream of peace, innocent music, innocent workman whose hands had not made bullets. In time of war hatred confused all the values, hatred fell upon cathedrals, paintings, music, rare books, children, the innocent passersby (*SHL*, p. 105).

Witness how skillfully this miniature umbrella is made to serve a didactic purpose.

> She could not keep pace with the angry pulse of the world. She was engaged in a smaller cycle, the one opposite to war. There were truths women had been given to protect while the men went to war. When everything would be blown away, a paper parasol would raise its head among the debris, and man would be reminded of peace and tenderness (*SHL*, pp. 105–6).

This is poetic prose of a high order, and of a kind that is relatively rare in English. Passages such as these, together with the validity of the book's total conception and its integrity of purpose, combine to make *A Spy in the House of Love*, if not the most successful of Miss Nin's fictions, by no means the least so.

IN 1960 Anaïs Nin completed her *roman fleuve*. The final volume, *The Seduction of the Minotaur*, appeared the following year under the Swallow imprint. The bulk of it, entitled *Solar Barque*, had previously been issued in a limited edition.[1] In this novel it is Lillian who is brought to the point of awareness, and the story differs from A *Spy in the House of Love* in that awareness is followed by action. Its symbolism is the most complicated of any of Miss Nin's longer works except perhaps for *House of Incest*, and at the same time it makes more concessions than any of the others, with the possible exception of *The Four-Chambered Heart*, to the tradition of the realistic novel: the result is a work of unusual richness, a fitting climax to what is one of the most remarkable continuous novels in the language.

Whether Paris or New York, the settings of her earlier books (like those of Kafka) were the merest of backdrops: the author's narrative interest, as we have seen, was neither in place nor in time, and these works have a curiously abstract quality, as if they had unfolded in a world from which the dimensions of the realistic novel had been excluded almost as if by natural law. The advantage of this was that it created an illusion of universality, and that (again as in Kafka) the symbols had greater force *as symbols* since their realistic correlatives were negligible.

But there was a sacrifice where excitement of a nonintellectual kind was concerned, and this sacrifice has not been made in *Seduction of the Minotaur*. For the first time the author relates setting to character, and the setting itself is used as a symbol. Also for the first time, some of the characters are provided with surnames.

The Lillian we meet in *The Seduction of the Minotaur* is not at all the same Lillian we knew in *Ladders to Fire*, any more than the Lillian we meet at the beginning of the present novel is the same whom we know at its end, after her encounter with the Minotaur. She has renounced her submissive relationship with Jay, as we learn from a flashback, and returned to her husband, Larry, and their children. They are all of them back in New York now. But the reconciliation is not entirely satisfactory, and when the novel opens Lillian has left New York once more and gone to Mexico, where she has accepted an engagement to play with a jazz orchestra at a hotel.

She would like to think that she has broken with the past and that she will be free to begin a new life in Golconda, the name she has given to the seacoast resort which is her new home.

> Golconda was Lillian's private name for the city which she wanted to rescue from the tourist-office posters and propaganda. Each one of us possesses in himself a separate and distinct city, as we possess different aspects of the same person. She could not bear to love a city which thousands believed they knew intimately. Golconda was hers (*SM*, p. 8).

Golconda to Lillian thus represents freedom, and all the details of the place, described with a wealth of sensuous images, support this impression of it. It is very different from any other place she has ever seen, and she has the illusion that she is beginning life afresh: "Everything was novel," the author tells us. Shortly after Lillian arrives she meets two men, Doctor Hernandez and an engineer named Hatcher, who are to play important parts in the story. The Doctor came to Golconda years ago in his last year of medical school and stayed on to practice; he is a hard-working man whose patients are wealthy tourists with imaginary illnesses and natives with genuine ones. Hatcher has apparently gone native: he wears the local costume, but something about him suggests that he is really not in tune with his environment: "On him the negligent attire still seemed a uniform to conquer, rather than a way of submitting to, the tropics . . . the tropics had not relaxed his forward-jutting jaw and shoulders."

Lillian finds the Doctor more sympathetic, and the two soon become close friends. Each senses a mystery about the other. Lillian tells him she is a convalescent, but that it is not physical illness from which she has suffered. Physical illness, she says, does not frighten her: "The one that does does not exist in Golconda," she confides, and the Doctor eventually discovers that her marriage has been a failure. Lillian, for her part, learns that the Doctor is troubled because his wife, who lives in the capital, refuses to share with him the hardships of his career. The Doctor is being harassed by a group of native addicts who want him to supply them with drugs.

The freedom for which Golconda is a symbol is illusory, for it is also suggested, almost from the beginning of the story, that it is the freedom of narcosis, of oblivion. "With the first swallow of air she inhaled a drug of forgetfulness well known to adventurers," the author tells us, and again and again she emphasizes the drug-like atmosphere of the place, which resembles the land of Tennyson's lotus-eaters. Because of her troubled past Lillian welcomes oblivion, and mistakes it for genuine freedom. A subtle connection is thus established between Lillian and the addicts, a connection which Doctor Hernandez, with his diagnostic intuition, is quick to perceive, for he warns her that individuals do not have the power to free themselves of the past.

> There are many kinds of drugs. One for remembering and one for forgetting. Golconda is for forgetting. But it is not a permanent forgetting. We may seem to forget a person, a face, a state of being, a past life, but meanwhile what we

are doing is selecting a new cast for the reproduction of the same drama, seeking the closest reproduction to the friend, the lover, or the husband we are striving to forget. And one day we open our eyes, and there we are caught in the same pattern, repeating the same story. How could it be otherwise? The design comes from within us. It is internal (*SM*, p. 19).

Significantly, the Doctor, in his laboratory, has made a profound study of "drugs of remembrance." At this point, however, Lillian is only half convinced. For years she has been haunted by a persistent dream, wherein she struggled to liberate a land-locked boat: "She was in this boat and aware that it could not float unless it were pushed, so she would get down from it and seek to push it along so that it might move and finally reach water. The effort of pushing the boat along the street was immense and she never accomplished her aim." Now, in Golconda, she feels that she has at last attained "a flowing life, a flowing journey." In earlier chapters we have traced the evolution of the boat image in this author's fiction; here the land-locked ship is Lillian's own inhibited self, which has sought unsuccessfully for liberation, for the stream it was destined for and on which it could float effortlessly. And water, as in *The Four-Chambered Heart*, symbolizes life, and more specifically the life of the unconscious, so that the process of flowing in obedience to its rhythms corresponds to the act of harmonious adjustment to the decrees of the "basic self." In Golconda it is not merely the water which seems to flow: "It was not only the presence of water, but the natives' flowing rhythm: they never became caught in the past, or stagnated while awaiting the future. Like children they lived completely in the present."

The symbolism of *The Seduction of the Minotaur*, however, is more complicated than in the earlier work. For now there are two kinds of boats.

She had read that certain Egyptian rulers had believed that after death they would join a celestial caravan in an eternal journey toward the sun. Scientists had found two solar barques, which they recognized from ancient texts and mortuary paintings, in a subterranean chamber of limestone. The chamber was so well sealed that no air, dust or cobwebs had been found in it. There were always two such barques—one for the night's journey toward the moon, one for the day's journey toward the sun (*SM*, p. 23).

Lillian sees in this the metaphor which applies to her own situation.

In dreams one perpetuated these journeys in solar barques. And in dreams, too, there were always two: one buried in limestone and unable to float on the waterless routes of anxiety, the other flowing continuously with life. The static one made the voyage of memories, and the floating one proceeded into endless discoveries (*SM*, pp. 23–24).

The nocturnal voyage, that is, is the voyage of memory, and is associated with stasis and death—and therefore with land—while the daylight voyage is the voyage of discovery, and is associated with freedom and life—and therefore with water. The book is full of marvelous water scenes (Lillian and the Doctor in a canoe, Lillian crossing a jungle stream on a raft, Lillian swimming with Doctor Hernandez in the hotel pool and on the beach), which, since Golconda represents a kind of freedom, is of course symbolically appropriate.

In one of their conversations, Doctor Hernandez tells Lillian,

In Eastern religions there was a belief that human beings gathered together the sum total of their experiences on earth, to be examined at the border. And according to the findings of the celestial customs officer one would be directed either to a new realm of experience, or back to re-experience the same drama over and over again. The condemnation to repetition would only cease when one had understood and transcended the old experience (*SM*, p. 30).

"So you think I am condemned to repetition?" Lillian asks him. "You think I have not liquidated the past?" And the Doctor answers, "Yes, unless you know what it is you ran away from." To her protest, "But I do feel new," he replies, "Maybe only the backdrop has changed." Lillian ponders this.

Lillian examined the pool, the sea, the plants, but could not see them as backdrops. They were too charged with essences, with penetrating essences like the newest drugs which altered the chemistry of the body . . . It was impossible that in this place the design of her past life should repeat itself, and the same characters reappear, as the Doctor had implied. Did the self which lived below visibility really choose its characters repetitiously and with only superficial variations, intent on reproducing the same basic drama, like a well-trained actor with a limited repertory? (*SM*, p. 30).

A trip which she makes down the coast to visit Hatcher and his native wife strengthens Lillian's increasing suspicion that the Doctor may be right after all. For she discovers that Hatcher, though he lives in an isolated spot and takes pride in identifying himself with the native way of life, has nevertheless surrounded himself with all the appurtenances of civilization; his storage room contains "every brand of canned food, every brand of medicine, every brand of clothing, glasses, work gloves, tools, magazines, books, hunting guns, fishing equipment." Lillian is profoundly disillusioned: "She could not sleep, having witnessed Hatcher's umbilical ties with his native land's protectiveness." Hatcher has previously been married in the States, to a woman he came to despise, and now it occurs to Lillian to wonder if he really loves his present wife for herself: "Did he truly love Maria, with her oily black hair, her maternal body, her compassionate eyes, or did he love her for not being his first wife?" To make matters worse, Hatcher, with his domineering ways, reminds Lillian of her own father.

Already she regretted having come. This was not a journey in her flowing barque. It was a night journey into the past, and the thread that had pulled her was one of accidental resemblances, familiarity, the past. She had been unable to live for three months a new life, in a new city, without being caught by an umbilical cord and brought back to the figure of her father. Hatcher was an echo from the past (*SM*, p. 75).

Is there, Lillian wonders, any similarity between the situation of Hatcher, who *thinks* he has freed himself, and her own; and might not Doctor Hernandez have perceived that she too, though less obviously, is tied to the past?

Hatcher's umbilical cord had stirred her own roots . . . The farther she traveled into unknown places, unfamiliar places, the more precisely she could find within herself a map showing only the cities of the interior . . . Was there no open road, simple, clear, unique? Would all her roads traverse several worlds simultaneously, bordered by the fleeting shadows of other roads, other mountains? She could not pass by a little village in the present without passing as well by some other little village in another country, even the village of a country she had wished to visit once and had not reached! (*SM*, p. 80).

Shortly after her return from the Hatchers', Doctor Hernandez is ambushed by addicts and murdered. Meditating on the conversations they have had together, Lillian is at last prepared to acknowledge that he had been right: examining the various relationships she has formed in Golconda, she realizes that they are echoes of previous relationships, that she has been repeating a pattern dictated by her inmost self. As the Doctor had said, "the design comes from within us." The problem, then, is to discover the design, to *know the self*. She regrets that the Doctor is no longer here to aid her in this "archaeology of the soul."

If only they had gone down together, down the caverns of the soul, with picks, lanterns, cords, oxygen, X-rays, food, following the blueprints of all the messages from the geological depths where lay hidden the imprisoned self (*SM*, p. 95).

Caverns of the soul: the phrase leads us naturally to the image of the labyrinth, which, as we know, is one of Miss Nin's favorites. And now Lillian decides that she will penetrate to the heart of the labyrinth, there to confront the Minotaur that she had feared would devour her.

> Yet now that she had come face to face with it, the Minotaur resembled someone she knew. It was not a monster. It was a reflection upon a mirror, a masked woman, Lillian herself, the hidden masked part of herself unknown to her, who had ruled her acts. She extended her hand toward this tyrant who could no longer harm her (*SM*, p. 111).

Lillian has recognized and come to terms with her basic self.

The author has ingeniously contrived to synchronize Lillian's journey of self-discovery with her return to New York: "Lillian was journeying homeward." On the plane everything becomes clear, and she sees her relationship to Larry in a new light. She perceives that in Golconda, so far from being separated from her husband, she had "either become him or looked for him in others." And Doctor Hernandez' death provides her with insight into her own situation: the Doctor had shown her only one of his selves, the smiling one, and now that he is dead she realizes that he had other selves of which she had been unaware. Similarly, her knowledge of Larry has been one-dimensional.

> It was as if having begun to see the true Doctor Hernandez, solitary, estranged from his wife and his children by her jealousy and hatred of Golconda immersed only in the tropic, troubled life of a pleasure city, she could also see for the first time, around the one-dimensional profile of her husband, a husband leaving for work, a father bending over his children, an immense new personality (*SM*, p. 98).

Golconda has thus served a therapeutic purpose for Lillian: "It had taken the true freedom of Golconda,[2] its fluid, soft, flowing life, to expose her own imprisonment, her own awkwardness." But now she is free at last, and Golconda is no longer necessary to her.

A study of the important characters in *The Seduction of the Minotaur* shows that they are all defined in terms of their commitment either to the principle of life particularized by details of movement, especially flowing movement, or to the principle of death, particularized by details of nonmovement, of stasis. Lillian, inert on her arrival, through immersion in the life of Golconda and removal of her false selves, is virtually reborn, so that in a sense it might almost be said that she disproves the Doctor's thesis. Hernandez, who *seems* alive, in reality is the victim of a death wish, and his shooting, as Lillian realizes, has something of the quality of a suicide: "Certainly at times his intelligence and knowledge of human nature must have warned him that he was courting sudden death." Hatcher's disguise is even more apparent: surrounded by comforts in the midst of a primitive setting, he too (like Port Moresby in Paul Bowles's *The Sheltering Sky*, another champion of the simple life) is death-oriented.

Fred, the University of Chicago student who hitchhikes to Golconda and cannot decide whether to return or to stay on in the company of Lillian and Diana, a vivid, overblown female who is emphatically a life symbol, is torn between the two principles, but his inhibitions, together with his indecision—he reminds Lillian of Gerard, the unsatisfoctory lover we met in *Ladders to Fire*—incline him in the direction of death. Fred will not take his shoes off at a native dance; he is fearful of contact with nature. And there is a scene at the seashore which might have come right out of Lawrence, where everyone strips and goes into the water except Fred, who refuses to share in the "baptismal immersion": "Fred stood further away, clinging to his locks and his clocks, to peripheries, islands, bridges."

Michael Lomax, the elegant, well-to-do youth whom Lillian visits in an "ancient city" in the interior, where he owns a decaying mansion, is another nay-sayer to life. Enroute, Lillian has a dream in which a native guide with a machete, guarding an Aztec tomb, asks her, "Would you like to visit the tomb?" When she arrives, everything reminds her of death: the city, which in former times had been half buried by a volcanic eruption, is in ruins, and the church bells toll persistently "although there was no ritual to be attended, as if calling day and night to the natives buried by the volcano's eruption years before."

With its rows of broken columns, it reminds Lillian of a painting by Chirico; there are no songbirds, only vultures, and not a breath of air is stirring: "The windlessness gave it the static beauty of a painting."

Michael is homosexual, and if the author's portrait of him is lacking in sympathy it is not lacking in shrewdness. Apropos of a celebration in the streets, Michael observes, "This is a fiesta for men only, Lillian. The men here love each other openly. See, there, they are holding hands." But Lillian knows better: "He wants it to be thus, this is the way he wants it to be." The scene in which the two friends are seated in Michael's patio is strongly reminiscent of the story "Under a Glass Bell" and the corresponding incident in *House of Incest*.

> "What a strange conversation, Michael [it is Lillian speaking], in this patio that reminds me of the illustrations for The Thousand and One Nights—the fountain, the palm tree, the flowers, the mosaic floor, the unbelievable moon, the smell of roses. And here we sit talking like a brother and sister stricken by some mysterious malady. All the dancing and pleasure are taking place next door, nearby, and we are exiled from it . . . and by our own hand" (*SM*, p. 67).

It is a sterile atmosphere, full of empty beauty, a climate from which the warmth of normal human love has been eliminated—though the moon is "unbelievable," it is without life.

Even minor characters are polarized in this fashion. A beauty queen arrives in Golconda, "a plastic perfection of hair, skin, teeth, body, and form which could not rust, wrinkle or cry," and chooses for her escort a handsome ex-Marine, "tall, strong and blond, with so rich a coloring he could not take the sun," who has been rendered impotent through exposure to atomic radiation. These two perfect mannekins stroll together, photographing everything in sight but without looking at each other "as the Mexican lovers did." And on the bus to Hatcher's Lillian observes an English schoolteacher: "Her English clothes were wearing out; they were mended, patched, but she would not change to Mexican clothes. She wore a colonial hat on her sparse yellow hair. The books she carried were yellow and brittle, the corners all chewed, the covers disintegrating." Anaïs Nin's tourists and expatriates (like those of Lawrence, Forster, and Bowles) are generally naysayers; like those authors, and like romantic writers generally, she associates primitive backgrounds with life and "civilization" with death. Except for Doctor Hernandez and Hatcher's guest, Doctor Palas, whose contacts with civilization have corrupted them (Doctor Palas carries a French novel), the natives are all in tune with nature, at ease with themselves and with one another. The contrast is especially apparent in the above-mentioned bus scene, and at the airport where Lillian, disembarking, notices the customs officials are shirtless.

> The absence of uniforms restored the dignity and importance of the body. They all looked untamed and free, in their bare feet, as if they had assumed the duties of receiving the travelers only temporarily and would soon return to their hammocks, to swimming and singing. Work was one of the absurdities of existence. Don't you think so, Senorita? said their laughing eyes while they appraised her from head to toes. They looked at her openly, intently, as children and animals do, with a physical vision, measuring only physical attributes, charm, aliveness, and not titles, possessions, or occupations (*SM*, pp. 6–7).

Here, on the other hand, are the civilized travelers.

> Their full, complete smile was not always answered by the foreigners, who blinked at such sudden warmth of smile as they did at the dazzling sun. Against the sun they wore dark glasses, but against these smiles and open naked glances they could only defend their privacy with a half-smile . . . Thus children and animals stare, with their whole, concentrated attentiveness. The natives had not yet learned from the white man his inventions for traveling away from the present, his scientific capacity for analyzing warmth into a chemical substance, for abstracting human beings into symbols. The white man had invented glasses which made objects too near or too far, cameras, telescopes,

spyglasses, objects which put glass between living and vision. It was the image he sought to possess, not the texture,
the living warmth, the human closeness (*SM*, p. 7).

This of course is purest Rousseauism, by way of Lawrence and innumerable late-nineteenth- and early-
twentieth-century novelists on both sides of the Atlantic,[3]
and rendered here with a wealth of detail that is at once
superfluous and overfamiliar. It seems a bit naïve nowadays, after the work of the cultural anthropologists who
have shown us what complex individuals these so-called
primitives really are, and how their lives, which we had
enviously imagined to be "free," are full of stresses and
strains of a kind with which we are happily unfamiliar,
and are hemmed in by an elaborate set of taboos which
(since they are not our own) we simply do not recognize
as such. Passages of this type undoubtedly weaken the
intellectual interest of the book—an interest which in any
case is not primarily intellectual—and they can be justified, if at all, only by the extreme stylization of its plan,
which requires that attitudes and identities, for dramatic
reasons, be sharply polarized.

More than one critic[4] has objected to the final pages of
*The Seduction of the Minotaur*, where Lillian, homeward
bound on the plane, reconstructs earlier scenes in Paris,
scenes which involve the other principal characters of
*Cities of the Interior*—Jay, Djuna, and Sabina. While
these scenes may puzzle readers unfamiliar with the earlier
novels, they are entirely necessary for the rounding off of
the series, as the reader who *is* familiar with them will be
quick to realize. One is particularly grateful for the flashback wherein Lillian views with a new objectivity the
course of her relationship with Jay, a relationship which
she abandoned when she came to understand that it did
not permit either the expression or the expansion of her
truest self. The pattern of her life with Jay—a pattern
which satisfied only two instincts within her (masochistic
and maternal) and which was therefore not representative
of her total self, the self of a complete woman—she is now
able to trace back to a series of childhood spankings in

which the pleasure of seeing her father was mixed with pain.

> As the rest of the time he did not talk to them, nor play with them nor cuddle them, nor sing to them, nor read to them, as he acted in fact as if they were not there, this moment in the attic produced in Lillian two distinct emotions: one of humiliation, the other of pleasure of intimacy. As there were no other moments of intimacy with her father Lillian began to regard the attic as a place which was both the scene of spankings but also of the only rite shared with her father . . . Thus the real dictator, the organizer and director of her life had been this quest for a chemical compound—so many ounces of pain mixed with so many ounces of pleasure in a formula known only to the unconscious (*SM*, pp. 111, 113).

It is thus via the route of memory, after all, that Lillian arrives at self-understanding: the lunar barque was as necessary as the solar, for the voyage had to be made in the one before the other could be freed of its land-locked condition. Therefore the negative associations with which, in Lillian's imagination, the "night journey" was associated are invalidated in the same way as her initial illusion of freedom (an illusion by which Doctor Hernandez was not deceived) is also dispelled: "She had been taken in by the myth of her courage, the myth of her warmth and flow. And it was her belief in this myth which had caused her to pass judgment on the static quality of Larry, concealing the static elements in herself." It is not until she is willing to undertake the lunar voyage that she is enabled to flow in genuine harmony with the rhythm of the natives, who symbolize nature, and with the rhythms of her own basic self.

Because of the realism of its setting, none of Miss Nin's books is so successful as this one in the evocation of natural scenes conveyed in images that, in the truest tradition of Surrealism, mix sight and sound, colors with musical notes.

> Just as every tree carried great brilliant flowers playing chromatic scales, runs and trills of reds and blues, so the

people vied with them in wearing more intense indigoes, more flaming oranges, more platinous whites, or else colors which resembled the purple inside of mangoes, the flesh tones of pomegranates (*SM*, p. 12).

By the device of pathetic fallacy (a favorite with Miss Nin), even the sense of taste is invoked.

The houses were covered with vines bearing bell-shaped flowers playing coloraturas. The guitars inside of the houses or on the doorsteps took up the color chromatics and emitted sounds which evoked the flavor of guava, papaya, cactus figs, anis, saffron, and red pepper (*SM*, p. 12).

Effects such as these are the peculiar monopoly of Surrealism. "Once or twice, her mouth full of fruit," the author tells us, "she stopped. She had the feeling she was eating the dawn."

Even more striking than these passages is the long one, sustained for the length of seven pages, with which the book ends; it is an extended astronomical conceit, worked out with the most complete thoroughness and consistency, in which man's knowledge of the moon is likened to Lillian's knowledge of her husband. It is an elaborate and astonishing tour de force, one of the most amazing passages in contemporary literature, and if we had not been prepared for it by similar but less ambitious conceits throughout the series we might find it a little ingenious, even a bit bizarre. But it comes, I think, as an appropriate climax to the five novels, which, as we have seen, are full of stylistic innovations. Nor does it serve a merely decorative purpose, for the author makes use of it to sound for the last time a theme which she has repeated at strategic intervals throughout the series.

It was the year when everyone's attention was focussed on the moon. "The first terrestrial body to be explored will undoubtedly be the moon." Yet how little we know about human beings, thought Lillian. All the telescopes are focussed on the distant. No one is willing to turn his vision inward . . . Such obsession with reaching the moon, because they had failed to reach each other, each a solitary planet! (*SM*, pp. 130, 136).

*The Seduction of the Minotaur* is in many ways the most finished of Anaïs Nin's books. The success with which she creates a thoroughly realistic setting, and the skill with which she relates it to her characters, were accomplishments for which the early fiction, remarkable as it was in its own way, had not prepared us. If this novel lacks the unity of *The Four-Chambered Heart*—and it might also be objected that the image of the boat and the labyrinth are not sufficiently integrated [5]—it is a far richer and more ambitious work. It is, indeed, the most ambitious of all the novels, and lacks the structural and stylistic flaws of *A Spy in the House of Love*. There is more symmetry in *Cities of the Interior* than is at first apparent, for the series begins and ends with Lillian. It is a journey from darkness to light, unawareness to awareness, confusion to order, incompletion to completion. The reader will remember that Miss Nin's concern in the first novel, *Ladders to Fire*, was with the "negative pole"; in *Seduction of the Minotaur* it is with the positive. In the intermediate novels the pattern is duplicated: the other women characters, Djuna and Sabina, take the same journey by different routes. The terms in which the problem of incompletion is presented naturally differ in each case, but the problem remains the same, and there is a similarity in the nature of the effort which each woman makes to solve it.

*COLLAGES*, Anaïs Nin's most recent book,[1] is, as its title might imply, a heterogeneous work. It is a difficult book to classify, for it is a novel only in the loosest sense of the word and might be more properly described as a collection of short stories with a single common character, a woman painter named Renate. The arrangement is spatial rather than temporal, and the character of Renate, unlike that of the women in *Cities of the Interior,* undergoes no considerable change or development; moreover, the various episodes tend to be interesting in their own right rather than because of the almost accidental way in which Renate happens to be involved in them. This is not to say that Renate is not interesting in her own right: she is, but the interest we have in her is not a continuing interest because Renate does not change, and it is soon exhausted. Fortunately, there are other interesting characters. And the setting, as befits a collage, is equally varied; it shifts rapidly from Vienna (where Renate was born) to Mexico, thence to Holland, thence to the French Riviera, thence to Southern California, thence to Mexico once more, and finally to New York.

There is thus not one story but many stories, and *Collages* falls somewhere between fiction and anecdote—a tenuous distinction, perhaps, unless we think of fiction as sustained anecdote and anecdote as incomplete fiction. The story which is sustained the longest is that of Renate and Bruce, a would-be writer who reminds her of a statue of Mercury which she remembers from her Viennese childhood. Bruce is not an articulate person, which of course is consistent with the sculptural image, but Renate senses that something is troubling him, and the reader will recognize one of Miss Nin's favorite themes in Renate's impression of him.

> Renate, having been trained for years to read the unmoving lips of statues, heard the words which came from the perfect modeling of Bruce's lips. The message she heard was: "What does one do when one is fourteen times removed from one's true self, not two, or three, but fourteen times away from the center?" (C, pp. 11–12).

She and Bruce go together to Mexico. Here, as in so much of this author's fiction, a voyage symbolizes a spiritual journey, and the purpose of Bruce's journey is self-discovery. They wish to leave clock time behind them; Bruce winds his alarm clock, sets it in the middle of the road, and leaves it there: "As they drove away, it suddenly became unleashed like an angry child, the alarm bell rang like a tantrum, and it shook with fury and protest at its neglect." Their relationship is not unlike that of Jay and Lillian. "He rebelled," the author tells us, "against all ties, even the loving web of words, promises, compliments. He left without announcing his return, not even using the words most people uttered every day: 'I'll be seeing you.'" Renate stays up nights waiting for him, and on one occasion, when she decides to go in search of him, she discovers him in the act of making love to a Mexican boy. This is not the self she had hoped to help him find, and she returns to California alone.

But Bruce follows her, and installs himself with his usual casualness in her Malibu home: "He laid his dusty and tired head on her shoulder, and sought in the darkest part of her hair, at the base of her neck, the place where the nerves most clearly carried messages of future pleasures." Renate is powerless to resist, and buys him a peace dove, but when they try to hang it the thread breaks. This is of course foreshadowing, and Bruce's comment ("Now I know why my buttons never stay on. You sew them with

such a weak thread") is a *double-entendre* which reproaches Renate for not being sufficiently the mother he is
seeking—the thread suggests the umbilical cord which
Miss Nin has used elsewhere as a symbol of parental
control and domination.

Their next adventure—and again a voyage is
involved—also proves a failure. At Bruce's suggestion they
go to Holland to buy a sailing boat; his plan is that they
shall sail around the world while she paints and he writes
a novel. But in their clumsiness they damage an historical
bridge on a Dutch canal and have to leave the country to
avoid prosecution—which they do by train, taking the
boat with them in another car to the South of France. But
the hot sun to which it is exposed on the train melts the
caulking, and when they attempt to sail it in the Mediterranean it almost founders. The symbolism here is similar
to that in *The Four-Chambered Heart*.

> "We'll sink if you don't pump out the water, Bruce." "Let
> it sink," he said and went back to sleep. Renate wondered
> if this were a symbolic indication of the pattern their
> relationship would follow (*C*, p. 26).

Back in California, Renate does a portrait of Bruce, not
as the Mercury of whom he reminds her but as the Pan he
thinks of himself as being. One day the house is threatened by a forest fire; her concern is naturally to save it,
which she does by—among other things—watering down
the roof with a hose, but Bruce, in whom the narcissistic
element looms typically large, is only concerned with sav-
ing his portrait. "So Bruce saved Pan, and Renate saved
the house, but the fire seemed to have finally consumed
their relationship." There is a sequel, however, for Bruce
conceives an ingenious plan for consoling Renate at those
moments (usually during his frequent absences) when she
is moved to question his love for her. He gives her a set of
Chinese puzzle boxes in each of which he has placed a
chapter from his personal history, and asks that she open
one each time she is in doubt. They turn out to be
confessions involving his relations with other young men,
experiments with drugs and with various forms of perver-

sion. But they do not have the effect on Renate that he intended, for after opening the second box she is revolted and sets fire to the remainder. Bruce is merely another one of the largely unsympathetic portraits in Miss Nin's gallery of half-men.

After her affair with Bruce, we see Renate in the company of various friends and acquaintances, and these provide the occasion for much of the anecdotal material of which the book is composed—the young man from California who has a love affair with his car; the eccentric nobleman, a fellow countryman of hers, who has left an ancestral castle to run a laundry in Malibu and whom she nicknames Count Laundromat; the girl model who complements the gentleness of her own nature by taking a raven for a pet; the old man who leaves his family to live among seals in an ocean cave and who comes to resemble the animals he loves so much; the Haitian negress who sings at the nightclub where Renate has taken a job as hostess; the cook, adopted son of Escoffier, whose complaint is that people have lost their palates and lack the vocabulary to praise him properly; the collage artist who lives on a Sausalito houseboat and whose daughter, a drab, sullen teen-ager, experiences a metamorphosis of character after exposure to LSD; the madwoman, Nina, who likes to mop floors with beer and paste silver paper on the walls; the Japanese actress whose kimonos are flowered according to the season of the year and who chooses writing paper according to the moods of the weather; the French consul's wife who, when he becomes absorbed in a movie actress, falls in love with the image of a long-dead Turkish hero and actually journeys to Turkey to take up residence with his living descendants; the Colonel who takes an instant dislike to the woman in whom Renate tries to interest him; the "financier" who offers to back Renate and her friends in a publishing venture and who, after all the arrangements are completed, turns out to be a rich man's gardener; and the Doctor whose hobby is seeking out and making friends of the women writers whom he most admires.

West Coast readers will recognize some of these portraits, such as that of the collage artist, Varda, but in most cases they, like the rest of Miss Nin's characters, are composites. The focus in these accessory pieces is invariably on them rather than on Renate, who serves merely as a link, in some cases a rather tenuous link, of connection. The most substantial stories—though not necessarily the most interesting or the best written—are those concerning Varda, the Consul's wife, the swindler, and the Doctor with his unusual hobby.

The Varda episode is full of verbal magic. Like the author, he chooses women for his subjects, and one feels there is a strong affinity between this collagist—who, working with fabrics, "small pieces of cotton and silks, scissors and glue and a dash of paint," depicts the various legendary aspects of woman—and Anaïs Nin, who, in another medium, explores feminine archetypes with sensitivity and in depth. The concern of both is with the alchemy of art. "He never painted homely women," the author tells us, "jealous women, or women with colds. He dipped his brushes in pollen, in muteness, in honeymoons, and his women were interchangeable and mobile." We have commented on this quality of interchangeability in Miss Nin's characters, and this passage may provide us with an explanation,[2] for she, like Varda, is interested in the creation of archetypes, and the number of archetypes is necessarily limited. "Nothing endures," says Varda, "unless it has first been transposed into a myth, and the great advantage of myths is that they are ladies with portable roots." Renate, it might be pointed out, is such a lady, for if she is not "interchangeable" (and she does somewhat resemble both Lillian and Sabina), she is nothing if not "mobile."

The value of the Varda story does not lie in its denouement, which is unconvincing—the reader's credulity is strained to accept the daughter's dramatic and drug-induced reversal of character—but rather in the skill with which Varda and his daughter (before her initiation to LSD) are portrayed and in the beauty of the images, many of which, as in *The Seduction of the Minotaur*, are synesthetic.

In his landscapes of joy, women became staminated flowers, and flowers women. They were as fragrant as if he had painted them with thyme, saffron and curry . . . Sometimes they were masked like Venetian beauties at masquerades. They wore necklaces or solar meteorites, and earrings which sang like birds. Violet petals covered their breasts and stared with enticing eyes. Orange tones played like the notes of a flute. Magenta had a sound of bells. The blues throbbed like the night (C, p. 59).

The passage describing the drug experience is also extremely interesting from this point of view.

On the walls appeared endless murals of designs I made which produced their own music to match. When I drew a long orange line it emitted its own orange tone . . . Each form, each line emitted its equivalent in music in perfect accord with the design. An undulating line emitted a sustained undulating melody, a circle had a corresponding musical notation, diaphanous colors, diaphanous sounds, a pyramid created a pyramid of ascending notes, and vanishing ones left only an echo. These designs were preparatory sketches for entire Oriental cities (C, pp. 67–68).

The image then becomes architectural; the subject has glimpses into the "Oriental cities" and ends, through the alchemy of drugs which resembles the alchemy of art, by identifying herself with the precious metal.

I saw the temples of Java, Kashmir, Nepal, Ceylon, Burma, Cambodia, in all the colours of precious stones illuminated from within. Then the outer forms of the temples dissolved to reveal the inner chapels and shrines. The reds and the gold inside the temples created an intricate musical orchestration like Balinese music . . . The temples grew taller, the music wilder, it became a tidal wave of sounds with gongs and bells predominating. Gold spires emitted a long flute chant. Every line and color was breathing and constantly mutating. The smoke of my cigarette became gold. Then I felt my whole body becoming gold, liquid gold, scintillating warm gold. I WAS GOLD (C, pp. 68–69).

Throughout this study we have noted that the author, following the practice of the Surrealist painters, frequently

fuses animal, vegetable, and mineral identities—a phenomenon characteristic of the dream experience, which
accounts for the interest it has always had for the Surrealists. Probably no single tendency in Surrealist art is so
typical of it as this, and it would be difficult to find a
better literary example than the following.

> After his scissors had touched them, his women became
> flowers, plants, and sea-shells.
>    He cut into all the legendary textiles of the world: dam-
> ask of the Medicis, oyster-white of Greek robes, the mixed
> gold and blue of Venetian brocades, the midnight-blue
> wools of Peru, the sand colors of the African cottons, the
> transparent muslins of India, to give birth to women who
> only appear to men asleep. His women became comets,
> trailing long nebulous trains, erratic members of the solar
> system. He gave only the silver scale of their mermaid
> moods, the new shell rose of their ear lobes, corollas, pistils,
> light as wings . . . He saw women as feathers, furs,
> meteorites, lace, campaniles, filigrees; and so he was more
> amazed than other fathers to find his own daughter made
> of other substances like a colorless doll lying inside a ma-
> gician's trunk, with eyes not quite blue, hair not quite
> gold, as if she had been the only one he had forgotten to
> paint (C, pp. 59–61).

The story of the Consul's wife is the one which connects most closely with Miss Nin's other fiction. The
Consul, a Marseillais, is a famous writer whose chief regret
is that his mother did not live to witness his triumphs: he
is yet another of this author's mother-fixated males, but
decidedly more virile than his forerunners, his weakness
being a passion for young girls. He and his wife, an Eng-
lishwoman who is also a writer (she has written a book
about four English women "who had wanted to escape
from England to the Orient, had wanted an adventurous
life and had all succeeded and fulfilled their desires richly
and fully"), live in Hollywood, where he is exposed to the
nubile attractions of various young actresses, with one of
whom he contracts a liaison.

In previous moments of crisis, when she and her husband were living in Turkey, the wife had consoled herself

with opium; now her Hollywood friends give her tranquilizers which merely make her feel that she is "turning into a white slug." She immerses herself in her new book, a biography of Shumla, a Turkish warrior, and falls in love with her subject.

> The man she carried in her mind at that moment was a Turkish hero, a dark and wild man. She was writing his biography . . .
> A romance with a man who had died long ago promised at least no pain, no separation, no betrayals (*C*, p. 91).

She flies to Turkey and takes a bus to the obscure village where Shumla lived. At the invitation of his descendants she stays on, sleeping in the bed of her imaginary lover and surrounded by his relics—his weapons, maps, and personal belongings. The book completed, she flies home, but the plane, upon landing, bursts into flames: "The plane was emptied without accident, but the fire raged after they left it, and in this fire burned the intimate personal data on Shumla which his jealous religion, his jealous gods, did not want to release to the press, to the world, to women like the Consul's wife who committed adultery in their dreams."

The story thus presents a contrast between physical desire, represented by the Consul's commonplace infidelities with ordinary persons, and the spiritual love which chooses for its object an extraordinary individual—and which does not require the presence of the beloved. The Consul's passion is human and realistic; his wife's is romantic and Platonic. The theme reminds us of John Crowe Ransom's famous dictum that lust is the science of sex; love, its aesthetic.

Few of the stories in *Collages*, however, are serious. It is Anaïs Nin's lightest book (the dedication to the American edition reads, "To R. P., the real gardener who created a world in which a humorous book could bloom"), and the story of the swindler, John Wilkes, is probably the most humorous in the group. Weary of painting and hostessing, Renate decides to found a magazine, and enlists the help of some of her more talented friends—a photographer, a film critic, a layout artist, a music editor, and several writers. Her only editorial principle is that the magazine "be alive."

> Renate was inviting contributions born of enthusiasm, inventiveness, novelty, exploration, of people in love with their media and whose love was contagious. What she banished was the bored critics, the imitators, the second-handers, the standardized clichés. Even the first dummy aroused in people a feeling they were at last to know, read, see everything other magazines neutralized, dissolved, synthesized, deodorized, sterilized, disguised, monotonized, mothproofed, and sprayed with life-repellents (C, p. 101).

She advertises for capital, and receives a telephone call from a man who identifies himself as an oil magnate who is bored with business and seeks a "new interest." He asks her to send him a dummy and a budget for operating expenses; she complies, and he calls back to say he is delighted with the dummy and that she should have her lawyer prepare a contract. Renate rents an office, makes commitments right and left, and her friends all give up their routine jobs. She and the "millionaire" spend three days with lawyers, and Renate is able to tell her friends, "He says yes to everything." They decide to give an office party: "It was such fun to buy champagne and fill in a slip which would be paid by the expense account," and while it is in progress Wilkes telephones to excuse himself; he has to attend a conference in Denver and will mail them his check. When it fails to arrive they become suspicious, and an investigation reveals that their benefactor is a gardener in Phoenix, a chronic mythomaniac who enjoys passing himself off as a patron of the arts. "There was no law," writes Miss Nin, "to jail a man who swindled one of illusions and not of money. The gardener watered other people's dreams. It was not his fault they grew so big and had to be pruned."

The final, and in some ways the most distinguished, of these stories is that of Doctor Mann, the heroine worshiper who spends his leisure time cultivating the friendship of his favorite women writers. He woos them with gifts, persuades them to autograph their books for his collection, and kisses them "only once, on parting." The more inaccessible they are, the greater the challenge, and the most inaccessible of them all is Judith Sands, author of a "poetic and stylized mythological novel" [3] which is justly famous. Miss Sands is a mysterious woman about whom no one seems to know anything definite, though the rumors and legends surrounding her are legion. Doctor Mann finally succeeds in tracking her to her Greenwich Village apartment, where he seats himself outside her door and begins the first of a series of curious monologues designed to convince her of the sincerity of his admiration. "I have grown grey hairs waiting to meet you," he declares, and adds,

> I know you do not like strangers; but, just as you are no stranger to me, I cannot be a stranger to you because I feel that, in a sense, you gave birth to me. I feel you once described a man who was *me* before I knew who I was, and it was because I recognized him that I was able to be myself. You will recognize me when you see me . . . Remember this, it is good for a writer to meet with the incarnation of a character he has invented. It gives him an affirmation, a substantial proof of his intuitions, divinations (C, pp. 114–15).

Eventually he wears down her resistance, and she opens the door to receive him, explaining that her solitude has been a deliberate withdrawal from life caused by fear of forming associations which might have the power either to inflict fresh emotional wounds or to open old wounds by resuscitating parts of herself which she has buried.[4] He replies that she and those she loved are not dead but live on in the form of their children, who, he assures her, are "scattered all over the world." They are, he tells her, "descendants in direct line from your creations." Through the alchemy of her art she has affected the lives of untold numbers all over the world, the readers of her book:

> those who read it and pretended they had never heard of it but proceeded to live their lives oriented by its flow; those

who succumbed to its contagion and searched for a similar atmosphere as if it were the only air they could breathe in; those who fell in love with your characters and searched for their counterparts. Those who quoted it to each other as a password to enter a unique and exclusive world (C, pp. 117–18).

Following this conversation the Doctor escorts her to the Museum of Modern Art, where an unusual spectacle has been scheduled for that evening: Tinguely's "Machine that Destroys Itself." [5] The machine turns out to be a fantastic collection of miscellaneous objects ingeniously wired together and surmounted by a giant roll of paper over which a brush hangs poised "to write on it as on a ticker tape." A fire chief stands by suspiciously, "wondering at which moment the suicide of the machine would become an attempt to overthrow the government," and at a given signal the machine bursts into flame and the brush begins to write the names of various artists "like stock market quotations." The fire chief reaches for his extinguisher ("Suicide is illegal") and, though the spectators hiss at him, attempts to put out the conflagration; his interference, however, proves ineffectual, and the machine is reduced to a heap of smoking fragments. Miraculously, a scrap of the roll of paper has survived, and on it, together with a few other names, the Doctor finds that of Judith Sands.

This Kafkaesque scene, which reminds us of "The Penal Colony," is of course allegorical. The machine symbolizes technology and, more specifically, its most awesome achievement, the atom bomb; and the didactic message is that a civilization dedicated to the mechanical principle must eventually destroy itself. The thick-witted fire chief personifies law and order, and his efforts to save the machine suggest the collaboration between technology and official authority—a collaboration of which the public, who acknowledge the inevitability of the spectacle, show their dislike by hissing. The reaction of the public is in fact healthy, for they are content that the machine shall accomplish its destiny of self-destruction. All that remains of this misguided civilization are a few names—and it is significant that they are the names of artists rather than of scientists or engineers.

The story has a trick ending. Judith Sands tells Renate and Doctor Mann she has something to show them, and takes them to her apartment where she gives Renate a manuscript to read. The opening words of the manuscript are also the opening words of *Collages*, so that the book ends where it began, a denouement for which we have been prepared by the remark, several times repeated, of an Arab in the story of the Consul's wife, that "Nothing is ever finished." Because of this preparation, the trick succeeds better in *Collages* than it did in *A Spy in the House of Love*, where the two night-club scenes become one. If we think in logical terms, Judith Sands and the narrator are thus the same individual, but I think (because the tone of the book is playful) that we are not intended to be quite so literal: we are once more in the presence of an archetype, and individual identities dissolve in the archetype which includes both the narrator and Miss Sands, both of them alchemists of art.

The fact that *Collages* was reviewed for the most part favorably both in England and America is evidence not so much of its superiority to her previous work—for it compares unfavorably with the best of it—as of the long-delayed recognition by critics (after many promptings and proddings from obviously knowledgeable quarters) of the fact that Anaïs Nin is an experimental writer of real originality and importance. "The best of collages fall apart with time," wrote Henry Miller; "these will not." *The Times Literary Supplement* called the book "a handful of perfectly told fables," and Elizabeth Jennings, in *The Listener*, praised the author's "sensitivity of mind and heart." Marguerite Young, poet, critic, and novelist, declared, "*Collages* . . . spills over into a new and curious thematic relationship with the reality of American character and life."

Nevertheless, *Collages* is an uneven book. One cannot escape the feeling that it would have been improved had the various episodes of which it is composed had had a common theme, or even if they had been divided, on the basis of separate themes, into several groups; for even a collage must be constructed with a total design in mind, and must be concerned with producing a total effect. As for the style, it varies between the kind of verbal magic of which I have given several examples in this chapter and passages of an almost embarrassing flatness. Compare, for instance, the awkwardness of "She had a . . . graceful way of standing and sitting creating an aesthetic delight" with the opening lines of the book, which in a series of statue images [6] marvelously evoke the atmosphere of Vienna and which are among the most successful this author has ever written.

*Collages* is not quite like anything Miss Nin has created previously, and there is a sense in which we should be grateful for this, for a fiction which merely repeats itself with variations on the same theme ends by ceasing to be of interest, and a talent which is incapable of change — even though that change may not invariably be for the better — is a frozen talent. The art of Anaïs Nin is dynamic, not static; the alchemical process is constantly at work.

FOR MANY YEARS it has been customary to think of Anaïs Nin as an artist whose literary virtue was its own—and almost its only—reward; her name has become virtually a byword for the kind of integrity that stubbornly resists the commercial compromise. Though championed almost from the first by a handful of critics and fellow writers (Edmund Wilson, Rebecca West, William Carlos Williams, Henry Miller), she has been consistently neglected by the great reading public, who remain either ignorant of or indifferent to her accomplishment. Mindful of Cocteau's dictum, *"Ce que le publique te reproche, cultive le—c'est toi,"* she seemed herself to accept her role as guardian of the ivory tower, for in 1946 she wrote, "No real writer should try to earn a living from writing because if his writing is valuable to society, it is surely not for immediate, agreeable, and harmless consumption . . . A real writer only wants his book read by those people who want to read it, and if there are one hundred of them it is enough to keep his work alive and sustain his productivity."

She has never been a popular writer, and may never be. The recognition she has received even from professional critics has been, as we have seen, by no means uniformly favorable, so that one is astonished to learn from Leslie Fiedler that she is "much overrated" [1]—as one is frequently astonished at what Fiedler has to teach us. It is even conceivable that she will be remembered ultimately for the *Diary* rather than for the fiction, though the recent republication of the latter in its entirety by Alan Swallow is an encouraging omen and is certain to result in a wider appreciation of her talents. But if Miss Nin lacks popularity she does not lack prestige; her audience, if small, is nevertheless select.

Her importance is not primarily intellectual. Many of her ideas—such as the belief that primitive man enjoys greater freedom than his civilized neighbor, and that woman has traditionally denied her true self in order to conform to the image imposed upon her by man—are derived from others—in this case Lawrence and Rank respectively—and are highly controversial. We may disagree with her on the relative importance (which many modern psychologists agree that Freud exaggerated) of the unconscious, and with her assertion that "nothing that we do not discover *emotionally* will have the power to alter our vision." We may be skeptical of the flat statement that "for the writer, the conscious mind is the great inhibitor, the great censor." We may question the sharp separation of mind and heart, intellect and emotion, that ends in the kind of total subjectivism which denies the possibility of objective motivation and criteria (thereby eliminating, incidentally, the possibility of responsible literary criticism), and we may feel that the polarization of the sexes in her fiction (man's concern being typically with the outer world, woman's with the inner) is unrealistic. We may, from the viewpoint of existentialist psychology (which holds, *à la* Locke, that a man's character is the sum of his experiences and that he defines himself by a series of conscious choices) challenge the concept of a basic self as mystical and idealistic. We may, in short, refuse to share the author's assumptions, but this does not mean we cannot share the fictional experience which she offers to us out of her gift as an artist. The act of reading any novelist who has definite convictions about life—and this means any novelist of interest—requires, for his fullest appreciation, a temporary abdication of our own convictions for the sake of an aesthetic reward which justifies the sacrifice. It is true that the sacrifice is greater in the case of some writers than of others, and here two factors are involved—the degree to which the author's convictions differ from our own, and the extent to which the assumptions are woven into the fictional fabric. In the case of Anaïs Nin, the fiction sometimes suffers because the narrative is made to depend too heavily upon the intellectual assumptions, so that they assume proportions which (particularly if we do *not* share them) may sometimes be incommensurate with the rewards of the sacrifice.

The intellectual value of Proust, of Joyce, and of Lawrence is also negligible, and of the three, Lawrence requires the greatest sacrifice for the reason just mentioned, that his assumptions are so much a part and parcel of the narrative; he cannot resist the temptation to thrust them upon the reader. I do not mean to imply that he was on this account the weakest of these novelists, for as an artist he was immensely gifted. The truth is that we do not read novelists primarily for their intellectual value, for the kind of truths that we can obtain in purer form from textbooks—or some speeches and sermons. From the artist we get another kind of truth, a kind that he alone can give us, and it is for this reason that we read him. It does not greatly matter whether the reader shares or does not share the author's assumptions; what matters is that the writer, working with such assumptions as are the product of his experience—and in no case will his experience exactly duplicate the reader's—produce a work of art. The fact that Tolstoy idealized the Russian peasant out of all resemblance to reality does not prevent *Anna Karenina* from being a great novel. In the last analysis the value of a work of art must be demonstrated on aesthetic grounds, and the literary critic can make no worse error than to praise an author because he happens to approve of his "message"—unless it be that of censuring an author because he does not. The honest critic will forever be on guard against errors of this type, which end in the kind of aesthetic blindness from which Tolstoy suffered when he pronounced *Uncle Tom's Cabin* an important novel; of which F. R. Leavis was the victim when he declared *Hard Times* to be the best of Dickens; and of which anyone is guilty who acclaims C. P. Snow as one of the most important of living artists.

If we judge Anaïs Nin on those grounds which, as an artist, she has every right to expect that we should, we shall find that she has an importance which is out of all proportion to her popular reputation. She has contributed significantly to the form of the modern novel, following the examples in English of Woolf, Joyce, and Djuna Barnes; and in France of Proust, Jouve, and Giraudoux. A pioneer in the application of cinematic effects to prose fiction, her efforts in this country parallel those of Robbe-Grillet, Marguerite Duras, and Natalie Sarraute in France; and she is, as Edmund Wilson has remarked,[2] perhaps the best of the writers in English who are working in the tradition of literary surrealism. For nearly a quarter of a century she has campaigned unremittingly in favor of a new form for the novel, a form which is closer to that of poetry than to the commercial item with which we have been made unhappily familiar. Concerning the effects upon fiction of the new psychology, she wrote in 1947, "The new dimension in character and reality requires a fusion of two extremes which have been handled separately, on the one side by the poets, and on the other by the so-called realists." The modern "poetic novel" undoubtedly owes much to her example. As Karl Shapiro, who is convinced that the poetic novel is the novel of the future,[3] has observed, "Technically surrealist, Anaïs Nin is one of those writers who erased the line between poetry and fiction."

I think it is not sufficiently realized how, as early as the late thirties, Anaïs Nin anticipated and articulated certain tendencies which are now taken for granted in that fiction which is truly contemporary. In *Realism and Reality*, a pamphlet published in 1946, she made a vigorous and coherent defence of the kind of fiction she had already been writing for several years.

> I intend the greater part of my writing to be received directly through the senses, as one receives painting and music . . . There is a purpose and form behind my partial, impressionistic, truncated characters. The whole house, or

the whole body, the entire environment, may not be there, but we know from modern painting that a column can signify more than a whole house, and that one eye can convey more than two at times. We know that in Brancusi's sculpture he achieved the closest expression of the flight of a bird by eliminating the wings [4] (*RR*, pp. 13–14).

I have said that Miss Nin's importance is not primarily intellectual, by which I mean that to many readers, perhaps to most, her ideas about life in general will seem arbitrary and inadequate. But when she is writing about the craft of fiction, her ideas are nearly always interesting. Consider for example the following on the subject of focus and proportion, which is interesting both in its own right, as narrative theory, and as a justification of her own practice.

The episodes to which we are accustomed to give much importance, such as the death of one of the principal characters, might well be expedited in five lines, whereas a detail may be treated at length and in full development. But this is because the values, the emphasis in our subjective life, do not obey the rules of our conscious life. They are dictated by feeling. If a death is not *felt* as important to the emotions, it is not made objectively important. This is the reality of subjective life. It is not the symmetry created by conventional feelings, the feelings we should have, but the asymmetry of the real feelings we do have (*Unpublished lecture by Anaïs Nin*).

Likewise, when she is writing about what has always been her favorite subject (the situation which is real rather than apparent, the predicament which is personal rather than social, the drama which is private rather than public—and private frequently to the extent that the individual involved is himself unaware of it), her ideas are invariably well considered, and their implications for the fiction of the future are very real.

If the writing has a dream-like quality it is not because the dramas I present are dreams, but because they are the dramas as the unconscious lives them. I never include the concrete object or fact unless it has a symbolical role to play

. . . These dramas of the unconscious to gain a form and validity of their own must temporarily displace the over-obtrusive, dense, deceptive settings of our outer world which usually serve as concealment, so that we may become as familiar with its inner properties and developments as we are with the workings of our conscious, external worlds . . . The world of the dream like the world of my books is actually the way we re-experience our life, and I expect people to recognize its contours or its lack of contours without fear (the most disturbing element of the dream is that it has no frames, no walls, no doors and no boundaries . . . like my novels) (RR, pp. 14–15, 16–17).

In her theory of fiction, the distinction which Miss Nin constantly makes between realism and reality is fundamental ("I intend the greater part of my writing to be received directly, through the senses, as one receives painting and music"), and the reproduction and the rendition of reality is an immensely complicated business involving unconscious as well as conscious levels of experience. It is her conviction—and few living writers have expressed it so emphatically and so consistently—that the one-dimensional novel with its static characters and situations belongs to the past; the conventions of realism and naturalism are inadequate for the communication of contemporary reality, and the modern novelist must concern himself not with single but with multiple and *changing* selves, and with experience as a flowing, constantly changing phenomenon. Lawrence, who attempted to depict "the changing rainbow of our living relationships," perceived this—as Frederick J. Hoffman, among others, has pointed out [5]—but the literary conventions of his time, against which he rebelled impatiently, did not permit him to realize his ambition. It is with these relationships that Anaïs Nin is chiefly concerned, and it is in the skill with which, abandoning traditional methods, she is able to depict them that her special talent lies. As Robert Gorham Davis comments, "What Anaïs Nin records are configurations of character, the fields of electric tension, movement and resistance in human relationships. She defines these with elegance and insight." [6]

She writes best about women, and explores the feminine psyche with a sensitivity and a thoroughness that make of her, as William Carlos Williams was quick to perceive,[7] a pioneer in this particular territory of fiction. Sometimes, however, she identifies so closely with her characters, or with certain of their archetypal aspects, that we regret the lack of distance which would enable us to view them as participants of a drama that is universal rather than personal, creations which are truly imaginary rather than projections of the author's multiple identities. And critics have justly objected to the lack of variety in her male characters; they are satellites at best, as if the only interest which the author takes in them is as they affect the destiny of the feminine protagonist. The men she describes most successfully are those "children of the albatross" who are the victims of parental — usually maternal — domination; whose characteristic attitudes are withdrawal and flight; who relate uneasily to the opposite sex; and who are narcissistic, hedonistic, and frequently homosexual.

Independently of the sex of her characters, Miss Nin's favorite theme — the quest for self, the search for identity — has come to dominate much if not most of the serious fiction which has been written in the last three decades; it is a contemporary obsession, a fact of which the literature of existentialism offers abundant proof. Where she differs from Sartre and the French existentialists is in the finality with which she rejects the outside world, the world of "current events," of political and ethical philosophy, of facts and circumstances, and in the importance that, true to her interest in psychoanalysis and surrealism, she assigns to dreams and symbols as clues to the essential self. In Sartre man defines himself through his choices ("To make oneself, and to be nothing but the self that one has made" is the motto of the French existentialists), while Miss Nin apparently believes that man must first know what he is not, before he knows what he is.

She writes an English that is curiously unidiomatic — the penalty, perhaps, of having learned it as a second language — but which is not unmusical and which, at its best, can sometimes, like that of Conrad, be peculiarly compelling. Her vocabulary is remarkable, and she is certainly one of the best imagists writing in this country today. The device of the conceit, neglected for nearly three centuries by English novelists who considered it a monopoly of poetry, has been revived by her and practiced with a brilliance which is unique in this generation and which, if it has a rival, is not to be found in English prose since the *Euphues* of Lyly.

Though her sincerity is unquestionable, her scope is narrow—dangerously narrow, perhaps. She is no Proust or Faulkner; her tendency is to probe rather than to range. Her intense preoccupation with the inner life, and the casualness—even the carelessness—with which she handles external action carry her at times into regions where the rewards of following her will not always be apparent to the reader of normal interests. There are whole areas of human experience—and important areas—about which she has not written, and perhaps could not have. These are severe limitations. In her work the subject too frequently becomes the object; one feels that, while writing ostensibly about fictional characters, she too often is, in reality (though perhaps unconsciously) writing about herself. But she does succeed, as do Proust and Faulkner, in creating a fictional world which, though it is very different from theirs, is nevertheless *sui generis*, and this is frequently the sign of a superior talent.

By choosing to concern herself with characters at only their most elusive levels, Anaïs Nin has cut herself off from much of the popular recognition that would otherwise certainly have been hers. But there must be few women novelists in any language who have searched so relentlessly and with such artistic effect into the ultimate sources of character, or who have concerned themselves so exclusively and so successfully with the nuances of emotional relationships, the myriad subtle influences—and all constantly changing—which human beings, consciously or unconsciously, exert upon one another.

All page references are to the following editions, which are thus abbreviated:

HI    *House of Incest* (Denver: Alan Swallow, 1961)
WA   *Winter of Artifice* (Denver: Alan Swallow, 1961)
UGB  *Under a Glass Bell* (Denver: Alan Swallow, 1961)
LF    *Ladders to Fire* (Denver: Alan Swallow, 1966)
CA   *Children of the Albatross* (Denver: Alan Swallow, 1966)
FCH  *The Four-Chambered Heart* (Denver: Alan Swallow, 1966)
SHL  *A Spy in the House of Love* (Denver: Alan Swallow, 1966)
SM   *Seduction of the Minotaur* (Denver: Alan Swallow, 1966)
C     *Collages* (Denver: Alan Swallow, 1964)
RR   *Realism and Reality* (New York: Alicat Book Shop, Outcast Series No. 6, 1946).

### 1—Genesis of a Fiction: The Diary

1. For Miss Nin's own account of these relations, see the pamphlet *On Writing* (New York: Alicat Book Shop, Outcast Series No. 11, 1947), pp. 20–24.

2. Public School Number Nine, in Manhattan.

3. *Winter of Artifice.*

4. An early article, probably written about 1945–50, a copy of which Miss Nin has retained. It was never published.

5. My discussion of this relationship is limited to the first volume of the *Diary*, that is, the portion covering the period from 1931 to 1936. This decision is not altogether arbitrary,

since this was the period when, intellectually, Miss Nin "came of age."

6. June Smith, Henry Miller's second wife.

7. One recognizes here the ideal of Walter Pater, to burn always with a "hard, gemlike flame," an ideal which, by way of the French Decadents and Symbolists, became an important part of Surrealism.

8. See chapter 2.

9. Compare James Harvey Robinson, *The Mind in the Making* (New York: Harper Brothers, 1921), p. 47: "Philosophers, scholars, and men of science exhibit a common sensitiveness in all decisions in which their *amour propre* is involved. Thousands of argumentative works have been written to vent a grudge. However stately their reasoning, it may be nothing but rationalizing, stimulated by the most commonplace of all motives. A history of philosophy and theology could be written in terms of grouches, wounded pride, and aversions, and it would be far more instructive than the usual treatments of these themes . . . And now the astonishing and perturbing suspicion emerges that perhaps almost all that had passed for social science, political economy, politics, and ethics in the past may be brushed aside by future generations as mainly rationalizing . . . This conclusion may be ranked by students of a hundred years hence as one of the several great discoveries of our age."

10. D. H. Lawrence wrote in his *Studies in Classic American Literature* (New York: Viking Press, Compass Book, 1964), p. 70:

One should be sufficiently intelligent and interested to know a good deal *about* any person one comes into close contact with. *About* her. Or *about* him.

But to try to *know* any living being is to try to suck the life out of that being.

Above all things, with the woman one loves. Every sacred instinct teaches one that one must leave her unknown. You know your woman darkly, in the blood. To try to *know* her mentally is to try to kill her. Beware, oh woman, of the man who wants *to find out what you are*. And, oh men, beware a thousand times more of the woman who wants to *know* you, or *get* you, what you are.

It is the temptation of a vampire fiend, is this knowledge.

Man does so horribly want to master the secret of life and of individuality *with his mind*. It is like the analysis of protoplasm. You can only analyze *dead* protoplasm, and know its constituents. It is a death process.

11. See Anna Balakian, "André Breton as Philosopher," *Yale French Studies*, xxxi (1964), p. 37; also (in the same volume) Henri Peyre, "The Significance of Surrealism," p. 23.

12. Peyre, p. 29.

13. The culmination of this tendency is seen in Keats's "Ode on Melancholy," where the assumption is that the wise man, the man whose "palate" is "fine"—i.e., who is a connoisseur of the emotions—will wish to make the most of the "melancholy fit" by seeking out objects that, so far from assuaging his grief, will, on the contrary, increase it. The aesthetic theory which is in part based on this assumption (and which resembles in certain ways the classical theory of the Sublime) is treated interestingly by Kenneth Burke in *The Philosophy of Literary Form*.

14. Gwendolyn M. Bays, "Rimbaud—Father of Surrealism?" *Yale French Studies*, xxxi (1964), p. 50.

15. Peyre, (p. 35) writes: "In its content . . . Surrealism must be regarded as a powerful Romantic offensive. Our age fondly imagines that it has buried the illusions of the Romantics beneath its own positive preoccupations, its cynicism, its resigned acceptance of man as a creature made up of animal impulses. It has only momentarily repressed its Romanticism and is unwittingly preparing a tidal wave of Romantic revolt, which is likely to put an end to all the pseudo-scientific claims of the novel, criticism, psychology, and sociology of the last few decades.

16. The notion that Proust's novels were not consciously architectured is now, since the elaborate structural studies of Germaine Brée, J. M. Cocking, Milton Hindus, Howard Moss, and Roger Shattuck (to mention only a few) generally discredited.

17. *Winter of Artifice*.

18. An unpublished early article, written about 1948, of which Miss Nin has retained a copy.

19. *Ibid*. "The endurance of Egyptian art, the very choice of form and material born of this sense of destiny, is reflected among modern people in the predilection for the autobiographical work. What the modern artist finds it impossible to do, because of the scope and complexity of his task, the biographer and the diarist often accomplish by deliberately turning

away from art. No one has yet given us the great American Novel, and no one probably will; on the other hand, the life of Barnum or the life of Brigham Young can tell us a great deal about the soul of America. If any one book ever approached this goal it was *Leaves of Grass*, and yet somehow it is not America; it is the soul of a unique American, a model all too quickly discarded."

## 2 – *The Room Without a Window:*
### House of Incest

1. Only 249 copies were printed; they are now collectors' items. The book was reprinted in 1947 by the Gemor Press in New York, and again, in a paperback edition with photomontages by Val Telberg, in 1958 and 1959 (Anaïs Nin Press).

2. As Stuart Gilbert observes: "The title refers, I think, to one of her discoveries in this uncharted land; that ultimately such experience is self-centered, the lover is thrown back on himself or herself, while the partner dwindles to a lay figure draped in the vestments of creative passion. Thus, in a sense, the beloved is a projection of the lover, a phantom born of his imagination; and the act of love becomes an act of incest." (*Reading and Collecting*, 1: 12, [November 1937], p. 23).

3. Thus, Harriet Zinnes writes in "Anaïs Nin's Works Reissued," *Books Abroad* (xxxvii [Summer 1963], p. 285): "It must be admitted, however, in an analysis of Miss Nin's work that her technique, which lends itself to excess, occasionally fails her. *The House of Incest*, an early book (which, like all of Miss Nin's works, is extremely moral), is an example of this failure. There is very little action (due in some measure to its being a "prose poem"), and the writing is over-rich and precious almost to the point of monotony. One misses those naturalistic moments where brute human action combines with dream metaphor to produce Miss Nin's characteristic style, a style that is rarely dull." Compare with this Stuart Gilbert (p. 23): "In this amazing work Anaïs Nin sets boldly out to describe those experiences which to most writers seem to lie beyond the range of words. She has succeeded, as nearly as success is possible—given the limitations of our modes of thinking and expressing thought—in the attempt . . . To my belief, nothing quite like this has been done before; previous attempts to scale these heights have had a way of falling into bathos. For, seen from the outside, such experience looks

merely grotesque; hence the absurdity of so-called realism in erotic literature . . . Inevitably there are no ready-made phrases for such an experience, which, like the ecstasy of the mystic, can be described only in metaphor, conveyed by implication."

4. In the pamphlet *Realism and Reality* (New York: Alicat Book Shop, Outcast Series No. 6, 1946), p. 21, Miss Nin writes: "The richest source of creation is feeling, followed by a vision of its meaning. The medium of the writer is not ink and paper but his body: the sensitivity of his eyes, ears and heart. If these are atrophied, let him give up writing."

5. Miss Nin's eyes are, in fact, a bluish green.

6. Alrunes were witches believed to be capable of reading the future in the blood of their prisoners. In Germanic mythology the word, with its several variants, has various occult meanings, all of them sinister. The name *Alraune* is somewhat misleading as applied to the character in *House of Incest*, who is not a consciously evil person, and among those who were misled by it was Otto Rank, who thereby misinterpreted the meaning of the book.

7. This concept of love is graphically illustrated by Picasso in the well-known painting in which two persons breathe from the same lung—though this, to be sure, may not have been the artist's conscious intention. Breathing images, incidentally, occur frequently in Miss Nin's work: suffocation is a fairly obvious symbol of the fatality of a love that is too demanding.

8. This and succeeding page references are to the most recent (paperback) edition, Denver: Alan Swallow, 1961.

9. Though the phrase belongs to contemporary psychology, recognition of the "vital lie" is as old as literature itself, e.g. Sophocles' *Oedipus Rex*. Some interesting modern illustrations of it occur in Ibsen's *Wild Duck*, James's "Tree of Knowledge," and Williams' *Streetcar Named Desire*.

10. In the first two editions the sister's name is Isolina— Italian for "little island" and therefore appropriate to the loneliness of the incestuous condition.

11. Similarly, in the fiction of Carson McCullers, the physical mutilations of the various characters symbolize the spiritual incompleteness that causes this isolation. (See my essay, "The Theme of Spiritual Isolation in Carson McCullers," *New World Writing* No. 1 [New York: New American Library (Mentor Book), 1952].) One remembers also Laura

Wingfield's limp in *The Glass Menagerie* and Brick's in *Cat on a Hot Tin Roof.*

12. See Mario Praz, *The Romantic Agony* (New York: Oxford University Press, 1956), p. 145.

13. Cleanth Books, *William Faulkner: the Yoknapatawpha County* (New Haven: Yale University Press, 1963), p. 329.

14. This visit is described in the *Diary.*

15. See note 13, this chapter.

16. It will be remembered from the first chapter of this book that Miss Nin herself suffered from this anxiety, which she describes vividly in the pages of the *Diary.*

17. For his physical description, p. 68, Miss Nin took the poet-playwright Antonin Artaud as her model, as readers of the *Diary* and of the story "Je Suis Le Plus Malade des Surréalistes" in *Under a Glass Bell* will recognize.

### 3 – The Figure of the Father:
### Winter of Artifice

1. In *Under a Glass Bell.*

2. "Stella," which in the most recent edition forms Part One of *Winter of Artifice,* is in this book discussed in the chapter on *Ladders to Fire,* of which it originally formed a part.

3. Pierre Brodin makes the same mistake: "Le père de la narratrice, dans *Winter of Artifice,* est à peine un personnage de fiction, car il procède certainement en droite ligne de l'image du père de l'écrivain, absent de la vie d'Anaïs Nin pendant ses années d'adolescence, retrouvé plus tard en Europe sous des aspects nouveaux." *Présences Contemporaines: Écrivains Américains d'Aujourd' hui* (Paris: Nouvelles Éditions Debresse, 1964), p. 116.

4. In this connection it is interesting to compare Miss Nin's theory of love with Carson McCullers'. In Mrs. McCullers' work the fact that the love object may be worthless by any standards except the mysterious ones cherished by the lover is irrelevant: love is valuable therapeutically *to the lover,* whom it transforms and ennobles for the time that he loves. It is true that the discrepancy between the reality and the illusion ultimately results in the failure of love on a physical level, but in Mrs. McCullers' work the physical level is negligible: the implication is that the illusion is *necessary to the love,* therefore good while it lasts. Miss Nin, on the other hand, considers the destruction of illusion the first step in the

direction of a successful love. Hers is a more optimistic view: mutual love is possible—permanently so, and on both a physical and a spiritual level—but only after the masks have been removed.

5. All page references in this chapter are to the Swallow edition (Denver: Alan Swallow, 1961).

6. *Partisan Review* (June 1948) 705.

7. Jean Fanchette writes in his preface to the French edition of *A Spy in the House of Love:* "Not enough has been said of the element of pity in the work of Anaïs Nin. Pity is one of the great themes inexplicably neglected by the modern novel. The pity which appears like a water-mark in the novels of Anaïs Nin is not pity for the feminine condition, but rather for those women who do not assume this condition fully, and whom it leaves behind or destroys. Some of the stories in *Under a Glass Bell* are especially revealing in this respect."

8. It is only fair to observe that this opinion is not shared by at least four critics: William Carlos Williams, *New Directors Annual*, " 'Men . . . Have No Tenderness': Anaïs Nin's *Winter of Artifice"* (Norfolk: New Directions, 1942), pp. 429–36; Emily Hahn, *"Winter of Artifice,* by Anaïs Nin," *T'ien Hsia Monthly* (Shanghai), ix (November 1939), pp. 435–38; Paul Rosenfeld, "Refinements on a Journal," *The Nation*, cxxxv, September 26, 1942, pp. 276–77; and Alfred Perlès, "Fathers, Daughters and Lovers," *Purpose* xii (January–March 1940), pp. 45–48.

9. A common phenomenon of the dream experience, as witness the paintings of Tchelitchew, Ernst, and Dali.

## 4—Houseboats, Veils, and Labyrinths: Under a Glass Bell

1. The original edition, published by the Obelisk Press in Paris in 1939, literally disappeared. The edition was completed on the same day the Nazis entered the city, and Miss Nin was able to smuggle only a few copies with her when she fled to New York. A copy of this very rare edition is in the possession of the Deering Library at Northwestern University, which owns all of Miss Nin's published works. The library also owns the typewritten manuscript (with marginal comments, criticisms and corrections by Henry Miller) from which the Obelisk edition was prepared. In 1952 it purchased thirty-nine of Miss Nin's original manuscripts.

2. For an account of Miss Steloff's relationship with Miss

Nin at this period see W. G. Rogers, *Wise Men Fish Here* (New York: Harcourt, Brace and World, Inc., 1965).

3. Copies of this edition are also quite rare and much in demand at the moment.

4. The foreword to the first American edition of *Under a Glass Bell* does not appear in the later editions.

5. This phase actually began with the Spanish Civil War, when Miss Nin, in common with many other artists and intellectuals on both sides of the Atlantic (especially those with Surrealist affiliations) professed Marxist sympathies, and continued through World War II. In the foreword to the early edition she wrote, "Because these stories were written before the Spanish War I thought first of all to destroy them, and then I understood a truth which it might be good to state for others. The stories must be placed in their proper light for those who fail to see the relation between fantasy and reality, the past and the present . . . These stories represent the moment when many like myself had found only one answer to the suffering of the world: to dream, to tell fairytales, to elaborate and to follow the labyrinth of fantasy. All this I see now was the passive poet's only answer to the torments he witnessed. Being ignorant of the causes and therefore of a possibility of change, he sought merely a balm-art, the drug . . . I did not stay in the world of the dream or become permanently identified with it. The Spanish war awakened me. I passed out of romanticism, mysticism and neurosis into reality. I see now there was no need to destroy the art which was produced under an evil social structure. But it is necessary to understand, to be aware of what caused the suffering which made such an opium essential and what this fantasy world concealed. And to this task I will devote the rest of my writing. I am in the difficult position of presenting stories which are dreams and of having to say: but now, although I give you these, I am awake!"

6. "Books," *The New Yorker*, xx, April 1, 1944, pp. 73–74.

7. One is reminded here of the situation of Djuna in "The Voice," who complains to her analyst, "I seem to be standing and watching this current passing and I am left behind . . . I stand for hours watching the river downtown." The Voice tells her she must not stand still but move with the current, i.e., participate in the flow of life rather than merely observe it.

8. In common with much modern poetry, many modern

films, especially on the Continent, have abandoned the logical presentation of a theme in favor of an associative type of presentation based on the strategic arrangement of certain images, symbols, or scenes.

9. It may be remarked here that when visiting Maupassant's former house at Etretat, Miss Nin heard from its occupants many stories concerning the opium habit from which he is supposed to have suffered. It is quite possible that these stories fused with the image of the fishing boat to produce what Kenneth Burke terms a "symbolic cluster," in which the boat itself has a narcotic function.

10. The situation in "The Mouse" is closer to that in "The Boarding House" (also in *Dubliners*) than in either Joyce's "Clay" or "Eveline," but the outcome of "The Mouse" is very different from Joyce's. In the foreword to the early edition Miss Nin wrote, "It is in 'The Mouse' that first appears the thread of humanity that was to lead me out of the dream: my feeling for the maid was human but I did not know what to do with her."

11. *Twice a Year*, No. 1 (Fall-Winter 1938), pp. 132–37.

12. "The Child Born Out of the Fog" was inspired partly by the circumstances of Richard Wright's marriage and partly by those of another couple (a Negro musician and his white wife). The characters do not resemble Wright and his family; the situation does.

13. A statement which recalls the *Diary*. See chapter 1.

14. In its lifelessness and unreality the world of Molnar's paintings reminds us of that inhabited by Jeanne and her brother in *House of Incest*, and of the story, "Under a Glass Bell," which is another version of the same situation.

15. One of the sources of the domestic situation described in this story was an aristocratic family with whom Miss Nin was acquainted in Paris.

16. The original of this story, a friend of Max Jacob, was brought, during the Occupation, by Henry Miller from Paris to New York, where he supported himself by casting horoscopes. Ultimately he returned to Paris, where he died in extreme poverty.

17. According to Gerald D. Klee, M.D., this experience is quite common among persons under the influence of hallucinogenic drugs. See his article, "Lysergic Acid and Ego Functions," in *Archives of General Psychiatry*, VIII (May 1963), pp. 461–74. See also Harold F. Searles, M.D., *The Nonhuman*

*Environment* (New York: International Universities Press, 1960), pp. 29–53 and pp. 143–77. *The Tibetan Book of the Dead* (London: Oxford University Press, 1927) is also rich in the description of such experiences.

18. At this point the portrait becomes a composite. Miss Nin did not see Artaud in a straitjacket, but another artist who had been so confined, and their dialogue, she has said, is reported practically *verbatim*. Likewise the circumstances of her visit (with the doctor and his aides looking on) are authentic.

19. The situation in this story bears a certain resemblance to that in Steinbeck's "The Snake" (from *The Long Valley*), in which the protagonist, for different reasons, enjoys watching the same spectacle.

20. The archetypal pattern of this story corresponds roughly to that of Tennessee Williams' *A Streetcar Named Desire*; in both cases we are made, by the special nature of the circumstances, to sympathize with the protagonist, who is alcoholic and death-oriented and who suffers confinement at the end.

21. William Carlos Williams' comment (*New Directions Annual*, " 'Men . . . Have No Tenderness' " (Norfolk: New Directions, 1942), p. 432) is relevant here, "Men have been far too prone to point out that all the greatest masterpieces are the work of males as well as of the male viewpoint or nearly so. Women swallow this glibly, they are the worst offenders."

22. Elizabeth Hardwick, "Fiction Chronicle," *Partisan Review*, xv (June 1948), pp. 705–8 *passim*.

23. This seems a curious charge to bring against the author of "Birth." Perhaps the difficulty is that Miss Nin achieves a *kind* of exactness to which Miss Hardwick, a very different sort of writer, is insensitive and which therefore seems to her vague. It is not, certainly, the exactness of ordinary prose. The charge of being "old fashioned," which is equally astonishing, is one to which Miss Hardwick, when she wishes to be particularly damning, frequently has resort; see, for example, her comment in "The Theatre of Decadence," *New York Review of Books*, April 28, 1966, p. 8: "Should we call it 'the end of an era'? In any case it was 'curtains' this season for one sort of American playwriting. Edward Albee, Tennessee Williams, and William Inge produced plays of startling antiquity."

24. Lawrence Durrell wrote this criticism in a personal letter to Miss Nin in 1937.

## 5 – The Search for Completion:
### Ladders to Fire

1. The other four novels are, respectively, *Children of the Albatross, The Four-Chambered Heart, A Spy in the House of Love,* and *The Seduction of the Minotaur.*

2. This edition was dedicated to Gore Vidal, the novelist, who in the mid-Forties was an editor at Dutton. He became one of Miss Nin's most intimate friends.

3. A thousand copies were thus manufactured, and bear the imprint Gemor Press. This volume includes "Hejda," which was later dropped from *Ladders to Fire* because it had appeared in the meantime in the Dutton edition of *Under a Glass Bell,* where it more properly belongs.

4. Elizabeth Hardwick "Fiction Chronicle," *Partisan Review,* xv (June 1948), pp. 705–8 *passim.*

5. See also, in *Seduction of the Minotaur* (Swallow edition, pp. 130–36), the brilliant image, sustained for several pages, in which man's knowledge of the moon is likened to the protagonist's knowledge of the lover.

6. A particularly successful example of dream symbolism is seen in *Seduction of the Minotaur* (Swallow edition, p. 23), where Lillian has recurrent dreams of a landlocked ship which represents her inhibited self. But the symbols which Miss Nin chooses to characterize her protagonists are not always from the world of dreams. Sometimes the characters form them in their conscious minds, and apply them quite consciously to their own situations. Thus, in *A Spy in the House of Love* (Swallow edition, p. 127), Sabina sees in Duchamp's famous Surrealist painting, *Nude Descending a Staircase,* a symbol of her own multiple selves; and in *Four-Chambered Heart* (Swallow edition, p. 177) Djuna's decision to sink the houseboat is the result of her realization that her love affair with Rango is doomed.

7. Unpublished lecture by Anaïs Nin.

8. See Anaïs Nin, *Realism and Reality* (New York: Alicat Book Shop, Outcast Series No. 6, 1946).

9. "Stella" was in fact removed from later editions of *Ladders to Fire.*

10. See note 10, chapter 1.

11. The same line uttered by the flower vendor in Tennes-

see Williams' *A Streetcar Named Desire*. Williams' heroine, to whom it applies, is also dead spiritually rather than physically. Stella is also the name of an important character in *Streetcar*, though there is no other resemblance between the two women.

12. This character bears no resemblance to the Lillian who appears in "The Voice"; the resemblance is rather to Lilith (in the same story) who in fact "becomes" the Lillian in *Cities of the Interior*.

13. The wording here is ambiguous. By "accomplished this" Miss Nin refers to the woman's working her will on the man.

14. Later Lillian asks Djuna, "Did you ever think how men who court a woman and do not win her are not hurt? And woman gets hurt. If woman plays the Don Juan and does the courting and the man retreats she is mutilated in some way." And Djuna replies, "Yes, I have noticed that. I suppose it's a kind of guilt. For a man it is natural to be the aggressor and he takes defeat well. For woman it is a transgression, and she assumes the defeat is caused by the aggression. How long will woman be ashamed of her strength?"

15. In a way, also, that reminds us of Frankie Addams, in Carson McCullers' *Member of the Wedding*. See my study of this novel in *The Ballad of Carson McCullers* (New York: Coward McCann, 1966).

16. This incident forms the plot of a story which Miss Nin had previously published in *Twice a Year* (Fall-Winter, 1940; Spring-Summer, 1941) under the title "Woman in the Myth," the chief difference being that the earlier version is told in the first person, with the narrator corresponding to Lillian.

17. The incident reminds us of that in "Birth"—another example, perhaps, of the overlapping we have come to expect of Miss Nin's characters.

18. For an account of the origin of this scene, see the pamphlet *On Writing* (New York: Alicat Book Shop, Outcast Series No. 11, 1947), pp. 28–29.

19. Edmund Wilson writes concerning this section, "The story is rather amorphous and there is little clue to whither it is leading, but the whole book is only an installment in a novel which is, I believe, to run to several volumes, and it is impossible to judge it on the basis of this first presentation of the characters." ("Books," *The New Yorker*, XXII, November 16, 1946, p. 130).

20. Diana Trilling, "Fiction in Review," *The Nation,* CLXII, January 26, 1946, pp. 105–7.

### 6—*The Phosphorescence of Faith:*
### Children of the Albatross

1. The book was first published by Dutton in 1947 and has been reprinted only once, in the Swallow edition of *Cities of the Interior* (1966).

2. See notes 6 and 7, chapter 5.

3. In *Ladders to Fire,* Jay remarks, "I suspect that when Sabina gives one so many lies it is because she has nothing else to give but mystery, but fiction. Perhaps behind her mysteries there is nothing."

4. We see now the significance of the title of Part Two ("Bread and the Wafer") of *Ladders to Fire,* for which this passage was perhaps originally intended and where, if the reader is not to be puzzled by the title, it properly belongs.

5. This is true only if we except the case histories which comprise the bulk of "The Voice."

### 7—*The Drowning of the Doll:*
### The Four-Chambered Heart

1. Published originally by Duell, Sloan and Pearce in 1950, and reissued in the Swallow edition of *Cities of the Interior* (1966).

2. See my analysis of this situation in *The Ballad of Carson McCullers* (New York: Coward McCann, 1966), pp. 126–43.

3. As if, also, *The Turn of the Screw* were a novel of character. James Korges evidently subscribes to the persistent heresy that the ghosts in James's story are not real but figments of a neurotic governess' disordered sexual imagination, a theory which reduces the novella to a mere case history and which has been discredited many times. See, for example, my essay, "James's 'Air of Evil': a Revaluation of *The Turn of the Screw,*" in *Partisan Review,* XVI (February 1949), pp. 175–87, and, for a history of the entire controversy, *A Casebook on The Turn of the Screw,* edited by Gerald Willen (New York: Thomas Y. Crowell Company, 1960).

4. *Sunday-Journal* (Providence, Rhode Island), January 29, 1950, VI, p. 10.

5. This theme is more characteristic of Miss Nin's work as a whole than of *The Four-Chambered Heart.* In the pamphlet *On Writing* (New York: Alicat Book Shop, Outcast Series No. 11, 1947), pp. 17–19, Miss Nin wrote:

I not only believe that we are suffering from a collective neurosis, but that this is precisely one of the most *urgent* themes for the novel today: the struggle between the forces of nature in us and our repressive and consequently destructive treatment of these forces . . . Today a novelist's preoccupation with inner psychological distortions does not stem from a morbid love of illness but from a knowledge that this is the *theme* of our new reality.

6. This story is exceptional in the McCullers canon, for the tramp actually does succeed in his quest—by first learning to love simple objects in nature, "a tree, a rock, a cloud." Its positive outcome may explain why, of Mrs. McCullers' various writings, this is one of Miss Nin's favorites. Mrs. McCullers' "holy tramp," incidentally, is somewhat similar to Jay, in *Cities of the Interior*, and both anticipate the type who became an indispensable fixture in the novels of Kerouac and other so-called Beat writers.

### 8—The War Among the Selves: A Spy in the House of Love

1. The rendezvous with Philip on pp. 47–52 (Swallow edition, 1966) is described as if it occurs in a single afternoon, or perhaps overnight. But we are told on page 52 that Sabina has been away from Alan five days—yet another instance of this author's indifference (which resembles Rango's) to "clock time." Most readers will feel that, since specific periods of time are occasionally mentioned, they should be consistent.

2. Harriet Zinnes writes ("Anaïs Nin's Works Reissued," *Books Abroad*, xxxvii (Summer 1963), p. 285): "It ought to be said here that there is nothing sensational or obstreperous about Miss Nin's writing on homosexual love. She is hindered neither by a sense of shame nor by pretension nor by a desire to shock. There is always the sureness of the poet writing. What other American writer could achieve such purity of language writing on a subject still uneasily perceived by our current novelists? (One has only to look at James Baldwin's new novel, *Another Country*.) Miss Nin writes with equal poetic integrity and ease as she describes physical love between men and women (or for that matter between woman and woman). It is that she writes with an understanding not of mere sex, but of the total motivation behind the encounter

of man and woman, of man and man, of woman and woman. This is the understanding of the poet."

3. A French translation was published in Paris by Stock in 1964.

4. Further confusion between Sabina and Djuna is suggested by the circumstance of both characters having preferred, as children, to live in a world of fantasy, and persisting in their habit of acting out their illusions.

### 9—Stasis and *Flow:*
### The Seduction of the Minotaur

1. Ann Arbor: Edwards Brothers, 1958.

2. But the freedom of Golconda has been shown to be illusory, which qualifies the effectiveness of the symbol.

3. The myth of the "natural man" can be traced at least as far back as the eighteenth century in France, where Chateaubriand's *Atala* was instrumental in circulating it. It plays an important part in the literature of English romanticism: for Byron, Keats, Shelley, and Leigh Hunt the Italian peasants corresponded to the primitive ideal as they later did for Samuel Butler, Lawrence, and Norman Douglas. It is central to the philosophy of New England transcendentalism, and is especially evident in the work of Emerson, Thoreau, and Whitman. Cooper, in New York state, had the advantage of contact with genuine aborigines, whom he greatly idealized. Tolstoy's healthy peasants are proof that the myth was not confined to America and Western Europe; Lawrence found his "natural men" not only in Italy but also in Mexico and New Mexico; E. M. Forster, in Italy; and Paul Bowles, in Morocco. The list could be expanded almost indefinitely; it is testimony to one of the great intellectual fallacies in the history of Western literature.

4. Patricia Hodgart, *The Spectator*, May 26, 1961, and *The Times Literary Supplement*, June 16, 1961.

5. Effective reconciliation of these two images, the one of land and the other of water, may in fact be impossible. The reader may also be disturbed, in the labyrinth image, by the implied equation between the "umbilical cord" of memory and the thread, whose purpose, in the myth, is to lead one *out* of the labyrinth. By the logic of the narrative, the Minotaur's lair should correspond to the source of the umbilical cord rather than to its trailing end.

### 10 – *The Alchemy of Art*: Collages

1. The book was first published (1964) in England by Peter Owen Limited and later in the same year reissued by Alan Swallow.

2. Explanation, of course, is not necessarily justification, where the decisive factor is the success or failure of the experiment.

3. We may speculate, because of the reference to T. S. Eliot, that the novel is *Nightwood*, and that "Judith Sands" is a composite suggested by its author, Djuna Barnes, who, as is well known, is a recluse.

4. The situation here is somewhat similar to that of the Reverend Hightower, in Faulkner's *Light in August*.

5. This machine, an invention of Tinguely's, actually existed. For a description of it, see G. Peillex, "L'Anti-Machine à l'Exposition à Lausanne," *Werk* (Winterthur, Switzerland), CI (July 1964), pp. 259–61.

6. In its association of water with birth the statue image in the first paragraph ("They stood in the heart of the fountains glistening with water as if they had just been born") reminds us of both *House of Incest* ("I remember my first birth in water") and the short story, "Birth," ("It has long eyelashes on its closed eyes, it is perfectly made, and all glistening with the waters of the womb").

### 11 – *Reality as Rainbow*

1. Leslie Fiedler, *Waiting for the End*, (New York: Stein and Day, 1964), p. 45.

2. "Books," *The New Yorker*, xx, April 1, 1944, p. 73.

3. Karl Shapiro, "Is Poetry an American Art?" *College English*, xxv (March, 1964), pp. 395–405.

4. See, in connection with this theory of significant omission, Kenneth Burke's discussion of the synechdochic function in literary art in *The Philosophy of Literary Form*, revised edition (New York: Vintage paperback, 1957), pp. 22–28.

5. Cited by Anaïs Nin in *On Writing* (New York: Alicat Book Shop, Outcast Series No. 11, 1947), p. 20.

6. "The Fantastic World of Anaïs Nin," *New York Times Book Review*, March 28, 1948, p. 24.

7. William Carlos Williams, " 'Men . . . Have No Tenderness,': Anaïs Nin's *Winter of Artifice*," *New Directions Annual* (Norfolk: New Directions, 1942), pp. 429–36.